DARKENING VALLEY

Dale Aukerman

DARKENING VALLEY

A *Biblical Perspective*
on Nuclear War

FOREWORD BY JIM WALLIS

THE SEABURY PRESS · NEW YORK

Second printing

1981
The Seabury Press
815 Second Avenue
New York, N.Y. 10017

Library of Congress Cataloging in Publication Data

Aukerman, Dale.
Darkening valley

Bibliography: p. 228
1.   Atomic warfare—Moral and religious aspects.
I.   Title.
BR115.A85A9   261.8'73   81-4380
ISBN 0-8164-2295-8 (pbk.)   AACR2

34, 221

Grateful acknowledgment is made to Literistic, Ltd. for permission to reprint "Requiem for the
Living" by C. Day Lewis. Copyright © 1964 C. Day

For Daniel Chris
"My God sent his angel and shut the lions' mouths,
and they have not hurt me"

Miriam Jane
"Sing to the Lord, for he has triumphed gloriously;
the horse and his rider he has thrown into the sea"

Maren Songmy
"A voice is heard in Ramah,
   lamentation and bitter weeping.
Rachel is weeping for her children;
   she refuses to be comforted for her children,
   because they are not."

What a din of hordes, what a din within the
valley of the Verdict! For the Eternal's day
is near, within the valley of the Verdict.
   Dark the sun and moon,
   the stars have ceased to shine,
   and the Eternal thunders out of Sion,
   loudly from Jerusalem;
   heaven and earth are shaking,
   but the Eternal is a refuge for his own folk,
   a stronghold for the sons of Israel.

Joel 3:14–16

Even though I walk through a valley dark as death
I fear no evil, for thou art with me,
   thy staff and thy crook are my comfort.

Psalm 23:4

CONTENTS

FOREWORD

"You have heard it was said, 'You shall love your neighbor and hate your enemy.' But I say to you, Love your enemies and pray for those who persecute you" (Mt. 5:43–44).

These are the words of Jesus which we shoved aside a long time ago. Recently I spoke to a conference on "The Soviet Threat." I began my remarks with this passage and felt quite unsure about the likely response. The scene was the Cannon Office Building on Capitol Hill. The words from Jesus' Sermon on the Mount seemed starkly out of place in a congressional conference room filled with all the trappings of power. To speak of loving enemies there, in that austere political chamber, is to risk being thought naive, unrealistic, and even foolish. I confessed to feeling a little insecure about that and proceeded to raise the question of where all of our realism had brought us. The tough and pragmatic approach, so common in those hallowed halls of Congress, had brought us to the brink of nuclear war and the increasing likelihood of a destruction none of us can even begin to imagine.

"But what about the Russians?" continues to be the most commonly asked question when one begins to talk about the nuclear arms race. Even in the churches, the Soviet threat gets much more attention than the words of Jesus. The question may indeed be the right one, but it is being asked in a tragically wrong way. What about the Russians? What about the Russian people, children, Christians, and churches? What would become of them in a nuclear war? They are among the hundreds of millions of God's children whom we seem quite ready to destroy in the name of freedom, democracy, and national security. What will our causes mean to us after they and we are all dead?

The question we should be asking is, "What has become of us?" What does it say about a people when they are prepared to commit mass murder, whatever the reason? For some things, there are no reasons good enough. We have elevated our nation, our system, and our principles above everything else, even the survival of the world. The Bible calls that idolatry. But we haven't been listening to the Bible.

Our country now worships at the altar of national security; it has become a demon among us. This false and alien god has entered into the household of faith and corrupted the worship of Christians. More than our survival is at stake here; the very integrity of our faith is at stake.

Dale Aukerman helps us to listen to the Bible again. *Darkening Valley* puts the nuclear question where it belongs: at the heart of Christian faith today. Dale rightly sees that at the center of the present controversy over nuclear weapons is a theological, more than a political, question. Where is our security finally rooted? Do we trust in God or in the Bomb? Will we follow Jesus or follow those who are leading us to nuclear oblivion? In persuasive and penetrating style, Dale Aukerman goes to the root assumptions of our present thinking and submits them to a searching biblical scrutiny. Throughout the book, the Cross is lifted up as the great countersign to the Bomb. The Way of the Cross or the Reign of the Bomb is posed as the most urgent choice with which we are now faced. This generation of Christians, in particular, must decide under which one we will live. The decision is crucial, both to the integrity of the gospel and to the future of humankind.

Jesus never said that we would have no enemies nor that they would never be a threat. There is no lack of realism here. What Jesus offers is a new way to deal with our enemies, a different way of responding which has the potential to break the endless cycle of violence and retaliation. That cycle has always brought an escalation of violence and now threatens us all with ultimate violence. Our present approach has not worked so well. What is realism now, in the face of nuclear war? Which strategy must we now call naive? To continue to think that both real and imagined threats can be successfully countered with nuclear weapons is the height of unreality and naivete. Nuclear weapons cannot defend us; they can only destroy us. We have reached a dead end. To continue down the same road is to court disaster.

We must be turned around. That has always been the promise of the biblical word and is the true meaning of repentance. Something entirely new must be tried. Jesus' simple exhortation to love our enemies has usually been given a place of reverent respect and then summarily dismissed as politically irrelevant. Some theologians have called it "a necessary but irrelevant ideal." With the growing prospect of nuclear holocaust, however, Jesus' long-ignored teaching is revealed to be supremely relevant and vitally necessary. If we fail to see a neighbor in the face of our enemy, the consequences will be unthinkable. To ignore Jesus now, in the name of political realism, is to allow our realism to destroy us.

We live in discouraging times. The country is controlled by fear and the world seems increasingly out of control. Some religious leaders now suggest that God needs the U.S. nuclear arsenal to wage war with communism, that the gospel must have the protection of the nuclear umbrella. Even more distressing, the rest of the church seems immobilized, unable to name such a doctrine as heresy. In the political arena, the present assumptions surrounding the debate over military policy are so constricted as to strangle the possibility of peace. If the churches limit themselves to speaking within those assumptions and acting within the acceptable political boundaries, the cause of peace will forever be diminished.

Our fearful situation needs a new word, a new approach, a new level of commitment. Dale Aukerman has laid the foundation for that very thing. The new vision we need will be found, as always, in the biblical vision. That is the gospel vision which pervades this book and which challenges all who would call Jesus Lord. Dale has done us all a great service. *Darkening Valley* takes us a step closer to peace.

To take a new approach is to take a risk. But to take that risk is to state that the risks involved in our present course are much greater. Will the church take the risk? Will we repent of our nuclear sin and no longer cooperate with the preparations for total war? Will the church declare that it no longer wishes to place its trust in nuclear weapons? Will the church be the first to demonstrate another way?

If we can answer yes, then there is indeed hope.

Jim Wallis

List of Abbreviations

Quotations taken from the Bible are from the Revised Standard Version unless otherwise designated by the following abbreviations

AV — *The Holy Bible: Authorized Version.* New York: Oxford University Press.

JB — *The Jerusalem Bible.* Garden City, N.Y.: Doubleday, 1971.

Moffatt — James Moffatt, *A New Translation of the Bible,* New York and London: Harper & Brothers, 1926.

NEB — *The New English Bible,* Oxford University Press; Cambridge University Press. New Testament, 1961; Old Testament, 1970.

Phillips — J. B. Phillips, *New Testament in Modern English.* New York: Macmillan, 1972.

Weymouth — Richard Francis Weymouth, *The New Testament in Modern Speech.* Boston: Pilgrim Press, 3d ed., 1909.

INTRODUCTION

In all these aspects the question of war must be asked and answered as a personal question. And perhaps the most important contribution that Christian ethics can make in this field is to lift the whole problem inexorably out of the indifferent sphere of general political and moral discussion and to translate it into the personal question: "What hast thou so far done or failed to do in the matter, and what art thou doing or failing to do at this moment?" Killing is a very personal act, and being killed a very personal experience. It is thus commensurate with the thing itself that even in the political form which killing assumes in war it should be the theme of supremely personal interrogation.[1]

Karl Barth

Less than half an hour away, there are specific missiles with nuclear warheads aimed at each one of us. These can be seen and touched; they are as real as an automobile swerving toward any one of us from the oncoming lane of a highway. They are weapons which, if fired, would bring for each one of us instantaneous obliteration or a slower dying. Integrated with each weapon are particular flesh-and-blood human beings who are ready to play a part or perform a function that will turn them into our murderers. And on "our side," not far from each of us geographically or in terms of what is deep within us, are their weapon and weapon-tender counterparts.

To the degree that each of us tends to proceed as the center of all things, we find that whatever is not within our immediate experience —starving children, the inner struggle of someone nearby, God, thermonuclear weapons and their potential victims—remains abstract and remote. A biblical word for absorption in the self, the sensory, the externals nearby, the manageable, and for the narrow focus that makes everything remote into something abstract, is *blindness.* Jesus in his rebuke to the Pharisees (Mt. 23:13–39) saw this blindness as closely related to murder. Isaiah saw blindness as bringing on "the furies of war" (42:17–25 JB).

With mighty acts, vivid images, stories, and intense dialogue, Jesus struggled to give sight to the blind. A guiding assumption in this book is that by returning to the biblical stories, images, and motifs we can be drawn out of this vacuous, abstract way of thinking and be given a new way of seeing so that the actualities of killing and war, especially thermonuclear war, can be seen for what they are.

If war has always been the most extreme disclosure of what is darkest in man, then with the development of thermonuclear weapons and the prospect of nuclear holocaust that disclosure moves to its culmination. "It only needed the atom and hydrogen bomb to complete the self-disclosure of war in this regard,"[2] says Karl Barth. Earlier there were limits to the evil which individuals and societies could perpetrate. With thermonuclear technology those limits have vanished. The unleashing of the atom has been the climactic unleashing of man. The contortedness and desolation within can now express its outward image as never before.

Christians discern in Jesus' advent, his ministry, Crucifixion, and Resurrection on the one hand God's fullest disclosure of Himself to man, and on the other, His most penetrating exposé of man. Here more than at any other time or place God in His being for us is revealed and we in our defiance of God are unmasked. The unmasking came preeminently in the judicial murder of Jesus. One implication of this is that in any killing of others and in the premeditations which lead to it, we can, more than in anything else, discern the darkness within. War, now nuclear war, is the key issue not only for survival but also for coming to grips before God with who we are.

The not very widely noticed unmasking that has come with the construction of nuclear weapons, epochal as the development is, and the stupendous further exposé so close at hand in the aftermath of the initial thermonuclear volleys, should, nonetheless, be seen as subsumed in that earlier unmasking. And even as we try to face up to the horrific dimensions of the current exposé, God's self-disclosure in Jesus should be what looms far larger for us.

On a Campaign for Nuclear Disarmament march in Scotland in the early sixties a Trotskyite boy asked me with regard to Christianity, "Does it show a way through?" In the deepening darkness of the nuclear age I seek to make clear in this book that Jesus Christ does reveal a way—for however many or few who take it.

In a book intended for use in convincing "the world of sin and of righteousness and of judgment" (Jn. 16:8), extensive treatment of the more somber aspects of the current human situation cannot be avoided. But such treatment, like the Passion narratives themselves, is meant to point to the Risen Lord, who leads us out of the old age, which must eventually collapse in total ruin, and into his New Age. As French pacifist theologian Jean Lasserre has expressed it, "Even if we talk of the nuclear peril, it must be also with a smile of joy at Christ's victory."[3]

DARKENING VALLEY

PART I

VICTIM

Chapter 1

THE PRIMEVAL MURDER

We must recognize, and clearly, that violence begets violence.
Does anyone ask, "Who started it?" That is a false question. Since
the days of Cain, there has been no beginning of violence, only a
continuous process of retaliation.[1]

Jacques Ellul

Cain felt a shadow, cast by his brother Abel, falling across his life.
How could he have his place in the sun with his brother's shadow in
the way? He did not realize that the shadow actually came from the
stalking form of sin close by him. God warned him: Subdue that
"crouching beast hungering for you" (Gen. 4:7 JB).

But Cain stalked and sprang upon his brother. Cain the plowman
turned to sow his brother's body. Into the deep furrow he cut, he
dropped his brother's body, a seed that for him would never spring up.
The earth yielded to Cain's swift wounding and took into its wound
the blood and body of Abel. The horror which was never to have been
under heaven was now underground. Below the earth's slowly healing
scar lay the decomposing corpse.

Blood and life are God's. Cain had broken into God's realm. Into the
ground he poured blood and life, not his, but God's and his brother's.
He attempted to hide not himself (like Adam) but what had been his
brother.

To God's question, "Where is Abel your brother?," Cain replied with
a combination of lie, half-truth, and witticism: I do not know. Am I
shepherd of that shepherd?

God said to Cain, "The voice of your brother's blood is crying to me
from the ground," crying to the sovereign Giver and Protector of life.
Response to that cry came in articulation of the curse. The earth,
pulled shut around Abel, lay open endlessly before Cain. Now there
was no brother to obstruct or burden his going, no longer a brother to
see as a threat to his place under heaven; but along with his brother
had disappeared even the uncertain place that was Cain's before. The
solitude he had willed he achieved beyond his expectations. The earth,

2

which he had drenched and scarred in doing away with his brother, became everywhere a witness against him, crying out the absence of Abel. "Then Cain went away from the presence of the Lord, and dwelt in the land of Nod [Wandering], east of Eden."

The story of Cain and Abel, like the other stories of Genesis 1-11, shows us with overwhelming vividness who we are. We are each to some extent Cain, rising up to do away with the brother whose inherently accusing and delimiting presence we cannot tolerate. And each of us is in some degree Abel, caught, uncomprehending, under the descending weapon of the brother. Our rising up to murder begins as drama deep within the mind ("sin at the door like a crouching beast hungering for you"), but presses outward to lay hold of whatever weapons are within reach, from words or silence to hydrogen bombs.

This story can be pondered in relation to the prospect of nuclear war. In the East-West struggle there are two sides. As each seeks the status of Abel—what Cain sought—it becomes Cain. Each side tries to have a fully confirmed place and to establish its own righteousness; but the other side is there to negate that attempt. This negation is too much to bear, and the two Cains draw each other into the open field where each stands over against the other with weapon raised high, a posture which makes it evident that here there is no Abel, only Cain.

Each side, though, is not only a Cain poised for slaying but also a conglomerate of persons about to be slain. And this conglomerate is partly Abel, for there are those whose place and righteousness God fashions, those who, as they are enabled to master the crouching beast, are more Abel than Cain, and those too young to help constitute the lineaments of Cain. And all the persons are breath (the meaning of the word "Abel"), slight, insubstantial, God-breathed, so very soon likely to pass into final exhalation. Cain's deed left for every human being the possibility of being murdered; that change in the human situation has now become unsurpassably ominous.

In the story the terrible dynamism that presses Cain toward murder is pictured as a crouching, hungering beast. We experience that dynamism on a vaster, more confounding scale in the mutually reinforcing psychopathologies of those engaged in the Cold War, in the enormous momentum generated by the military-industrial-political complex of each side, in the unending proliferation of nuclear weapons, weapons that outwardly image the interior "crouching."

Adam grasped the promise, "You will be like God." Cain tried to actualize that promise by reconstituting the world—without the brother. Any murder is a repetition of that attempt. The genocidal nuclear slaughter which is contemplated and totally prepared for would be the most extensive such attempt imaginable.

In the story there is a bleak sense of the vacuum which results from Abel's being killed. Isolated murders in the midst of a society can hardly bring a vacancy comparable to what followed the primeval murder. But a nuclear war would. It would create vast stretches of radioactive desolation without another human being.

Remarkable in the story is the way the murder brings an awesome alienation of Cain from the ground, the good earth out of which he, like his parents, had received his being and sustenance by the hand of God: "And now you are cursed from the ground, which has opened its mouth to receive your brother's blood from your hand. When you till the ground, it shall no longer yield to you its strength; you shall be a fugitive and a wanderer on the earth." With Adam's sin the alienation hit. With Cain's sin it became still more acute. The slash that severed the tie to his brother severed also the tie to the nurturing earth. In the technological pollution of the planet and in the escalating desolation of nature carried out in the twentieth century wars, mankind in huge impersonal collectivities[2] has been pressing that alienation further and further. And now nuclear Cain can make not only that which grows on the earth but even the earth itself into a sprawling corpse.

Cain, without the brother whom he had feared might displace him, is gripped by a new fear: "Whoever finds me will slay me." As he had done to his brother, a non-brother would do to him. The cry of that spilt blood would recruit an avenger. But the Lord says to him: "Not so! If any one slays Cain, vengeance shall be taken on him sevenfold." And he "put a mark on Cain, lest any who came upon him should kill him." God does not strike down or forsake the murderer but takes him under His special protection. He checks the escalating desolation of retaliation initiated by Cain's deed.

From this it can be seen that, even when an individual or a collectivity plainly bears Cain's image, we must not resort to lethal punishment. God assigns to Himself, and ultimately to no one else, the matter of dealing with murderers. If we usurp God's role, we become agents of escalating violence and expose ourselves to a judgment still more severe than that which we would presume to carry out. God's mark on Cain was no guarantee that he would not be slain but rather an emphatic warning to any who would seize God's prerogative.

God's mercy to Cain is His mercy to us all. "Any one who hates his brother is a murderer" (1 Jn. 3:15). There is within each of us some portion of the dark dynamism from which the horror of nuclear weapons and the insanity of their proliferation have arisen. If nuclear war has not yet engulfed us, we can only attribute this to the mercy of God. For He has put His mark on the contending Cains (each side guilty of a sequence of mass murders, actual and contemplated), and has ruled and overruled in the midst of the Cold War to hold back till now that vast impending reciprocal slaughter. But that mark is no guarantee and stands in dialectical tension with the threat of sevenfold vengeance.

Gerhard von Rad has observed that throughout Genesis 3 to 11 human sin swells like an avalanche, from the sin of the first human beings to the building of the Tower of Babel, and that the song of Lamech, descendant of Cain, marked the stage beyond the sin of Cain in the downrush of that avalanche:[3]

> *Adah and Zillah, hear my voice,*
> *Lamech's wives, listen to what I say:*
> *I killed a man for wounding me,*
> *a boy for striking me.*
> *Sevenfold vengeance is taken for Cain,*
> *but seventy-sevenfold for Lamech.*
>
> (Gen. 4:23-24 JB)

Lamech was the first proponent of massive retaliation.

The history of the twentieth century can be seen as a swelling avalanche of fear, violence, guilt. To an avalanche belongs not only the hurtling down but also the preceding buildup of subsurface strains. Similarly for human violence, individual and collective, there have been throughout history the alternations of building up (with only premonitory rumblings and marginal slides) and obliterating descent. Wherever what has fallen settles, another cycle of building up begins. At present we live with all the past avalanches of violence compacted in one dread mass up-slope from our world village.

But what has still greater weight and momentum is the reality of God's chief way of dealing with the Cain in us: He has come to us as the Second Abel, given Himself to our lethal blows, and then returned to offer us the power to leave off our flight with Cain and share the marks and destiny of the Second Abel.

Chapter 2

CURSING

When a godless man curses his enemy, he is cursing himself.
Ecclesiasticus 21:27 (JB)

As King David was fleeing from Jerusalem after Absalom's coup, Shimei the Benjaminite, only a little way off, "uttered curse after curse and threw stones at David and at all King David's officers, though the whole army and all the champions flanked the king right and left. The words of his curse were these, 'Be off, be off, man of blood, scoundrel! Yahweh has brought on you all the blood of the House of Saul whose sovereignty you have usurped; and Yahweh has transferred that same sovereignty to Absalom your son. Now your doom has overtaken you, man of blood that you are'" (2 Sam. 16:5–8 JB). Cohering elements of that cursing can be identified: the "away with you"; condemnatory names hurled like projectiles (the stones being hardly more than incidental symbols of the intangible attack); the promotion of doom from on high falling on a person seen only in the aspect of repellent wickedness.

Jesus told his disciples, "Bless those who curse you" (Lk. 6:28); and Paul echoed that command in the words, "Bless those who persecute you; bless and do not curse them" (Rom. 12:14). To curse is to call down doom. But cursing, like blessing, is first of all an attitude out of which words come. Blessing and cursing are the two utterly contrary attitudes we can take toward those with whom we are in contact. Around the world and throughout history cursing has had its variegated traditions of formulation and procedure. But the cursing which Jesus and the apostles prohibit for Christians is not so much the handy formulations as the lurking attitude from which they arise.

James in his indictment of the tongue writes, "With it we bless the Lord and Father, and with it we curse men, who are made in the likeness of God" (Jas. 3:9). He thus indicates that cursing is something common even among Christians, though "this ought not to be so." I may carefully avoid directing a *God damn you* or the like at anyone, half playfully or in thought. But I can so easily and with self-deceiving

6

subtlety curse without such formulations. My thought, "She won't get away with it" or "It would serve him right," may parallel someone else's "God damn you."

It is good if Christians do not use words like "damn" and "hell" casually to avoid trivializing that most terrible possibility. But how preposterous if we staunchly refrain from saying these words, and yet in attitude or in act, such as support for nuclear weaponry, we press upon others the earthly counterpart of the damnation these words point to.

"A man's words flow out of what fills his heart" (Mt. 12:34 JB). My unspoken thoughts too can suggest what is in the depths from which they emerge. News comes that a person I have found very irksome has died or has experienced terrible misfortune. There flares up in me an instantaneous elation which, even if I suppress it, has already disclosed within me a lurking curse that has now found fulfilment. What I had been feeling toward the person was "Out of my way—away with him." In attitude I had already been striking secretly at his existence, and now the outward stroke has come.

Jesus identifies what flows out of the heart and suggests its teeming character by naming each sin in the plural: "evil devisings, murders, adulteries, fornications, thefts, perjuries, slanders [abusive speech]" (Mt. 15:19 in more literal translation). Heading the list of specifics is murder, the most decisive attack on the existence of another. Closing it are two main verbal forms of that attack. The evil devisings, intermediate between the darkness within and wickedness carried out, take shape as initiatives against others or as disregard for them. Anger and abusive name-calling (diminishing a person to the worthlessness expressed in the name) are forbidden (Mt. 5:21–22) because they involve the same movement as murder against the existence of others.

Jesus said, "But what I tell you is this: Do not set yourself against the man who wrongs you" (Mt. 5:39 NEB, in a quite literal translation of the key Greek verb). There is, I think, no more crucial negative command in all the teaching of Jesus than this, none by which we need more often test ourselves. For in a great variety of subtle or crass ways we slip into setting ourselves against others. Most of the breakdown in human relationships, small scale and large scale, comes because individuals and groups set themselves against others.

When with decisiveness I set myself against a person or a group, I curse. Doom in many forms hangs over me, and that doom has such an ominous quality, not so much because of the particular shape it may take, but because others are the promoters of that doom. In varying

degrees their cursing me, their "Away with him," registers in me. I
counter by promoting their doom with my secret cursing even as they
in turn counter again with theirs. It is from this fearful escalating
reciprocal cursing that Jesus brings deliverance.

Hydrogen bombs and their missile carriers can be seen as an
extraordinary concretization of human cursing. They too arise from
the darkness that fills hundreds of millions of hearts, from the
fundamental curse "Away with them." In formal cursing great care
was (and for some cultures still is) taken through ritual and proper
formulation to insure the fulfilment. The curse once uttered took
on a certain autonomy between those cursing and those cursed.
There was ordinarily the period of interim anticipation before the
fulfilment. Modern man does not need malignant spirits to carry out
his wish, "Away with them." Precision with words and ritual has
become precision in nuclear weapons technology. Man could, if he
wanted, inflict immediately the doom he would call down. But he can
wait. Yet the curse, concretized, still assumes an autonomy apart from
those who willed it. There seems hardly any way to call back a curse
once willed.

Cursing as fearful reciprocity is there. Each side is set against the
other with technologically concretized curses poised against their
counterparts. Each side counters the doom promoted by the other by
promoting the doom of the other—and thus the endless escalation.
The horror of all that has, till now, not been fulfilled. But the
counterpoised curses merge toward one engulfing curse.

In blessing we ask that the mercy of God and the goodness of life
rest upon others. In cursing we seek to exclude them from that, and
thus slip into a fateful error: for only by God's mercy can the doom
thus unleashed be held back from any of us. It is possible to forgive the
person who makes life hard for me if I see that each of us desperately
needs God's mercy and the other's compassion and that each of us,
frail as we are, needs least of all any promoter of doom.

The same can be said, must be said, of the United States and the
Soviet Union in the nuclear arms buildup. Jesus' focal commentary on
his model prayer ("For if you forgive men their trespasses, your
heavenly Father also will forgive you; but if you do not forgive men
their trespasses, neither will your Father forgive your trespasses"—
Mt. 6:14–15) applies to the nuclear superpowers and their allies: Only
if there is a turn to some rough collective approximation of forgiveness and blessing of each side by the other—Americans, after a
fashion, bless the Dutch and the Swiss and have forgiven the English

and the West Germans—can the heavenly Father extend to us the forgiveness and blessing that averts doom.

As Jesus was on his way to the final encounter in Jerusalem, he tried to enter a certain Samaritan village (Lk. 9:51–56). Because of their nationalism "the people would not receive him." James and John in an uncharacteristic burst of "faith" (which they had been told could uproot trees or eliminate mountains) said to Jesus, "Lord, do you want us to bid fire come down from heaven and consume them?" Jesus turned and rebuked them. The words of the rebuke, though found only in certain ancient manuscripts, may incorporate a recollection that goes back to the incident: "You do not know what manner of spirit you are of; for the Son of man came not to destroy men's lives but to save them."

When the Samaritan villagers said, "Off with you!" James and John, partly in their own aroused nationalism, wanted to outdo them totally. God was to become their agent in carrying out the fire curse they were about to utter. The one right thing they did was to ask Jesus first. He rebuked them. Once again they had failed completely to understand his mission. Hoary Old Testament precedents and bans of utter destruction[1] might be pointed to; but Jesus had come that men might live, and for disciples of his to destroy human beings was unthinkable.

Religious cold warriors, high or low, live as successors to the James and John depicted in that incident: with corresponding nationalism, collective self-righteousness, and presumption in taking over God's prerogatives. But any who ask the Master can know that to invoke or assent to the curse of fire in nuclear weapons (or the curse in any weapons) is out of the question. Still more decisive than his ethical prescriptions is the imperative implicit in the mission of Jesus who came so that human beings may truly live. There might be exceptions to particular ethical commands as many claim, but for those drawn by Jesus into his mission of bringing life there can be no furloughs for doing the opposite of that mission.

Jesus, by going to Jerusalem, went beyond that rebuke of the two brothers. The annihilation which James and John (and we with them) wanted to call down, Jesus let fall upon himself. He absorbed the cursing, the curse, the doom. During his last hours, the verbal onslaught gave some expression to the essence of what was being perpetrated. The Roman battalion struck his head with a reed, spat on him, went down on their knees to do him homage, made fun of him. The mob shouted, "Away with him!" At Golgotha "the passers-by jeered at him .... The chief priests and the scribes mocked him among themselves . . . . Even those who were crucified with him taunted him" (Mk. 15:29,31,32 JB). Yet when Jesus experienced their cursing, even in its most extreme degree, he would not reciprocate: "When he was reviled, he did not revile in return; when he suffered, he did not threaten" (1 Pet. 2:23).

Jesus stepped into the no-man's-land between cursing antagonists: between Samaritans and Jews, between Jews and Romans, between man and gods. What is referred to in the Bible as God's cursing is, with closer scrutiny, seen to be the recoil of man's cursing. God points emphatically to that recoil within his sovereign ordering of human affairs; this pronouncement is his cursing. There is the remarkable fact that Hebrew does not have a word simply for punishment; the two main words that can denote the evil act "can also denote its evil result, and therefore punishment, because the two things are basically the same."[2] Already in the story of Cain God does not hurl his curse but somberly describes the recoil upon Cain himself of what he had thought and done. Jesus, who alone of all human beings did no wrong, stepped into the totality of all the recoil throughout human history and was crushed.

God said to Abram: "I will bless you. . . . I will bless those who bless you, and him who curses you I will curse" (Gen. 12:2,3). Jesus universalized the promise and the warning. Not only those who curse Abraham and his descendants but those who curse any of their fellow human beings incur the recoil. And only as persons bless others are they open to receive God's blessing.

Jesus became "a curse for us . . . that in Christ Jesus the blessing of Abraham might come upon the Gentiles" (Gal. 3:13,14). Because he accepted annihilation, the result of the accumulated recoil of human cursing and of all sin, God could give His blessing—His reversal of that annihilation—and let it surge out to embrace all who turn from their cursing to be blessed and bless in return.

Cursing is the brink of the abyss. If we press others to that brink, we teeter there ourselves. The nuclear arms race is the stark, unprecedented, outward imaging of our teetering condition. And the all-pervasive recoil of Cold War cursing shapes the nations and disfigures our deepest selves. But there was One who let himself be cast into the abyss and did not drag with him those (us) who pushed him over the brink. Rather he returned out of that dark place to lead us back from the dreadful rim where we would otherwise continue to teeter and eventually fall.

In Revelation 16 there are visions of catastrophes that suggest nuclear holocaust. Three times it is said that in the midst of successive disasters men cursed God. Thus in verses 10–11: "men gnawed their tongues in anguish and cursed the God of heaven for their pain and sores, and did not repent of their deeds." Man's habit of blaming God which came with the Fall ("It was the women you put with me"—Gen. 3:12 JB) reaches its ultimate expression in this final enveloping doom: "Away with you, God, you the guilty one, you the cause!" Doom is flung back (supposedly) at God, seen as the originator of doom. Ruin can come with such overwhelming immensity (and in the aftermath of thermonuclear volleys this would be the case for hundreds of millions) that human beings are driven to identify as the source of their ruin something comparable to it in magnitude. It is not God, but the unimaginable recoil of human cursing that is the root of all destruction. Fortunately for us God is greater than our cursing.

Chapter 3

UNDERLINGS
OF THE PROSECUTOR

They went each to his own house, but Jesus went to the Mount of Olives. Early in the morning he came again to the temple; all the people came to him, and he sat down and taught them. The scribes and the Pharisees brought a woman who had been caught in adultery, and placing her in the midst they said to him, "Teacher, this woman has been caught in the act of adultery. Now in the law Moses commanded us to stone such. What do you say about her?" This they said to test him, that they might have some charge to bring against him. Jesus bent down and wrote with his finger on the ground. And as they continued to ask him, he stood up and said to them, "Let him who is without sin among you be the first to throw a stone at her." And once more he bent down and wrote with his finger on the ground. But when they heard it, they went away, one by one, beginning with the eldest, and Jesus was left alone with the woman standing before him. Jesus looked up and said to her, "Woman, where are they? Has no one condemned you?" She said, "No one, Lord." And Jesus said, "Neither do I condemn you; go, and do not sin again."[1]

John 7:53–8:11

Concurrent dramas of prosecution darken our world: the massed fingers pointing against this minority or that; millions of marriages breaking up through reciprocal prosecution; put-down, accusation, come-back so often characterizing the behavior of children; monolithic societies pursuing self-justification by decrying the parallel sins of the other side. War is the climactic human effort at carrying through prosecution, sentencing, and execution. Prosecution is what any retaliation comes down to. Prosecution, so dominant in the clash of individuals and groups is, I believe, the term that best conveys to us what Jesus referred to as "judging."

In the story of the Fall the chief dynamism that enters into human interaction is that of accusation, prosecution. The Old Testament is filled with it. The prosecution motif runs through the gospel narratives. Scribes and Pharisees continually loiter around Jesus to scavenge for evidence, to set their traps, to scrutinize his every word and move "so that they might accuse him" (Mk. 3:2). Their night finally comes with its furious crescendo of accusations against God's Son to be followed by the long-desired sentencing and execution. Throughout Luke's account of the early church the grim forces of prosecution enter repeatedly, and in Acts 24 we are given an abbreviated speech by prosecutor Tertullus.

People of faith came to understand that there is a source, an initiator, a cohesion behind human agents of prosecution. The Hebrew word *satan* has the basic meaning, "accuser, prosecutor." The trials of Job were brought on by the infernal initiative of the prosecutor. The word *devil* derives from the Greek term used in biblical times to translate *satan*. The puzzle in the Bible about the evil we are up against being rooted in Satan alone and yet finding manifold expression in the demonic hosts can be solved if we see prosecution as *the* primary dynamism from which all other evil dynamisms issue. The goal of the frantic prosecutor is chaos, death, doom for all human beings.

Throughout the Bible we discover that God is no prosecutor and has no prosecutor. "Who will be the accuser of God's chosen ones? It is God who pronounces acquittal: Then who can condemn?" (Rom. 8:33 NEB). Many Old Testament passages appear to express prosecution by God, as do the "woes" Jesus addressed to the scribes and Pharisees. But God's hope at every juncture was not that sinners would die but that they would heed this warning and turn before destruction sweeps them away. The charges were aimed not to achieve a judicial conviction which would bring the death penalty but rather to expose the awfulness of their sin and thus their need for God's rescue. God is Judge, but He calls for no witnesses against anyone. All the evil within each person He already knows—and is intent on dismissing. The witnesses He calls have a very different assignment.

The exultant band of Pharisees and doctors of the law arraigned before Jesus their prize prisoner, a woman caught in adultery (Jn. 7:53–8:11). They came as the prosecutors, witnesses, volunteer executioners. They stood there as self-appointed agents of God's wrath. But Jesus, who was really the primary target of their prosecution, was to be the judge. If he condemned the woman to death, he would probably alienate many of his followers, and he would be taking over a prerogative that the Roman governor reserved for himself. On the other hand, if he did not condemn her to death, he would be openly contradicting the Law of Moses—a clear indication that he could not be the Messiah.

Confronted by this ingeniously set trap, Jesus did not challenge the severity of the law. As Jean Lasserre brings out,

> He confirms the condemnation of the woman to death: "He that is without sin among you, let him cast the first stone at her." He definitely cannot be made to say the opposite of the Law, He confirms the death penalty and apparently its legitimacy.... But He discreetly introduces a new clause, in the name of common sense and equity, for it would indeed be inequitable that a man worthy of death should condemn anyone else to death.[2]

With the requirement that a prosecutor/executioner be without sin, he struck away all basis for their (or any human) prosecution. The Divider (biblically judgment is division) did not prosecute even the prosecutors; he exposed them—to themselves. They fled away from the exposure, and in doing so gave an intimation of the dreadful possibility of fleeing at the End.

Jesus, the sinless Agent of God's severity and mercy, looked up at the woman: "Neither do I condemn you; go, and do not sin again." The One who could have hurled the first stone communicated to her instead: "I receive you. Turn from ruin. Enter life." This was exposure too, exposure experienced as irradiation by the Light. Thus there was the *dividing,* the contrasting two-sidedness of God's judgment: His rescuing from ruin—His conceding to a person's rejection of that rescue. Any contemplation of God's judgment could hardly do better than to begin with this story.

Those who give themselves to the Cold War assume a stance comparable to the one taken by the prosecuting scribes and Pharisees. Only the "righteous" dare pass the death sentence of nuclear (or any modern) war on enemy multitudes "caught in the very act of" despicable wickedness (Jn. 8:4 JB). Cold War prosecution coincides with mass sentencing and presses toward hot war execution. Only those who see themselves as hallowed by a collective right understood as absolute, or at least as absolutely determinative, can proceed to build nuclear guillotines set to swing down through entire populations. *Overkill* was an attitude before it became a technological achievement.

Revelation 12 pictures war raging in heaven until "the great dragon was thrown down, that ancient serpent, who is called the Devil and Satan, the deceiver of the whole world." And the cry of triumph rings out that God's Kingdom has come, "for the accuser of our brethren has been thrown down, who accuses them day and night before our God" (vs. 9,10). The prosecutor banished from heaven's throneroom! But how can earth contain his energies? Though this imagery may seem weird and remote to us, those energies of prosecution rage and reverberate through history. If there is such surging power in the malice of a single individual (something we have each experienced as subject and as object), what colossal power toward destruction there must be in the collective malice of hundreds of millions of people. In a more monolithic way than ever before, the prosecutor is incarnate in the cold-warring masses and material stockpiling of nuclear arms. That prosecutor God banished from His presence. If in private or global cold wars, we unwittingly align ourselves with him as his underlings, we will find that banishment coming upon us as well.

Cold warriors do not need to see their side or themselves as perfect or without blemish, but rather as constituting a collective right so unquestionable that all those caught in the evil of opposing it are justly to be condemned. The men who dragged the adulteress to Jesus would hardly have asserted that they were perfectly good and she totally wicked. But their collective judicial righteousness gave them such a sense of their own goodness confronting evil that they felt no hesitation to pick up stones. And so it is with those who aim missiles.

There are astute theological apologies for the military which, in rejecting this black-white thinking, solemnly confess the sin of their own side, but at the same time their proclamation of their country's relative righteousness proves nearly as serviceable for warring and cold-warring as the less subtle black-white thinking they rejected. These apologies lie in a continuum with the cruder attitudes. The bright gray versus dark gray has the same function for thoughtful warriors that white versus black has for the unthoughtful. If, for the thoughtful, the difference between the two sides is not absolute, it is nonetheless absolutely determinative for policy and provides grounds enough for the same sentence.

The Cold War, however, is readiness to execute coupled with stay of execution. The death sentence is held back but not commuted (as is evident from continued possession of the weapons); progressive preparations for carrying out the sentence are countermanded by successive stays of execution thus giving those who grant them the appearance of magisterial grace. In the East-West struggle this apparent demonstration of clemency confirms the sense of collective goodness and righteousness which undergirds the readiness to execute: we do not want to annihilate the other side; we would be delighted if the nuclear penitentiary turns out indeed to be a reformatory and the execution never needs to be carried out. But even in periods of so-called *detente* when Cold War passions have to some degree subsided, the earlier prosecution and verdict still dictate the roles of the executioners and the condemned.

Those scribes and Pharisees threw out their shrewdly conceived challenge to Jesus: how could he render a verdict contrary to theirs? Cold-warring protagonists, especially in the West, still do that. His response remains the same: "Let him who is without sin among you be the first" to proceed with what you are so intent on. But the current protagonists, unlike their predecessors, fail to hear his words, and so another saying of Jesus emerges to sum up the present and future of the Cold War: "With the judgment you pronounce you will be judged, and the measure you give will be the measure you get" (Mt. 7:2).

"The wages of sin is death" (Rom. 6:23); and one dimension of the judgment upon my sin is that my life can be crushed or extinguished by those I am in conflict with, by those who might presume to render and execute that judgment. I have sinned, and my life is laid open to death and killing. But no human being nor any collectivity has been appointed as paymaster of those wages. The One who could have qualified as paymaster took to himself the whole infernal payroll. Jesus told his antagonists, "Do not think that I shall accuse you to the Father" (Jn. 5:45). The single righteous One, instead of becoming Prosecutor-Messiah as he was tempted to do in the desert and again in Gethsemane, laid his life open to death by execution. My life is inevitably laid open in spite of whatever defenses I turn to. With him I can choose to lay it open.

* * *

The deepest source of our fear of being prosecuted lies in the fact that all prosecution intimates the ultimate threat, God's possible final No to any one of us. This fear is not well understood. As long as we refuse to face that worst threat we shall never come to discover that it has been overcome by God's Yes to us in Jesus Christ, and we shall continue to be caught up in the escalating reciprocities of human prosecution. We try to fend off in the lesser threats that most terrible one, which, even if quite unrecognized, is still vaguely sensed. Yet this continued compensatory fending off by prosecution, the result of a deafness to God's Yes, is the only thing that can finalize God's No to a person—which is in fact merely His conceding to a person's final No to Him. The sin which cannot be forgiven is the unyielding prosecution of the very Spirit of God (Mk. 3:28–30 and parallels).

When someone praises another person, the person complimented will typically feel glad but along with this, might think, "That's beyond what I deserve; I'm quite unworthy of such an appraisal." We often express our hesitation about praise that has been offered us. We so long for it; yet when we receive the opposite of prosecution, there comes the unreasoned, spontaneous sense that it doesn't really fit. That experience is parallel to the utterly crucial response to God's Yes to us in Jesus Christ: we know that He considers us to be much better than we sense ourselves to be now. Within the new life of union with Jesus Christ, God's affirming appraisal of us brings us to recognize, as no condemnation could, what is not yet right in us; but this recognition makes way for a joyful hopefulness and further turning because of God's declared intent for us. We can live in the splendor of His Yes only when it is counterpointed for us by the No to much of what we have been. The No is heard as a result of His Yes or as prelude that impels us to listen attentively for His Yes.

Chapter 4

HITLER AND THE WOMAN
CAUGHT IN ADULTERY

> In the kind of world that I see in history there is one sin that locks
> people up in all their other sins, and fastens men and nations more
> tightly than ever in their predicaments—...namely the sin of self-
> righteousness.[1]
>
> *Herbert Butterfield*

For vast numbers of people in the twentieth century Adolf Hitler has
functioned as the equivalent of the woman caught in adultery for the
Pharisees and doctors of the law: a case of human depravity so gross
that one's sense of righteousness is powerfully bolstered when con-
trasted to it. The search for such cases begins locally, and in every
locality those who seek find. The search culminates in the identification of global villains who, as we point at them, provide strong
reassurance of our contrasting goodness.

For Western societies and groups within them there has in recent
decades been a succession of villains: fascist leaders, communist heads
of state, terrorists, Third World dictators with the grimmest atrocity
records. But looming larger than all these is Adolf Hitler. No other
person who ever lived has been so universally and totally condemned
as the supreme example of evil. In the closing months of World War II
the biggest onrush of military might in history converged toward
Hitler. This drive was infused with the greatest surge of condemnation and hate ever directed against a single human being.

The most pernicious effect of Hitler's career and the Nazism
centered in him has probably been the tremendous impetus given to
collective and individual self-righteousness in the Allied countries. It
has seemed so clearly a matter of the good cause combatting the evil
cause. With the sins of Hitler and the Nazis so brazen, horrifying, and,
in the end, undefended, all wickedness on the other side could, in the
standard illogic of conflict, be taken as confirmation of the goodness of

the victorious side (though this self-confirmation soon split again between the new power blocks).

I do not intend to provide here an apology for Adolf Hitler or a revisionist assessment of his political career.[2] Rather I want to challenge the assumption that there is a sharp discontinuity between who we are and who Adolf Hitler was, and the parallel assumption of discontinuity between our particular society and Nazi Germany. It is crucial for us to recognize not only the continuity between the darkness deep in each of us and the darkness in Hitler, but also a continuity between positive impulses and longings within us and those, even if to a large extent atrophied, within Hitler.

The evidence that substantiates this dark continuity is manifold: many of the experimental findings of contemporary psychological studies of aggression and violence; any introspection which owns up to lethal sentiments, murderous fantasies, and racist presumptions within us; the final stages of World War II in Europe during which the Allied nations outdid the Axis powers in unleashing violence; the prevailing popular attitudes in Allied countries toward the Nazis then and now. The attitude that Hitler and those around him were so wicked that they simply had to be done away with, was identical with the darkness that was being combatted: a readiness to do away with those seen as enemies, a driving need to annihilate those reckoned unworthy to live.

It is most of all in the scriptural witness that we are shown the nature of this dark continuity. Jesus said, "If you then, who are evil..." (Mt. 7:11): not our cherished dichotomy between the righteous and the wicked. Paul in Romans 5:12–21 pictures the reign of sin and death over the human race as a corporate unity. We have each been subject to that reign. But the most revealing passage is again the story of the woman caught in the act of adultery. The Pharisees and doctors of the law could come as they did because they recognized no continuity between who they had been and were and the publicly exposed adulteress. Jesus, moving to save the woman from execution, sought also to save her accusers from perdition and to bring them to a recognition of this continuity. It may be that most or even all of the accusers had not committed adultery as a physical act. But he who in the Sermon on the Mount probed into the depths from which such acts emerge was doing the same here. He wanted to express to his antagonists that a conspicuous example of wrongdoing, rather than reinforcing an exultant self-righteousness, was to bring awareness of the sin common to all human beings and of the shared need for forgiveness and conversion.

The implications of this incident relate directly to our attitudes toward Hitler and other global villains. If much of the prevailing significance of Hitler and comparable persons corresponds to that of the adulteress in the minds of her accusers, we too, confronted by Jesus, must recognize our corporate bond with Adolf Hitler. He too was a human being, formed in our common humanity. He had been a child on his mother's lap and "a boy playing in a field."[3] There came for him that terrible impinging drivenness and his own dark yielding. When I see the sinister extreme to which Hitler went, I am jarred into recognizing, in my own worst impulses, fantasies, and vagrant thoughts, a largely hidden darkness contiguous to his. I am in jeopardy. There but for the grace of God, absence of comparable drivenness, and lack of means, go I.

We need to recognize that the strong tendency to see just one or a few as *the* perpetrators of vast crimes—Hitler, Stalin, Nixon—is the attempt to put the locus of wickedness and guilt at a further remove from our common humanity. Historically there has always been the complicity of the many, the complicity of most. And any who resist one complicity fall (with perhaps occasional exceptions) into another.

As for the continuity between the underside of the United States and Nazi Germany, American and Nazi racism proceeded side by side right through those war years, though the Nazi implementation was far grimmer. What the United States—and each of us in varying degrees—wrought in Indochina issued out of a blood relationship with the Nazis. Many other parallels could be pointed out; most nations and ethnic groups have perpetrated huge atrocities, if not in this era, then in an earlier one.

Terrorists in sensational, episodic fashion produce the same pernicious effect as Hitler: all attention is directed to the flagrant inhumanity of a few, and virtually none is left over for discerning inhumanity anywhere else. When several terrorists, holding a planeload of people as hostages, capture national and international attention, people hardly recognize that this in essence is a small-scale parallel to the nuclear terrorism practiced by the superpowers—with overriding popular assent.

When we recognize the continuity that exists between us and the most violent of persons or groups, we turn away from all readiness to go to war, for we can no longer claim a superior rightness which would legitimate our fighting, and we come to discern a worse danger than any which an adversary may pose for us. In Adolf Hitler and those around him, including the German people as a whole, we can see the awesome dynamism of evil, its horrendous power to drive individuals and peoples to perform ghastly inhumanities. We can see the dehumanizing drivenness pointed to in Jesus' warning, "Every one who commits sin is a slave to sin" (Jn. 8:34). But if we sense that dark continuity and our comparable jeopardy, individually and collectively, we must say a total No to war. If we do not, we come inevitably under the domination of that terrible dynamism. This has plainly happened for the Allied countries in World War II and in their policies leading to the nuclear arms buildup.

Jesus said in one of his most drastic images, "If your right eye causes you to sin, pluck it out and throw it away; it is better that you lose one of your members than that your whole body be thrown into hell" (Mt. 5:29). As we sense the incipient dynamism of sin within ourselves, we must, rather than yielding any further, make the most determined move imaginable for breaking with it. It can be seen throughout our world how much that call and warning of Jesus applies to readiness for war: Where there is not the determined plucking out of the eye that looks, however hesitatingly, toward killing, the whole person and the whole society are plunged toward the inferno of thermonuclear murdering and being murdered.

Theologians who have reiterated a just war or a war-of-liberation position have not adequately reckoned with this dynamism. For them a limited sinning (for which grace abounds) is permissible when a preponderantly good outcome is to be expected. Such positions have often been elaborated in the context of declaring with great emphasis the sin and guilt of all human beings. Because the sin and guilt are so encompassing, it is supposedly necessary, proper, and forgivable to add to them at times by going to war. Such positions are possible only for those who have no real comprehension of the biblical understanding that in sin and sinning a mighty dynamism strives for total dominion over those who in any way choose to commit sin and that God's grace moves not only to blot out guilt but, even more crucial, to hurl back that dominion. The history of our century, probably more than that of any other, corroborates the biblical awareness of sin's dynamism. Jesus said to the adulteress, "Go, and do not sin again." Only as we strive to hear and obey that directive with regard to our readiness to kill, can we be freed from this aspect of sin's dominion.

A prominent American clergyman asked me once, "What's the matter? Are you afraid of getting a little blood on your hands?" I *am* — not because I'm so good, but precisely because I'm not. I am in jeopardy, exposed before the power of evil impinging upon me and lurking within me; the little blood on my hands would inevitably become much, much blood. I can acknowledge a continuity in the depths between myself and that clergyman and still recognize that the dynamism toward the vast shedding of blood was manifested when he gave the dedicatory prayer at the launching of a nuclear submarine with the potential for killing more human beings than the six million Jews killed in the Nazi death camps.

All the desolation of nature, the razing of cities, the slaughter of millions of human beings carried out by Nazi Germany was only a limited foreshadowing of the desolating, razing, annihilating which the peoples of West and East are prepared to carry out. During years of residence in West Germany, I often wondered how decent, good-hearted Germans could have gone along with Nazism. Some of the answer comes through asking the same question about Americans (including myself at a certain level) and nuclear weapons. There is the drivenness of both those who lead and those who are led; fear of determined adversaries; emptiness within individual and society; the lure of power; the drive to be center of the universe; the infernal darkness within, which the Dark Powers from without align with themselves. The Yes to nuclear weapons by good-hearted Americans who are distraught by the death of a pet and full of altruism toward neighbors recapitulates that earlier yielding to the Dark Powers by Adolf Hitler and those who moved in concert with him.

When there is a keen awareness of that dark continuity, there can rightfully be a discernment of discontinuity. In John 7:53–8:11 there is, looming larger than shared human sinfulness, a great division: on the one hand the woman faced Jesus, accepted forgiveness, was ready to be drawn into transformed living, and on the other the Pharisees and doctors of the law walked away from Jesus into the solitude of their jolted but persisting self-sufficiency. The woman still had in common with them that underlying corporateness of human frailty and sinning which drags us down into death; but unlike them she was now being drawn toward a higher corporateness, a vital union with the Lord of Life and those who are his.

Here, though, was no inverted dichotomy between the righteous and the wicked, but rather the contrast of countermovements: from lostness into Life; and from lostness into death. Grounded in this contrast is the great and highly significant difference between a Martin Niemöller and an Adolf Hitler: not the difference between a wonderfully good man and a supremely wicked man, but that between one who was being drawn out of lostness into Life and one who was driven into an ever greater extremity of lostness. We dare not point the finger or clench the stone, but we must point to these immensely contrasting countermovements.

With regard to having committed adultery—if not physically, then in the underworld of lust—the woman and her accusers were on common ground. With regard to annihilating millions—if not physically, then in the underworld of lethal thoughts—we each are on common ground with Adolf Hitler. Only as we turn to Jesus, do we find ourselves on new and higher ground. But must not this transposition bring with it the determined relinquishment of all lethal projectiles (from thoughts to ICBM's) held in readiness over against the "unrighteous"? Without that relinquishment we cannot really be turned toward Jesus, and only through that steadfast turning can there come the continued letting go.

"But what about Hitler?" is often put as the weightiest possible argument against Christian pacifism. If, however, we recognize the dark continuity between him and us, we find ourselves without a righteousness that could give us the prerogative to execute the unrighteous. And with a sense of sin's fearful dynamism, we know that our opposition to a tyrant is to be in continuity, not with the dynamism that compels tyranny, but with the transforming dynamism that is God's grace.

In connection with all this, I acknowledge my own tendency to make of my No to war and my pacifism the key confirmation of my righteousness over against the unrighteousness of those who align themselves with or assent to the military. This tendency can disfigure me as it has often disfigured anti-war and peace movements. I need to be reminded again and again of the dark continuity between me and the men in the Pentagon, between me and the church people who bless the cursed weapons. Because that darkness lurks also in me, I am, like them, in jeopardy—most of all before God. There is for me no achieved righteousness of my own for countering that peril. There is only the One who, as in that Temple scene, interposes himself between me and the onslaught of doom and is leading me with others out of it. The more I sense the oneness of our jeopardy, the better I can point the unlikeminded to the Christ who clarifies what the jeopardy is and shields us from it.

Chapter 5

THE SOURCE OF KILLING

The root cause for murder is most significantly pointed to by Jesus in his confrontation with the Jews of the Jerusalem establishment in the Temple, recorded in John 8:12–59. We need to look closely at the central portion of that account.

> They answered, "We are descended from Abraham and we have never been the slaves of anyone, what do you mean, 'You will be made free?'" Jesus replied:
>
> *"I tell you most solemnly,*
> *everyone who commits sin is a slave.*
> *Now the slave's place in the house is not assured,*
> *but the son's place is assured.*
> *So if the Son makes you free,*
> *you will be free indeed.*
> *I know that you are descended from Abraham;*
> *but in spite of that you want to kill me*
> *because nothing I say has penetrated into you.*
> *What I, for my part, speak of*
> *is what I have seen with my Father;*
> *but you, you put into action*
> *the lessons learned from your father."*
>
> They repeated, "Our father is Abraham." Jesus said to them:
> *"If you were Abraham's children,*
> *you would do as Abraham did.*
> *As it is, you want to kill me*
> *when I tell you the truth*
> *as I have learned it from God;*
> *that is not what Abraham did.*
> *What you are doing is what your father does."*
>
> "We were not born of prostitution," they went on, "we have one father: God." Jesus answered:
> *"If God were your father, you would love me,*
> *since I have come here from God; yes, I have come from him;*

24

not that I came because I chose,
no, I was sent, and by him.
Do you know why you cannot take in what I say?
It is because you are unable to understand my language.
The devil is your father,
and you prefer to do
what your father wants.
He was a murderer from the start;
he was never grounded in the truth;
there is no truth in him at all:
when he lies
he is drawing on his own store,
because he is a liar, and the father of lies.

(Jn. 8:33–44 JB)

Jesus uses the word "murderer" (literally "manslayer") as primary designation for the devil. As a further explanatory designation he uses "liar"—a point that is given fivefold repetition. It is as liar, as the subverter of God's truth, that the devil became and remains the murderer. He was the father of Cain and Cain's deed (1 Jn. 3:12). But before that he brought death upon the first human beings by seducing them into acceptance of his lies: "Did God really say?...No! You will not die!...You will be like gods" (Gen. 3:1,4,5 JB). And he sought to make conclusive his original triumph over humanity when he approached Jesus in the desert with a reformulation of the same threefold lie—asking Jesus if God really named him as His Son; urging Jesus to cast himself down as he would not die; tempting him to assume godlike power over mankind and history (Mt. 4:1–11).

From Genesis 3 through the Gospel of John, the powerful, seductive lie subverts God's truth and brings killing and death. Echoes of Genesis 3 and 4 fill John 8.

"Did God really say?" The Jewish religionists confronting Jesus refused to recognize in him the authority of God's truth: Could the God of Israel possibly be speaking through such a fellow?

Jesus warned them,

You will die in your sins.
Yes, if you do not believe that I am He,
you will die in your sins.

(Jn. 8:24 JB)

On other occasions he made explicit his certainty that their rejection of him would lead inevitably to their mass slaughter by the Romans. But *"No! You will not die!"* They refused to heed Jesus' warning; such would not happen to them individually or collectively.

"You will be like gods (God)." Theirs was a vaunted ethnic superiority, an effortful knowledge of their own Godlike goodness in contrast to the evil of outgroups (including the local proletarian riff-raff—Jn. 7:49). Within this context there emerged the lure of messianic glory and sovereignty to be seized by the nation—and also the drive to do away with one who, rather than mobilizing and leading them in a still fuller savoring of the threefold lie, challenged all their presumption.

These aspects of the primeval lie stand out in all nationalism, militarism, and war making, but now climactically in the nuclear arms buildup. As Richard J. Barnet has well pointed out, "The very meaning of sovereignty which states guard so jealously is the magical power to decide what is or is not a crime."[1] In that comes the frontal countering of God's rule.

Many christendom/post-christendom ethicists and church people have been taken in by the lie: Jesus could not have meant what he said in Matthew 5 about our responsibility to enemy groups. Only by the realism of leaving aside these obviously impractical commands can we enjoy sovereignty, freedom, and the superior position that is ours. Only by taking the sword (now a huge arsenal of hydrogen bombs) can we survive. We shall not die, we shall not go under, for the military might which has brought us through till now and the Deity, duly impressed with our rightness, can be depended on to bring us through from here on. Ours is a goodness adequate for our sovereign pinnacle position, a goodness sufficient for our wielding superhuman powers.

In Genesis 3 and John 8 the grim result of the choice to be "like gods, knowing good and evil" is being a slave under the domination of evil. In the endless proliferation of nuclear weapons the slavery that results is more dramatically exemplified than perhaps ever before in history. Most Americans, like the Jews in the Gospel passage, exult in their "freedom"; but their present readiness to kill discloses their enslavement. Now, too, as in Genesis 3 and John 8 an inner dying propels us toward the terminal triumph of death.

The overarching deception, "No! You will not die!" has not yet for nuclear protagonists met the climactic refutation.[2] But to those ensnared in nuclear "defense" the Risen Jesus says quite simply, "If you do not believe that I am He, you will die in your sins." In the doing (much of it already done) and in the result a nuclear world war would be the most extreme reenactment of the Fall. On the day of that

Adamic transgression we would surely die—immediately or in the pervasive awesomeness of an immense, accelerated dying. Out of even the vestigial garden we would be driven, and the ever-widening swath of a radioactive sword would bar any return.

The establishment Jews of John 8 insisted on finding their righteousness in their own national group as "children of Abraham." It was precisely by doing this that they set themselves against Jesus and his righteousness. In that presumption they moved to kill the One who called it into question. They tried to stone him at the close of this confrontation and again in John 10:31. Soon after that they were successful in arranging to have him executed.[3]

The underside to that presumption, something that runs through the John 8 narrative, is clearly delineated in 1 John 3:12: We are not to be "like Cain who was of the evil one and murdered his brother. And why did he murder him? Because his own deeds were evil and his brother's righteous." Underneath that presumption by the establishment Jews was a most vigorously repressed awareness of an unrighteousness in themselves which negated their presumption. This repression and concealment were terribly threatened by the discernment, rebukes, and righteousness of Jesus. Like Cain they moved to do away with a brother whose contrasting righteousness they could not stand. That readiness to kill and the killing itself, though intended as uttermost defense of their claim, was the full disclosure of the concealed evil within them (and the nation) and the total refutation of their claim.

In John 8 the central opposing themes of the New Testament—being right by virtue of ethnic descent or being made right by turning to Jesus—come into starker juxtaposition than even in the letters of Paul; and collective "rightness"—climactic form of the threefold lie in Genesis 3—veers toward its culminating expression in the murder of the Messiah.

Out of the same stance came the Jewish persecution of the Early Church, as is so clear in Acts 21 and 22. Paul, in the custody of Roman soldiers who had just saved him from death at the hands of a Jerusalem mob, was able to speak to that mob until he spoke the word *Gentiles;* "then they lifted up their voices and said, 'Away with such a fellow from the earth! For he ought not to live!'" (Acts 22:22). Jesus and his early followers decisively rejected the prevailing in-group presumption of the Jews who saw themselves over against the outgroup; that stand was seen as intolerable.

All this has, through history, its continual recapitulations as the delusion of rightness in any collectivity affords main justification for violence and war.

Individuals, hard-pressed and faltering in solitary pursuit of self-justification and superiority, can align themselves with the presumed righteousness and superiority of their nation state. The collective presumption is not so slight and vulnerable as the private one. Joining in the collective presumption provides corroboration, reinforcement, and anchorage for each individual.

Collective "righteousness" is fabricated as broad cover over the sinkhole of social and individual evil. So great is the need people have to share in this "rightness" that any evidence that detracts from it generally goes unnoticed. Immense effort is required to maintain such a lie, and the most feverish aspect of that effort is the countering of the threat posed by those who deny and reject it. Underneath is an insecurity and unrighteousness so great that communists or capitalists (or their counterparts in other cold or hot wars) can be fill-ins for Abel or Jesus as most extreme threats to the presumed "rightness." Fearfulness before God (Gen. 3:10) in those who have swallowed the lie becomes fear and hatred of any who will not confirm the lie (Gen. 4:5).

In the global cold-warring of our time these dynamisms reach unprecedented proportions: the collective "rightness" that divides the whole of humanity into friends or enemies and justifies preparations for mass slaughter on an unimaginable scale; the frantic, collective self-exaltation that covers the abyss disclosed in the readiness for that killing; the reciprocity of fear and hatred in those who counter one version of the lie with another.

What Jacques Ellul has stated as the fifth law of violence is followed both individually and collectively: "the man who uses violence always tries to justify both it and himself."[4] In Western history the most serviceable means for justification has been provided by the tradition of the just war in both Rome and christendom.

A special irony with regard to the just war doctrine is that those who have most emphatically echoed Paul's (and Jesus') indictment of humankind as sinful have typically taken the lead in exempting their own group from that indictment. Churches, while proclaiming for individual sinners justification through faith in Jesus, have stood in solidarity with the "rightness" of their particular collectivity and thus had justification for sanctifying the status quo and going to war. Protestant state churches or the American transmutations have tended to be a bundling together of justified sinners, with little emergence of the new corporateness God creates—thus the fatefully unanswered yearning for a corporately shared righteousness and salvation.

Any just war stance, whether in the pew or from behind seminary lecterns, amounts to a negation of justification for the unrighteous through faith in Jesus Christ. As with the establishment Jews of John 8, to align oneself with a collective "righteousness" in its readiness to kill and its killing is (at least on that side of things) to reject Jesus in his Lordship and Jesus as the One through whom alone we are made right. And as in John 8, all present Cold War "rightness" and readiness to kill are delusion, adherence to the primeval liar, and progression into slaying the unrecognized Messiah: "You want to kill me because nothing I say has penetrated into you."

Individually or corporately, the stance of the tax collector, "God, be merciful to me a sinner!" (Lk. 18:13),[5] when infused with biblical readiness to turn fully around, *metanoia*, eliminates all basis for going to war.

In the United States the God-and-country patriotism that sees America as implicitly or explicitly the New Israel lies in continuity with the collective presumption that the New Testament writers recorded and struggled against. Our attempt to counter this, as we find it in ourselves and in fellow believers, can be modeled on the decisiveness with which Jesus and Paul countered the Judaic boasting of their period. At stake is the gospel of salvation through Jesus alone.

Chapter 6

"THEY DO NOT KNOW WHAT THEY ARE DOING"

One of the greatest deficiencies of our time is the failure of the imagination or the intellect to bring home to itself the portentous character of human sin.[1]

Herbert Butterfield

After examining other Old Testament passages where the phrase, "good and evil," occurs, Gerhard von Rad comments on the serpent's promise in Genesis 3:5, "you will be like God, knowing good and evil":

"Good and evil" is therefore a formal way of saying what we mean by our colorless "everything"; and here too one must take it in its meaning as far as possible. The fascination of this statement is in its lack of restriction, its intangibleness; it is intentionally mysterious, and after it has brought the thoughts of man into a definite direction, it is again open on all sides and gives room to all whispering secret fantasies. What the serpent's insinuation means is the possibility of an extension of human existence beyond the limits set for it by God at creation, an increase of life not only in the sense of pure intellectual enrichment but also of familiarity with, and power over, mysteries that lie beyond man. That the narrative sees man's fall, his actual separation from God, occurring again and again in *this* area (and not, for example, as a plunge into moral evil, into the subhuman!), i.e., in what we call Titanism, man's *hubris*—this is truly one of its most significant affirmations.[2]

A boundary was set by God in his movement toward man; the Edenic prohibition was an expression of this. And fellow human beings constitute limits. These bounds, though, are not constrictive barriers but frontiers where human beings are to meet God and one another. The absurd desire to have no boundaries is pursued by turning away from those who constitute them.

For Adam and Eve there was no understanding that this boundlessness could only mean a plunge into the abyss. For the boundary corresponded to the form given man, and to break through this boundary was inevitably to burst that form, and with it came a plummeting as grain pours out through a torn hole in a sack. What they hoped would be the attainment of godlike stature proved to be only this pathetic effusion.

They hoped for a new existence where there would be no more limit. But the God-given limit they negated became their all-negating limit of death. To move into the center and press beyond God's bound into the unknown was to discover only death in its infinitude. As God had warned, death did come in the day they transgressed an inner death presaging the ultimate physical one. They had hoped for a new godlike knowledge, but came instead into a pitiful unknowing. As the mystery of physical death shuts off our comprehension, so too does this inner death.

With the spilling of Abel's blood came the further spilling out of Cain's humanity. When Yahweh asked Cain, "Where is Abel your brother?," and Cain replied, "I do not know," there was in that first affirmation of human ignorance unintended truth alongside the lie. Cain had savored the sundering of the limit. He had experienced an orgiastic wielding of boundless power. He had grasped the weapon but could not grasp the fact. Through his own inner dying he was deaf before to the plea inherent in Abel's humanity, so close to his own, and afterward to the cry of his blood. The incomprehensibility of his brother's death was a mockery of the promise of godlike knowledge and power.

When God asks, "What have you done?," He who did comprehend what had been done indicates His anguish at the horror of it. And He calls Cain out of his ignorance into at least some knowledge.

It was in the midst of the agony of the crucifixion that Jesus said, "Father, forgive them; they do not know what they are doing" (Lk. 23:34 JB). In what ways did they not know? Both the Jewish governing elite and the Jerusalem populace did not recognize Jesus as God's Messiah; they did not see in him the fulfilment of the Old Testament prophecies, and through this failure they brought on the climactic fulfilment of those prophecies (Peter in Acts 3:17–18; Paul in Acts 13:27). They did not at all understand what type of Messiah God had promised and sent. Least of all did they know that the one being crucified was God's Son, the eternal Word of the Father in human form. But closely related to and underlying that was a more elemental blindness: lack of feeling for a fellow human being; a refusal to see him, if not as Messiah, then at least as a brother. Failure to recognize a brother goes with failure to recognize God, as surely as Jesus' second commandment goes with the first. The ruling elite, the soldiers, and, to a lesser extent, the participating populace were hardened to the horror of torture and killing there or anywhere.

"Father, forgive them; they do not know what they are doing." The salvation of all mankind hinged on those words of Jesus and what lay behind them. Jesus was not seeking to persuade the Father. His prayer expressed and brought toward realization his Father's intent. The decisive factor in the prospect of forgiveness for the crucifiers was not their ignorance but rather the character of Jesus and thus of the Father: his acceptance of the worst his enemies could do to him, his refusal to retaliate, his compassion for them in their blindness.

These words of Jesus were the utter opposite of all prosecution. His crucifiers—and no line divides the race into those who were and those who were not—had some knowledge of and guilt for what they did. ("This is the heir; come, let us kill him, and the inheritance will be ours"—Mk. 12:7). There was guilt for the blindness, the refusal to know. If the crucifiers rather than initiating, were being driven by the infernal powers, they at least acted in complicity with those powers. (These aspects had been laid bare in the John 8 confrontation.) Jesus pointed not to these dimensions but rather to what within the others intimated that there could be a turn back from the terrible wrong and a restoration of relationship. Source for the forgiving was the readiness of Jesus and the Father to reach out in love to the crucifiers; but that forgiveness could be consummated only if accepted. With the words, "they do not know what they are doing," Jesus looks in hope toward those others as redeemable: their unknowing, *agnosia*, leaves open the prospect that the divine initiative will triumph in spite of everything that weighs so heavily against this possibility.

I say something that deeply hurts a friend. The person afterward says to me, "You were under a lot of pressure just then," or "I know that wasn't really what you wanted to say to me." And I find myself freed from the need to excuse or justify myself. My friend has not provided me with justification or even quite with excuse, but with a way back. Out of the highly complicated mix of who I am and thus the specific mix that went into that affront, my friend has focused not on my guilt or on my perversity as the totality of who I am, but has recognized a faltering better part of me and has reached out to reassure me that there is for me a way back from a wrong into a healed relationship. This prayer of Jesus comes to us in much the same way. The words are meant for us to overhear. We need no longer pathetically defend our behavior, for the One on whom all depends takes our side. We need only accept him in his coming to us to give us a way back.

Peter in his second sermon to a Jerusalem multitude transposed Jesus' prayer into an appeal to them: "And now, brethren, I know that you acted in ignorance, as did also your rulers. But what God foretold by the mouth of all the prophets, that his Christ should suffer, he thus fulfilled. Repent therefore, and turn again, that your sins may be blotted out" (Acts 3:17–19). From Jesus and his messengers comes not prosecution but a way back.

Full knowledge of evil can be had, not through the doing of it (inner dying prevents that), but through rejection of its appeal and the willingness to give oneself as its victim. Jesus' knowledge of evil, which developed decisively in the temptations, reached its fullness on the cross. In the murder of the God-Man, man achieved the most extreme obliteration of all boundaries with a resultant fullest extremity of unknowing; simultaneously for God, it was the most penetrating moment of knowledge about man.

In these biblical motifs nuclear weapons and nuclear war receive explication.

The scene just before the first atomic explosion at Alamogordo, New Mexico, in July 1945—the test had been given the code name "Trinity"—was described like this in a letter from Brigadier General Thomas F. Farrell to President Truman in Potsdam:

> The scientists felt that their figuring must be right and that the bomb had to go off, but there was in everyone's mind a strong measure of doubt. The feeling of many could be expressed by, "Lord, I believe; help Thou my unbelief." We were reaching into the unknown and we did not know what might come of it.[3]

As Robert Oppenheimer watched the dazzling reflection of that first atomic blast and then the rising fireball,

> a passage from the Bhagavad-Gita, the sacred epic of the Hindus, flashed into his mind

> *If the radiance of a thousand suns*
> *were to burst into the sky,*
> *that would be like*
> *the splendor of the Mighty One—*

Yet, when the sinister and gigantic cloud rose up in the far distance over Point Zero, he was reminded of another line from the same source:

I am become Death, the shatterer of worlds.

Sri Krishna, the Exalted One, lord of the fate of mortals, had uttered the phrase.[4]

There at the dawn of the nuclear era, Oppenheimer, amazed and confounded by this demonstration of godlike power, rightly sensed that it would prove to be for its human wielders the fateful dynamism that could ultimately bring their end.

The predominant attitude toward the scientists who produced the atomic bomb has been described like this:

The godlike magnitude of their performance had given them the standing of mythical figures, more than life size, in the imagination of the public. They were called titans and compared with Prometheus, who had challenged Zeus, the controller of the Fates. They were also called "Devil Gods."[5]

It needs to be recognized that the refugee physicists who played the decisive role in persuading the Franklin Roosevelt Administration to press for development of the atomic bomb were impelled mainly by the fear of Nazism and what such weapons in Hitler's hands could lead to. But then and ever since, fear has led to endeavors and achievements infused with the expansion of this dark Promethean impulse.

In *Brighter Than a Thousand Suns* Robert Jungk has given the title "For They Know Not What They Do" to the chapter on the Alamogordo explosion and the decision to drop the bomb on Japanese cities. This unknowing is very evident in accounts of the top decision-maker, President Harry Truman. When handed the bulletin that the bomb had been dropped on Hiroshima with "complete success," Truman "took a deep breath and said: 'Captain Graham, this is the greatest thing in history.'"[6]

The first human beings, as they grasped for the boundless, set a precedent for all their descendants. For what they did continues in what we all do. The persons who played key roles in the development of the first atomic weapons have set an analogous precedent for their contemporaries and those coming after. There was a high degree of historical appropriateness in the fact that the United States, in first producing those weapons, assumed this precedent-setting role for all nations. What D. W. Brogan has called "the illusion of American omnipotence"[7]—nurtured and bolstered by the expansion to the Pacific, a triumphant, proliferating technology, the spectacular productivity and standard of living, the absence until the second half of the twentieth century of national reversals and defeats common to other nations—provided the superlative context for that climactic delving into omnipotence.

As Sir Thomas Browne perceived, "Cain was not therefore the first Murderer, but Adam, who brought in death."[8] The developers of atomic weapons achieved immense concretized magnification of what Adam had done—and this prior to the Cainite strike at Hiroshima.

More than any other event in history the worldwide human experience of those August days in 1945 was a recapitulation of the primeval Fall. Here again we discern the lure of boundless power; the headiness that came with the assimilation of the forbidden, although at the same time sensing a vast, imminent threat; the effort expended in collective reassurances that with this too we could live, and that death wasn't to be the penalty after all. But there was probably in those first days clearer discernment within the unknowing than there has been anytime since. Adam understood more in the first evening after his disobedience than after years of inner dying.[9]

A failure of imagination with regard to nuclear weapons and nuclear war is often pointed to: the inability of the human mind to take in the magnitude of the physical destruction the bombs can produce, or the immense physical, mental, and social desolation that would overwhelm survivors, or the near certainty that any of us in the North Temperate Zone would be among those casualties. Extraordinary intellectual brilliance has gone into the design and the preparations for delivery of these weapons. In this dimension the serpent's promise of breaking through the bound into godlike knowledge and power has received horrific fulfilment. But dwarfing all this is death in its near-sovereign imminence, not only as close ahead but as hidden dominion within, impinging upon us all.

The one thing God and nuclear weapons have in common is magnitude beyond what human intellect and language can take in. God has entered into the bounds of human existence and concepts in such a way as to open that delimitedness out toward Him. But the inadequacy of words and images, even those intended to unmask the lie, confirms tightening constriction of this weaponry.

Failure of imagination results from more than the inherent limitations of the human mind. Simone Weil in her study of the Iliad wrote:

"Force is as pitiless to the man who possesses it, or thinks he does, as it is to its victims; the second it crushes, the first it intoxicates." Force has a "petrifactive quality." It changes a person into inert matter, a corpse, or into an abject slave or suppliant completely subject to the determinations of force; or it changes the wielder of force into an unfeeling, driven entity. Everyone who falls under the dominion of force undergoes the death of the soul, the change into a thing, a stone.[10]

In the nuclear arms race there has been the descent into ever greater drivenness, unreason, callousness, intoxication. Beyond the overstepped bound there is no bound, nothing on which to reestablish limits; thus the general failure of all disarmament or arms limitations talks and the amassing of still more preposterous numbers of nuclear weapons. "Since 1945, American and other diplomats have met at least 6,000 times to discuss disarmament and arms control, but not a single warhead has been destroyed as a result of all these meetings."[11]

For Americans this petrifaction by violence results from so much in the American past, from the inundation by the mass media (with everything from Mickey Mouse to auto races), from the web of lies centered in national "security." The color television coverage of the Indochina War demonstrated and deepened that petrifaction—a contemporary fulfilment of words Isaiah at his commissioning as prophet was told to say to the people: "see and see, but do not perceive" (Is. 6:9). As Simone Weil wrote, "If the existence of an enemy has made a soul destroy in itself the thing nature put there, then the only remedy the soul can imagine is the destruction of the enemy."[12] A killing within must necessarily precede a killing without.

Scottish churchman George MacLeod has written: "What upsets every scene, domestic or political, is not man's desire to be bad. So far I have never met a man who wanted to be bad. The mystery of man is that he is bad when he wants to be good."[13] Most murder, most slaughter of others, lies within that mystery; it is committed as an undesired deed. In the nuclear arms buildup the leaders and the led have wanted to be good. If certain persons and groups play the decisive roles in starting World War III, they too will almost certainly proceed with some idea that they are trying to do something good. The global drivenness toward the dreadful climax of human wickedness is suffused by this ineffectual longing to be good.

God's most direct word against all militarism and against all participation in the military was spoken by Jesus in Gethsemane during the violent commotion of his arrest: "Put your sword back into its place;

for all who take the sword will perish by the sword" (Mt. 26:52). Jesus' reason for sheathing the sword contains no implication that it is dependent on the special circumstances there in that garden. It is an insight about a universal constant in human affairs. Throughout history the rationale for resorting to weapons has been that of coming through, of *living*, in one sense or another. For Jesus that rationale is an illusion: to take up weapons is to perish.[14]

The Greek verb translated here as "will perish" in the warning, "for all who take the sword will perish by the sword," is generally understood in the sense of "will get killed, will die physically." Most of the more recent English translations have "will die." But if this is the only meaning the warning is clearly not true; many persons and groups who have taken the sword do not in turn get killed by others. The usual New Testament meaning of this Greek verb in the middle voice (when it does not mean "be lost") is "perish": the focus, rather than just on physical dying, is on the movement into perdition, ruin, destruction, in both the physical and spiritual sense. Jesus' statement is true only when we take the verb in its full meaning of *perish*; there seems no good reason for doing otherwise.

Many Christian martyrs met death by the sword but did not *perish* by the sword. Not all who take up weapons are killed by others; but for all who take them up there is a recoil, an inner petrifaction, which Simone Weil has so well described. Jesus calls his disciples away from that movement into perdition which is typically evidenced in getting killed but is much more encompassing.

For collectivities (and the "all"of the warning is more collective than individual) there does come sooner or later the outer catastrophic corroboration of the inner perdition. The crowd within earshot when Jesus spoke were people who had taken up weapons; their armed action was a step in a progression that reached its end in the destruction of Jerusalem in 70 A.D. The perdition Jesus warned against permeates the atmosphere of the current human situation— these days prior to holocaust. Biblically, the awesomeness of perdition lies in the human plunge away from God.

There is one who held out against the petrifying dominion of violence. He did not yield to the temptation to make use of violence; and even when violence was doing its uttermost against him, it could not do its worst. "When he suffered, he did not threaten; but he trusted to him who judges justly" (1 Pet. 2:23). He did not become an abject suppliant. He did not even accept the numbing drink of wine mixed with myrrh. Governmental violence could bring about the effusion of his blood but not of his being who he was. Precisely because he accepted the outer form of impotence and death, Jesus broke at that point their petrifying reign within. That triumph found its fulfilment in the act of the One who, judging justly, provided a way back for Jesus and for all those for whom he interceded.

One dimension of that way back is the readiness to share with Jesus outer impotence and inner triumph. That readiness, though accepted by some, remains nearly as obscure in the world as it was in 30 A.D. So it is that we would need to listen, even in the very midst of thermonuclear volleys for those words of Jesus, "Father, forgive them; they do not know what they are doing." For those who blundered into that ultimate war would not know the hundred-million fold agony of their victims, the immensity of the desolation and guilt even as it envelops them, or more profoundly the central Victim who suffers in the midst of the stricken multitudes. They have not recognized God's Messiah and have not turned to his way.

Blessed are those who on that day, if it comes, remember those words and know that forgiveness is offered even for this, that he gives a way back even out of this, that the One in whom the eternal Son trusts will undo even this seeming triumph of death.

Chapter 7

"WHAT HAVE YOU DONE?"

"It hasn't bothered me a bit."
A crewman in the bombing of Hiroshima

"In my dreams I often see women and children running in and out of fires. That isn't pleasant."
Claude Eatherly[1]

Michiko Ogino, a girl ten years old and 1.5 kilometers from hypocenter in Hiroshima on August 6, 1945, later wrote:

It was a clear day without a speck in the sky. I was playing house with my sisters upstairs.

Mother had gone to the field to get some eggplants. As she was going out, she told us:

"Make a fire in the clay charcoal stove at eleven." But we were so excited that, even when the clock struck eleven times, none of us stood up. We were totally absorbed in playing.

Casually I looked up at the window. Just at that moment, there was a lightning-like flash.

"Oh—" I said. My body staggered. The next moment, I was pinned under the house. I could not move at all. The harder I tried to escape, the more pain I felt. I had to keep still and watch for my chance. Then I saw my two elder sisters outside. I was so glad. In my joy I cried:

"Help me! Help me!"

They immediately came running and tried to pull me out. But the latticed bamboo which supported the mud wall separated us. Pulled or pushed, it could not be removed.

My eldest sister encouraged me in a faltering voice:

"Be patient, will you? Mother and Father will be back soon. I'll bring someone to help us. Understand?" She ran away.

A small portion of the outside world could be seen through the latticed bamboo. I stared at it with my eyes wide open, waiting for Mother and Father.

Some time later, my eldest sister came running with several sailors. I was rescued by their help.

39

Standing outside, I was astonished. Although it had been such a beautiful day, it was now a terrible day, with black clouds winding and wriggling all over the sky.

I tottered and tried to walk towards the air-raid shelter. Then a low cry came from under the house:

"Help me!—Somebody!"

It was the voice of my younger brother.

My eldest sister seemed to be the first one to notice his cry. She immediately went running to the spot and pulled him out after removing a lot of roof tiles.

Then, a baby's cry came from the opposite direction. It was the voice of my two-year-old sister, trapped by falling walls. I hurried to the spot and found her crying fiercely, her legs pinned under a huge beam.

Together with the sailors, we tried to remove it, but the beam would not move an inch. With pain in her squeezed legs, my sister was crying and wriggling, her arms floundering. What in the world should we do—?

The sailors began to give up.

"We cannot make it." Some of the neighbors came to ask for their help, and they went running away to the nearby crushed house to rescue other buried men. Only we children were left behind.

What in the world was Mother doing in the field? Please, please come back soon. Why didn't Father come back? My little sister's legs would be torn off—. I was completely at a loss, and the only thing I could do was to look around on my tiptoes.

I saw someone dashing towards us in the distance. Disheveled hair. A woman. Looked naked. A purple colored body. She called to us in a loud voice.

Oh my!—It was Mother.

"Mother—" we cried. We felt so reassured.

Here and there, the houses began to flame up.

One of our neighbors appeared from nowhere, and pulled the beam up with all his might and main, trying to remove it from across my sister's legs. But it remained as firm as a rock. He drew a deep breath of disappointment and said in a sincerely sorry tone:

"I'm sorry but we must give up." He bowed and went away.

A blaze came up quite nearby. Mother's face went ashy pale. Father had not come back yet. Mother was looking down at my little sister. Tiny eyes looked up from below. Mother's eyes looked around, investigating the way the beams were piled up.

Then Mother got into an opening left beneath the beam and, placing her right shoulder under a portion of it, bit her lower lip tightly.

"Uhhhhhh—"

She strained herself. Rattling sounds came out, and the beam was lifted a little. My little sister's legs were freed. My eldest sister quickly pulled her out. Mother came out with a leap and hugged her tightly to her breast.

After a while, as if we suddenly realized what had happened, we children burst out crying. At that, Mother squatted on the ground with an air of abstraction.

Then I realized for the first time how my mother looked. She had been hit by the blast as she was picking eggplants to feed us at lunch. She was almost naked. Her coat and trousers were burnt and torn to pieces. Her hair had turned to reddish-brown, and was shrunken and torn as if she had had too strong a permanent. She got burnt all over the body. Her skin was red and greasy. The skin of her right shoulder, the portion which bore and lifted the beam, was gone, revealing bare flesh, and scarlet blood which was constantly oozing out.

Mother fell exhausted on the ground. At that moment, Father ran staggering up to us. He had been seriously burned, too.

Mother began to feel pain. After groaning and struggling, she passed away that night.[2]

* * *

The child stirs faintly in his sleep as I watch from the doorway. Late in the night at least, his room is a peaceable kingdom. His hands are spread wide on the bed as if in benediction. A low breathing measures out the long pause in his play. Calm suffuses his face. This one, who when awake is already armed with his power stratagems, lies there now so frail and exposed.

Tonight no dream monster stalks him—but rather an actual one. He sleeps as part of the target area of at least one specific thermonuclear warhead mounted on a distant missile. Here he lies near the end of the computerized half-hour trajectory of that poised, leashed fury. He has already learned to aim with pointed finger and to deal with a succession of fingers aimed at him. But he does not understand that massed millions of fingers are pointed his direction, all of which converge into those few fingers deputized to send the targeted metallic ones hurtling toward him. It is by no means clear what he has done this time; but I can recognize, as I stand there, that the movement of a single hand on the other side of the planet would within minutes dissolve his sleep into annihilating fire. The invisible bow across the sky is not God's but man's, and after it, rather than before, would come the fateful rain.

That hand with such dreadful power belongs to a man, a man (and quite possibly a father) like myself—flesh and spirit, hopes and frustrations, guilt and love. He may pray at times to a sovereign Father as I do. But that man, Russian brother of mine, could with the touch of his fingers annihilate this sleeping child and a million others. He has no eyes to see them. He simply cannot know what he could so easily do. And only by a most difficult trajectory of thought do I discover him.

In Eastern Europe also I have on occasion watched a little boy sleeping and could conceive a United States' warhead and missileman with the same relation to him as that Soviet warhead and missileman have to the child of mine. Children of the Warsaw Pact countries are in no less jeopardy than our own.

Perhaps the most significant proposal for preventing World War III, if there is the persisting unwillingness to move toward general disarmament, is a little noticed one made by W. H. Ferry a number of years ago. He recommended that the President of the United States and the Premier of the Soviet Union enter into "a solemn pact to murder fifty children before giving the order to fire the first thermonuclear weapon." There would be an annual exchange of fifty ten-year-old children. They would live close to the White House and the Kremlin, and each head of state would commit himself to kill the fifty with his own hand before issuing orders that would bring death to vast numbers of people.[3]

* * *

If my moral sensitivity were not as dulled as my imagination, there would be for me something more staggering than the prospect of nuclear holocaust: the actuality of our total collective preparedness to inflict that annihilation on others. Even if Cain, because of some fear, had held back from the lethal blow and had contented himself with murder fantasies and pantomimes when Abel's back was turned, the ghastliness of his intent would have remained. With megakill, too, an unspeakable ghastliness of intent for a hundred-million fold murder is there. The United States alone has the firepower to kill all human beings more than a dozen times over. Each day that passes, the readied nuclear weapons *are being used* for threat and the projection of global power.

Already now whole populations have been incapacitated by a stage of atomic sickness more lethally determinative than that which would follow the outbreak of nuclear war. Intimation of hell is to be found not so much in scenes of extermination in gas chambers or nuclear flames but rather in the perpetrators' lack of feeling, the petrifaction Simone Weil speaks about. And this is already with us prior to any firing of the weapons.

In a nuclear war the horror perpetrated would for most people in the belligerent nations be comprehended as the horror enveloping them. For the initial survivors, the global horror in its unsurveyable expanse would be present in the intensity of destruction immediately sur- rounding them. The near would lie in horrid continuum with the far. The mass murder committed on the other side of the earth would have its mirror image in the devastation close by. The awesomeness of the horror at hand would tend to blot out awareness of the faraway horror or a sense of guilt for it. But, as in Hiroshima and Nagasaki, people would soon be overcome by guilt for having turned away from others around them in that chaos of human need and anguish. For this petrifaction, if not for that which fed into the outbreak of the war, guilt would loom.

Chapter 8

THE CENTRAL MURDER

If it is our death that Christ died on the cross, there is in the cross the constraint of an infinite love.[1]

James Denney

From the teaching of Jesus and from his crucifixion we learn that murder is the central negative motif in human history. There is murder at the beginning, at the middle, at the close: the righteous son is killed; God's righteous Son is executed; followers of the Son are slain. Jesus, crying out to the doctors of the Law and the Pharisees (Mt. 23), could summarize the history of Israel, negatively seen, as the ever-repeated rejection and killing of the men of God, from Abel in the first book of the Hebrew Scripture to Zechariah in the last (2 Chr.). Jesus saw that the sequence was about to reach its culmination in what would be done to him. This summary was given still more vivid expression in the parable of the wicked husbandmen who mistreat or kill one representative after another sent by the owner of the vineyard and finally kill the owner's son (Mk. 12:1–9 and parallels).

Jesus stressed that his followers should expect treatment comparable to that given him. Stephen confronted his antagonists with a similar survey of Israel's history, including its culmination in Jesus' crucifixion. In Stephen's death by stoning, the murder sequence was continued. In the gospel apocalypses and Revelation, the close of history is depicted as a time filled with catastrophe and mass slaying, especially of the people of God.

In the two great commandments Jesus called his followers to love God and their fellow human beings. John later emphasized the inseparable unity of the two commandments with attention to the negative side: "If any one says, 'I love God,' and hates his brother, he is a liar; for he who does not love his brother whom he has seen, cannot love God whom he has not seen" (1 Jn. 4:20). The dual drives to be rid of God and the countering brother—the opposite of the dual loves to which we are called—coincided completely in the drama of the murder of Jesus. Malice toward the visible brother formed a continuum with

44

rejection of the unseen God; the judicial murder of the brother was at the same time an attempt to do away with God. "As it is, you want to kill me when I tell you the truth as I have learned it from God" (Jn. 8:40 JB). All their sin entered into the murder, the supreme expression of the totality of their sinning. Behind the desire to murder any human being looms that most terrible possibility: "blasphemy against the Holy Spirit, in other words, the murder of God in us."[2]

Still, as Christians we can at times discern in ourselves the dual drives to be rid of God and our enemy. The desire to be rid of God lies behind all of my sinning; the desire to do away with an enemy is the identifiable extreme of what is wrong with me. This means that any manifestation of the drive to be rid of a fellow human being—the hostility-hatred-murder continuum—carries with it inseparably the drive to be rid of God and veers back across the centuries into that crucifixion of the Christ.

Paul wrote: "We are convinced that one has died for all; therefore all have died" (2 Cor. 5:14). James Denney, pointing to the second half of the statement, explained: "This clause puts as plainly as it can be put the idea that His death was equivalent to the death of all. In other words, it was the death of all men which was died by Him."[3]

Taken into his dying was the death of Abel and Stephen and Martin Luther King, Jr. Taken in also was the death of Cain and Caiaphas and Adolf Hitler. Comprehended in the death of that Victim was the death of every other victim of the hostility-hatred-murder continuum. When one person kills another, he inflicts a death which entered into Jesus' dying. When anyone, in hatred or apathy, hands over another into dying, the result was present already in that betrayal long ago. The massacre of multitudes in war was a component in the one death. The words of the Son of Man on the judgment throne apply also to evil inflicted: "As you did it to one of the least of these my brethren, you did it to me" (Mt. 25:40).

Pragmatic readiness to sacrifice other human beings pervades history. This was given most cogent expression in the words of Caiaphas to his fellow oligarchs: "it is better for one man to die for the people, than for the whole nation to be destroyed" (Jn. 11:50 JB). The dire alternative was envisioned "If we let him go on in this way everybody will believe in him, and the Romans will come and destroy the Holy Place and our nation" (Jn. 11:48 JB). The argument, based on obvious common sense, that in certain situations some (and from an adversary group unlimited numbers) be given over to death for the survival and well-being of the many would seem here to be supremely persuasive: the death of only one is required to save the whole nation from being destroyed. The danger pointed to was an actual possibility, not something imaginary or fabricated. The oligarchs were chiefly concerned, not about the many, but about their own position and power whose base depended on the multitude. But still, whether for the many or for the privileged few, what more reasonable and natural course of action could there be than to sacrifice just one person?

Most of the subtleties and persuasiveness of all arguments through-out history (the theological ones also) for the sacrifice of some on behalf of the collectivity are compacted in that formulation by Caiaphas. Such arguments reckon that the numbers of victims (from within the collectivity) will be acceptably limited when viewed in comparison with the supremely important good at stake. Outra-geously stretching Caiaphas' point nuclear gamesmen proceed accord-ing to this "logic."

The pragmatic readiness to sacrifice human life, which found superlative expression through Caiaphas, took as its focal Victim, Jesus of Nazareth. But there was something that outweighed that readiness, even the totality of it within all of history: the willingness of Jesus to become Victim of that pragmatism and thus *"identify Himself* with the countless victims of wars, with all those who have been deliberately sacrificed to the Political Necessities and Social Duty, to [with] the millions of human beings who have been slaughtered and constrained to slaughter each other by being more or less persuaded that their deaths would be serving Justice and Law. By His readiness to become the victim of such a belief, Jesus unmasked its monstrous falsity, and showed His disciples in advance that they could never adopt it themselves."4

On a ruined wall in Hiroshima is dimly etched the figure of a human being who was standing next to it when the flash came. The body, though instantaneously vaporized, stopped enough of the awful light to leave that abiding epitaph. When German theologian Heinrich Vogel gazed at the dim silhouette, the thought gripped him: Jesus Christ was there in the inferno with that person; what was done to him was done to Christ; the horror he had no time to experience, Jesus felt.5 The Light of the world stood uncomprehended, comprehending, and undone by the hideous splendor of man's stolen fire.

We can envision the Risen Jesus there in the foot of that cross of atomic cloud, the Victor as Victim. But the death of the person next to the wall, the death of those Japanese multitudes, already weighed upon Jesus at Skull Hill. What the Crucified One took to himself at the midpoint of history, the Risen One, drawing near, takes to himself hour after hour, disease by disease, enmity by enmity, war by war in the sequence of history.

We can recite numbers or call up mental images of Auschwitz or Dresden, the Black Death or the slave trade, Julius Caesar's massacres or Tamerlane's, Stalin's or the Pentagon's in Indochina. But the awesome magnitude of such horrors remains a mystery impenetrable unless we approach it through the Man of Gethsemane and Golgotha. I can meditate on the vaporization of a few in Hiroshima and Nagasaki; but my mind cannot visualize the snuffing out of 250,000 human beings. There is, though, the slain One, whose mind, heart, and body in A.D. 30 and A.D. 1945 took all that in. Because the fullness of God dwelt in him, he could take to himself and know the full magnitude of human hate, killing, and death. We can know more of Jesus' agony when we begin to see that the slaughters, the hate and guilt of multitudes throughout all history converged on him. And reciprocally, by contemplating his agony, we can better grasp the magnitude of what has been inflicted on others.

What is currently being prepared for and what would be fought, would come as war against all human beings, not just against those in "enemy" countries. Everyone would be to some extent a casualty of such a war, and quite possibly everyone would die, over a period of time, as its victim. In Hebrew thought a single murder cast an imperiling shadow over the entire faith community; the gravity of the disorder it constituted touched upon all within that corporateness. In that perspective, how ominous and vast is the shadow over the United States, resulting from innumerable murders, from media violence, from past military slaughters. But that shadow in its greater breadth looms over all humanity in its corporateness—looms as a dreadful dynamism which has taken embodiment in the nuclear arsenals. It is as the central Person of all humanity that Jesus Christ is presently threatened by this guilt and doom.

God, in order that we might meet Him, made Himself vulnerable in Jesus. But Jesus also, in his vulnerability as one human being, represented the totality of humankind. He was formed that our vision might rest not only on this focal expression of the invisible God but also on this singular image of the neighbors we have been too nearsighted to see and of the myriads of human beings we have had no sight to see. This latter dimension is indicated by Jesus' words in the judgment scene pictured in Matthew 25:31–46. Though we cannot envision all who should be within our view, we are able to see him who is focus and head of that vast throng.

That 300,000,000 persons or a billion or four billion might be killed in a nuclear world war is beyond the imagination of any mortal. My nearest approach to the magnitude of that horror comes when I realize that Jesus would be the central Victim in the midst of the annihilation. Each victim he would know; each passion, each death he would feel. He in whom God has drawn near would be there in a thousand infernos with the least of all who are his. The slain Brother would be there with every brother and sister, with every terrified child as the slower ghastliness of radiation sickness spreads across the continents. A darkness more enduring than that on a long ago Passover would cross the world. From innumerable parched lips would come some echo of the cry, "My God, my God, why hast thou forsaken me?" (Mt. 27:46); for that elimination of intolerable neighbors would bring with it an apparent doing away with God. But the One who gave supreme utterance to that cry, the Neighbor-Brother-God, who was done away with, would be there in the midst.

This means that all the nuclear weapons delivery systems of this world point toward a target that comprehends all human targets: Jesus. The cold warriors of West and East, with no eyes to glimpse the "enemy" multitudes, see the One least of all. But Christians must understand that no nuclear weapon is aimed without pointing toward him: "As you did it to one of the least of these my brethren, you did it to me."

It is not given us to know whether a nuclear world war, if this comes, will constitute the engulfing terminal murder of all human beings. We can know that it would come as the greatest crucifixion of humankind and as such, the worst recrucifixion of Christ. Therefore the awesome magnitude of the guilt in nuclear terrorism (even apart from holocaust) is second only to that of the guilt in the crucifixion of Jesus.

PART II

JUGGERNAUT

Chapter 9

JAGANNATHA

The cult [of national sovereignty] has become mankind's major religion.... Today, the national state is a god (for sovereignty, when one analyzes its implications, means divinity, nothing less).[1]

Arnold J. Toynbee

In a traditional Bengalese ritual, devotees of Vishnu the Preserver, the all-wise, the supremely powerful, the incomparable, have had a way with their god. At festivals the throne and image of Vishnu are set on top of a high tower on crude, bulky wheels. Obscured by the magnificent apparel covering the carved wooden figure is the hideous face, painted black, with a distended blood-red mouth. Hundreds must strain and tug on the ropes which angle out from the tower and base to bring the wheels into creaking motion. Around the hundreds are thousands cheering them on and ready to take their turn. As the multitude cheers and tugs, the massive engine moves, gains momentum, rolls. It may move slowly, festively, ordering the masses to itself, although a few fall under the ponderous wheels or heedless feet. But when a downward slope is reached, the engine may pick up speed and hurtle forward to crush all in its path. No matter how many perish, Vishnu as Jagannatha (lord of the world) and Preserver must have his rolling juggernaut.

Whatever in human affairs is looked to as the "Preserver" must also be regarded as Jagannatha, lord of the world. Vishnu demands a coterie to tend, feed, bathe, and clothe him. But other Jagannathas can be still more demanding. When people mass in devotion to a "Preserver," an engine of power emerges. That focal embodiment of what people look to for security and survival moves in much the same way as Vishnu's chariot tower. The word *juggernaut* in recent decades has been used primarily with reference to Nazism, and generally without awareness of its origin in this Bengalese ritual. The background image is, though, highly suggestive for understanding a syndrome more universal than Nazism. Vishnu was said to have sixty million devotees, but there is a Preserver with far, far, more devotees than he, the nation-state.

God has revealed Himself under the name I AM WHO I AM, I WILL BE WHAT I WILL BE (Ex. 3:14, RSVB, with footnote). Human beings in collectivity seize that name for themselves. That the collectivity must and will survive is the claim behind all other claims, and this constitutes the presumption, WE ARE, WE WILL BE. Man, although he is stalked by death, in collectivity presumes to approximate the I AM of the eternal God. Babylon could say,

> I am, *and there is no one besides me;*
> *I shall not sit as a widow*
> *or know the loss of children.*
>
> (Is. 47:8)

With the Syrian Antiochus IV, the most evil ruler depicted in the Old Testament, the usurping claim to deity became furiously personal. He is described in Daniel 11:36 as one who "shall exalt himself and magnify himself above every god, and shall speak astonishing things against the God of gods." He sought to wipe out the people of God by forced acculturation or by slaughter. Antiochus took for himself the name *Epiphanes* ("the Manifest [God]"); his opponents, however, called him Antiochus *Epimanes* ("the Mad").

The *Epiphanes/Epimanes* correlation remains as contemporary as daily newscasts. The presumption to divinity, whether centered in a ruler or not, always manifests itself in madness. As with Antiochus IV, the cultic displacement of the Lord of history leads to crazed desolation of life and land (for example, Indochina). A collectivity, through repression, acculturation, cold or hot warring, presses toward wiping out any person or group that counters its *Epiphanes* claim. All countering of the claim aggravates the madness.

These biblical motifs pervade history. They loom large in the nation-states of our time, and largest in those that are most imperial. History is the tension between God's intention and man's pretension. According to the prophetic word the nations are as dust on God's scales (Is. 40:15). Totally unwilling to accept themselves in this valuation they seem bent on proving it nonetheless. Their mad presumption can lead only to annihilation in radioactive dust.

Each of the empires of biblical times liked to see itself as what we might now call "the engine of history." That essentially was the boast of the Assyrians (as in Is. 10:13–14), of Nebuchadrezzar, of the Roman

Empire. Americans or Russians or Chinese do not claim that their nation or leader is God. That would be too unsophisticated. But they do, by and large, see their ideological nation-state in its centered rule as the engine of history. ("McGeorge Bundy, borrowing from Dean Acheson, liked to talk about the United States as the 'locomotive at the head of mankind pulling the "caboose" of humanity along behind.'"[2]) Through power-block thinking, citizens of second- and third-class nation-states can share in the same presumption. Any engine-of-history outlook, however, requires the displacement of the One who is Lord of history. Every engine of history becomes inevitably a juggernaut crushing all who stand in its path.

The Roman totalitarianism that surrounded Jesus and the early Christians has been described like this:

> By Roman theory the State was the one society which must engross every interest of its subjects, religious, social, political, humanitarian, with the one possible exception of the family. There was no room in Roman law for the existence, much less the development on its own lines of organic growth, of any corporation or society which did not recognize itself from the first as a mere department or auxiliary of the State. The State was all and in all, the one organism with a life of its own.[3]

Jacques Ellul has delineated the contemporary equivalent:

> Finally, technique causes the state to become totalitarian, to absorb the citizens' life completely. We have noted that this occurs as a result of the accumulation of techniques in the hands of the state. Techniques are mutually engendered and hence interconnected, forming a system that tightly encloses all our activities. When the state takes hold of a single thread of this network of techniques, little by little it draws to itself all the matter and the method, whether or not it consciously wills to do so.
>
> Even when the state is resolutely liberal and democratic, it cannot do otherwise than become totalitarian. It becomes so either directly or, as in the United States, through intermediate persons.[4]

Herods today proceed most effectively, not by beheading a John the Baptist, but by filling the minds of Johns, Ivans, Hanses and Jeans with the ideas of Herod as their very own. Ironically, techniques to achieve this have been better perfected in Western countries than in communist ones where the methods of thought-control tend to be more obvious and shrill. Even more decisive than the development of the

technological means to immolate the "enemy" have been the technological means developed for instilling into the emptiness within the
Johns and Ivans a readiness to immolate and be immolated.

The absolutist posture of any collectivity finds its most direct
expression in the military, a command structure which is inherently
totalitarian. Persons taken into the military have no "inalienable
rights" to "life, liberty, and the pursuit of happiness." In war, "any
form of government becomes destructive of these ends"—most
dramatically for those on the opposing side, but more subtly for its
own soldiers sent into combat. In the nuclear arms buildup the general
public has granted to the government the authority to enter into
immense sacrificial destruction of those rights for any or all of its own
people, not just for soldiers. This is an ultimate expression of the
worship given to Jagannatha.

* * *

It is usually thought that idolatry among the Hebrews was a simple
turning from worship of Yahweh to worship of other gods. A number
of Old Testament passages indicate that those Hebrews involved in
idolatry did not reject Yahweh in favor of the Canaanite gods, but
were usually trying to worship both Yahweh and the other gods. In
fact, the first of the Ten Commandments prohibits the worship of
gods in addition to Yahweh; it does not speak directly against dropping
the worship of Yahweh in favor of something else. Some sense of the
reality and power of Yahweh remained, and so there was some effort
to worship Him, even though competing gods needed to be given their
due as well. To get along well in life one had to keep on good terms
with Yahweh—and with other gods. Often they were worshipped as in
the Greek pantheon, with Yahweh in all likelihood heading the
pantheon.

Aaron, after building an altar in front of the golden calf, proclaimed
to the people, "Tomorrow will be a feast in honor of Yahweh" (Ex. 32:5
JB). Solomon in his old age became a follower of certain gods of his
wives and thus no longer "a wholehearted follower of Yahweh" (1 Kg.
11:4–6 JB); that is, at least some of his efforts were still directed
toward following Yahweh. Elijah on Mount Carmel said to the huge
Hebrew crowd: "How long do you mean to hobble first on one leg then
on the other? If Yahweh is God, follow him; if Baal, follow him" (1 Kg.
18:21 JB). Clearly they wanted to have both Yahweh and Baal as their
gods. Jeremiah stood at the gate of the Temple and called out God's
word to those streaming in: "Will you steal, murder, commit adultery,
swear falsely, burn incense to Baal, and go after other gods that you

have not known, and then come and stand before me in this house, which is called by my name, and say, 'We are delivered!'—only to go on doing all these abominations?" (Jer. 7:9–10). God's warning through Zephaniah came to "those who bow down and swear to the Lord/ and yet swear by Milcom" (Zeph. 1:5).

When people who see themselves as followers of Christ are lured into absolutizing the nation, we have a situation analagous to this ancient attempt to have both God and another god: Well-being depends on giving God His due—but also on giving the nation-state its due in terms of full allegiance, support of military "defense," and readiness to kill and be killed in war. There is the ludicrous hobbling first on the leg of praising the God and Father of Jesus Christ and then on the leg of a military nationalism whose dictates are in total contradiction to His. Americans have outdone all others in a syncretistic merging of the two kinds of worship.

Gerhard von Rad describes the religious situation among the Hebrews in the period after David's reign:

> Looked at from the outside, almost everything connected with the cult was still what it had always been. The altars sent up their smoke, the customary prayers were offered, and the religious language and concepts which spoke to men's minds of Jahweh's self-revelation and of his acts may scarcely have changed. But were people still worshipping *Jahweh?* Was it not rather Baal, with his control over the blessings of the world of nature, who was now in their minds? For Baal was nonetheless Baal, even when invoked by the name Jahweh. Or was the object of worship some indeterminate third party who belonged somewhere between the two?"[5]

These questions, somewhat altered, could be asked about American religion; for any syncretistic merging of biblical and nonbiblical worship drastically transmutes the former, even though its outer forms may remain largely intact. Because of the absolutizing of the nation-state as Preserver, a "God" seen as Patron of the Preserver and of that "way of life" will have secret preeminence over the One pointed to in the biblically derived usages.

The Yahweh-*plus* worshippers of the Old Testament period, especially those such as von Rad describes, must have found it hard to see what they were doing wrong. Why those stern condemnations, allegedly from Yahweh? They *were* worshipping Yahweh, worshipping Yahweh very intently. For church people in the United States and in other countries it is comparably hard to see that insofar as they practice a Christianity-*plus* worship of the nation-state, they transmute and negate what in outward appearance is the faithful worship of God. As Gabriel Marcel points out, "an idolatry..., to be sure, is not recognized as such, its very nature excluding such recognition."[6]

John Howard Yoder has identified the key indicator:

> The idolatry of patriotism, believing that any one nation's or people's cause is so worthy that to it human lives—whether of "friend" or of "foe"—should be sacrified, must be unveiled not first when it has actually led to open warfare, but already when the possibility of such slaughter has been accepted in government plans. Not the taking of life, but the idolizing of one's own interest which leads finally to killing, is the deepest sin of militarism. Whether the sixth commandment absolutely forbids all killing is still debated; in any case the first forbids nationalism.[7]

Because of this idolizing, any nation-state is inherently totalitarian. Its claim and demand upon its people are total (though the explicitness, rigor, and brazenness of this can vary greatly).

The rituals for idolizing the collectivity have varied, from bowing down before the golden image at "the sound of the horn, pipe, lyre, trigon, harp, bagpipe, and every kind of music" (Dan. 3:7), through the offering of a pinch of incense to Caesar, to the American pledge of allegiance to the flag and the parallel practices in communist countries. This is not to say that the pledge to the flag or corresponding rituals are inevitably idolatrous. A person pledging allegiance can avoid nationalist idolatry only by rejecting the stance that the nation must survive and that the nation's cause is so worthy that to it human lives must be sacrificed. But if we reject that stance, we can hardly participate in a ritual which is collectively intended to express and confirm the stance.

* * *

God willed and there was light. Man wills and there is light. But the glow of candle, neon sign, and blast furnace is not interesting enough to hold his attention for long. He must have fireworks and fire spectacles. With fireworks man has seemed able to call down fire from heaven or set a little of the sky ablaze. Now Fourth of July patriots and their counterparts can set off far more godlike fireworks. They can produce on earth, ever so briefly, the sun's fire; they can ignite the firmament, rend the heavens. The earlier nuclear weapons-test spectacles and the space flight launchings assumed the character of national liturgies with the ancient elements of altar, priests, oblation, fire, and smoke. God takes light, refracts it into its component parts, and gives us a rainbow—a breath-taking, ephemeral sign of His love. Man takes atoms, smashes the components apart, and produces the fireball and mushroom cloud—the counterpoised sign of his presumption and fear.

Part of the meaning of war lies in its being the chief ritual of nationalist religion: human sacrifice on a grand scale, altar, blood, priests, fire, and smoke. The radio and newsreels during World War II and, with still more vividness, television during the Indochina War enabled tens of millions to congregate before the altar. The bombings of Hiroshima and Nagasaki were experienced by Americans as an awesome nationalist ritual. Conventional bombs, bombing raids, and nuclear weapons derive much of their fascination from being such spectacular developments within the ancient tradition of immolating sacrifice.

The original meaning of the word *victim* was that which was offered in sacrifice to a deity. Victims of war (or of exploitation and other covert systemic violence) still fall within that generally forgotten etymological meaning. The fact that *holocaust,* which literally means a whole burnt offering, is so often used to designate the vast fire slaying that would occur in a nuclear war grimly suggests that such mass slaughter would come as climax in history's long progression of the war sacrifices of nationalist religion.

Nuclear holocaust would be a parody of Pentecost: instead of the rush of a mighty wind and tongues as of fire from heaven resting on the few as a sign to the many from diverse nations to enter the unity being created by God—ultra-sonic winds and surges of fire leaping into the heavens which would be in actualization of a multinational sameness brought on by Satan. Only if God's people constitute a multitude of living sacrifices suffused by the Spirit's fire, can the worldwide death sacrifice be avoided.

After the battle of Gilboa the Philistines cut off Saul's "head and stripped off his armor, and sent messengers throughout the land of the Philistines, to carry the good news to their idols and to the people. They put his armor in the temple of Ashtaroth; and they fastened his body to the wall of Bethshan" (1 Sam. 31:9–10). To national idols and their adherents there is always proclaimed a comparable good news— wars won, adversaries laid low, preeminence achieved, superior military strength in readiness to do the same again—news utterly opposite to the Good News of the raising of a later Anointed One after he had been slain. In almost every country, the school texts, media, military training, and nationalist liturgies hold up war trophies for collective view.

It may be that the absolutizing of the nation-state, in the United States for example, is not greater now than in 1943 or 1917. The same can be said for the long shadow cast by this stance—the absolutizing of whatever adversary is perceived as chief threat. But nuclear weapons technology has brought to consummate expression the infernal essence of that idolatry: So worthy is the nation that there is no limit to how many millions or hundreds of millions of "foe" or "friend" may have to be sacrificed to it; it may even be necessary to offer up the nation itself in final demonstration of its righteousness and worthiness.

The Cuban Missile Crisis of October 1962 foreshadowed the nuclear end by revealing, as never before nor since, the dynamisms which impel the nations toward nuclear disaster. In both the American leadership and the populace was a belligerent self-righteousness, a do-or-die resolve to force the Russians to back down, a determination to press ahead even if that would mean nuclear war. The American cause was for most citizens so totally right that they were prepared to run the great risk of incinerating multitudes and of being incinerated themselves. Nuclear war was avoided "only by the grace of God and Nikita Khrushchev," as pacifist thinker John Swomley remarked soon afterward.

If the flag is one representation of deity, nuclear weapons are another. In the grim bolt-uprightness of rockets with their H-bomb warheads lurks an intimation of dour pagan idols. Philistines must have their Dagon fish images. Entire societies dance in fascination intermingled with obliviousness before the chief protector idols; for even the grimmest of gods, upon receiving the demanded oblations, permit their devotees to be gay. And these are not jealous gods. They are secure in their preeminence. To them come the richest offerings (what American church people pay in taxes for the military is many times more than what they give for church work); to them belong the most learned and numerous priesthood and the most esoteric rites. So they even allow their adherents a syncretized adulation of Jesus Christ. If from the first Easter Sunday through all the centuries until the present, $250,000 or the equivalent had been given *each day* to the Christian church for the work of God's Movement on earth, the total amount would add up to less than what the United States, with the approval of most professing (taxpaying) Christians, spends on the military in one year.

Psalm 115, after elaborating on the *senselessness* of idols that have

> *noses, but never smell,*
> *hands, but never touch,*
> *feet, but never walk,*

concludes:

> *Their makers will end up like them,*
> *and so will anyone who relies on them.*
> (Ps. 115:6–7,8 JB)

In Jeremiah 2:5 (JB) God says of ancestral idolaters,

> *Vanity they pursued,*
> *vanity they became.*

The climactic example of this has come with nuclear weapons. The bombs and their carriers have no feeling, no conscience, no imaginative sensitivity for the human beings toward whom they are targeted. Neither does the nation-state as such. Human beings feel, think, envision, but when they rely on the mindless nation and its unsensing weapons, they give way to enveloping insensitivity, hardness, emptiness. There is in the nation and its weapons something like a gravitational field which draws to itself devotees and absorbs them into that senselessness whose ultimate fulfilment would come in nuclear obliteration.

Idolatries have generally afforded some sense of power over deities. The occasional Old-Testament taunts about how idols are totally and ridiculously dependent upon their human creators and ministrants, bypass the fact that the appeal of idolatry lies to a great extent in this very dependency and the correlative human ascendancy. Primitive idolatries, however, have ordinarily been pervaded by an awareness of how precarious that human ascendancy is. Sophisticated idolatries usually lack any comparable awareness and are in this respect more naive than primitive ones. We have made the towering rocket images; they are ours. Mighty the powers we invoke; yet mightier still are we, for with our technological incantations we control them. Devotees and ministrants in their routine genuflections do not recognize that there lurks in these images a perverse insatiability and erratic vengefulness far surpassing that of the deities of old.

* * *

Scripture affirms that God will bring history to an end, His End. He will at last overwhelm the unruliness of man and history by meeting it and absorbing it fully in Jesus.

As man in collectivity tries to play God and lord it over history, that unruliness looms up to mock him. But now as never before, man has his own cataclysmic means for crushing and putting an end to that unmanageableness, even though he would thus make of it a sort of petrified finality. If man cannot bring off a credible imitation of God's End-fulfilment of history ("Thine alabaster cities gleam / Undimmed by human tears!"), he seems to have the real option of a coup that could bring the speedy end of history. If man cannot seriously compete with God's creating, he is presently in a position to outdo anything that till now could be regarded as God's destroying. But God, through Jesus' Resurrection triumph, would have His way of dealing with that terminal unruliness.

Chapter 10

THIEVES, ROBBERS, AND THE WOLF

Jesus said, "For judgment I came into this world, that those who do not see may see, and that those who see may become blind." Some of the Pharisees near him heard this, and they said to him, "Are we also blind?" Jesus said to them, "If you were blind, you would have no guilt; but now that you say, 'We see,' your guilt remains.

"Truly, truly, I say to you, he who does not enter the sheepfold by the door but climbs in by another way, that man is a thief and a robber; but he who enters by the door is the shepherd of the sheep....

"Truly, truly, I say to you, I am the door of the sheep. All who came before me are thieves and robbers; but the sheep did not heed them. I am the door; if any one enters by me, he will be saved, and will go in and out and find pasture. The thief comes only to steal and kill and destroy; I came that they may have life, and have it abundantly. I am the good shepherd. The good shepherd lays down his life for the sheep. He who is a hireling and not a shepherd, whose own the sheep are not, sees the wolf coming and leaves the sheep and flees; and the wolf snatches them and scatters them."

John 9:39–10:2; 10:7–12

The central contemporary idolatry is the absolutizing of the nation-state. But we are also confronted with an intermeshing of idolatries. If we discern the political implications of the above verses from John 9 and 10, we can better understand that intermeshing.

The "thieves and robbers" phrase has usually been thought of as referring to false religious teachers and false messiahs. But this interpretation is too narrow and misses the strong political dimension present in the dialogue.

Throughout the Old Testament God's people had been pictured as His sheep, His flock. Leaders of the people were called to be shepherds carrying out His shepherding. This role is implied for Moses as well as Joshua in Numbers 27:15–17. God had commanded the judges "to shepherd my people Israel" (2 Sam. 7:7); and to David He said, "You shall be shepherd of my people Israel, and you shall be prince over Israel" (2 Sam. 5:2). But the prophets repeatedly cried out God's warning to false shepherds—not only religious leaders, but the broader exploiting oligarchy of the period. Thus in the classic passage, Ezekiel 34: "You eat the fat, you clothe yourselves with the wool, you slaughter the fatlings; but you do not feed the sheep" (v. 3). Jesus' words in this dialogue are within that earlier tradition as he issues his warning and claims fulfillment of the Old Testament promise that God would raise up a true shepherd.

Because of the chapter division, John 10:1–21 is usually read with no recognition of the context disclosed in the preceding verses. It is a part of the confrontation between Jesus and the Jewish authorities resulting from the healing of the blind man (Jn. 9:1–12). The words recorded were not spoken to the disciples in quiet retreat. They were spoken in the intense thrust and counterthrust of an exchange with representatives of the Jerusalem religious-political-economic establishment. The Romans ruled here as elsewhere through a collaborating local oligarchy. It was this oligarchy that was moving against Jesus, not simply Jewish religious leaders separated from political and economic power. "And the chief priests and lawyers were bent on making an end of him, with the support of the leading citizens" (Lk. 19:47 NEB). "Thieves and robbers" refers to that governing elite. That oligarchy was the current configuration in the shabby sequence of priestly rulers and power wielders who dated from Maccabean times. Earlier still there had been the succession of unworthy, self-seeking rulers denounced repeatedly in the Old Testament. "All who came before me are thieves and robbers."

It is most significant that Jesus described his oligarchic opponents as thieves and robbers. Theirs was the covert violence of economic arrangements for oppressing and fleecing the poor majority. Jesus said that they had made out of the Temple "a den of robbers" (Mk. 11:17 and parallels). Like their Old Testament predecessors they were ruthlessly exploiting the people and did at times resort to overt violence. Like the false shepherds of Ezekiel 34 they were slaughtering "the fatlings," sacrificing people to their own greed. Their "cup and dish," so carefully polished for the public view, was filled inside with "rapacity and self-indulgence" (Mt. 23:25 Moffatt—a good rendering of the Greek words): Their affluent life style could be maintained only by relentlessly taking from others. Those who in their official status were at the furthest remove from the thieves and robbers on the fringes of the society were the custodians and beneficiaries of institutional arrangements for massive theft and robbery.

In the Old Testament larger carnivores were often a significant threat to domestic animals and thus became an image for threats to human life. God's sheep "were scattered, because there was no shepherd; and they became food for all the wild beasts" (Ezek. 34:5). "Her princes in the midst of her are like wolves tearing the prey, shedding blood, destroying lives to get dishonest gain" (Ezek. 22:27— cf., "steal and kill and destroy").

A hireling *"sees the wolf coming and leaves the sheep and flees; and the wolf snatches them and scatters them."* The wolf represents Satan, the dynamic power of destruction. But the good shepherd, who unlike the hireling does not flee, lays down his life as he defends the flock by facing the wolf. Thus, in this passage, the Jewish oligarchy with the Roman imperial power behind it is the wolf, the incarnation of the power of death, and Jesus, confronting it, gives up his life.

The Greek word translated *snatch* means to seize suddenly and carry off and is used with reference to wild animals or violent men. Rather astonishingly the wolf is not pictured as killing the sheep. It seizes them, scatters them; and without a shepherd the sheep are completely exposed to the ravages of the wolf. Here, as in a number of Old Testament passages, the scattering is the most decisive element in the activity directed against the sheep. The wolf, the ruthless oligarchy, in its destructiveness tries to break up any unity set over against it. The people find themselves to be helpless, isolated victims who are snatched, co-opted to become part of the wolf. The Jerusalem oligarchy feared Jesus, not just in himself, but because they saw people beginning to unite around him into a group threatening their power. They succeeded in scattering the sheep for a short period after Jesus' arrest (Mk. 14:27; Mt. 26:31). The later Jewish and Roman persecutions of the church were motivated by the fear that any such grouping was a direct threat to their authority and status.

Jesus came once for all "that they may have life, and have it abundantly." "The thief *comes*," the wolf *comes* to all places continuously throughout the centuries.

> There is no point in human history which lies beyond the horizon of the thieves and robbers of the parable. Wherever men have claimed to announce the gift of life, or shall claim to announce it, apart from faith in Jesus, they proclaim themselves as thieves and robbers, and their activity has been, and is, and will be, a destructive activity.[1]

The thieves-robbers-wolf confronting Jesus had their predecessors, contemporaries, and successors. The ruling elite of all nations throughout history have, to some extent, made that announcement, and their policies can be understood in terms of the threefold image Jesus used as he stood against the Jerusalem establishment. When religious leaders and structures have played their part in an oligarchic domination of people, they are to be seen as thieves-robbers-wolf.

Though there have been many groups which for different reasons have been seen as a threat to the power elite, the central group counterpoised against these elites through three millennia has been the community drawn together as God's people. The persecution of Jews or Christians, whether by imperial rulers before the birth of Jesus, by Roman or christendom oligarchies, by communist governments, or by dictatorships in the technologically less developed countries has come because the wolflike oligarchy feels and *is* extremely threatened by this most resilient and subversive of groups. Jesus, with his telling characterization of the Jerusalem power structure as thieves-robbers-wolf, denied it any ultimate status or even any real legitimacy. And that denial, repeated by God's people in every age, tends to bring out in any governing elite a fear and fury comparable to that depicted in the gospels.

Jesus could hardly have given better images to help us understand the multinational corporations, the coalition of rich Western nations with their ruling elites, and the United States' power elite, "the military-industrial-academic-labor-congressional-government complex" as Sidney Lens calls it.[2] *"The thief comes only to steal and kill and destroy."* Corporate greed results in carcinogens, toxic wastes, nuclear power plants with all their blighting of the environment. Corporate greed revels in military contracts, arms sales, the endlessness of smaller arms races and the big one. For the poorer countries corporate greed fosters repressive governments and economies made subservient to Western consumption. This is not to say that the multinational corporations are purely evil or that the people in them are simply wicked. But they are caught up in the steal-kill-destroy dynamisms whether they will it or not. Thieves are intent on getting all they can, preferably by cunning, stealth, covert violence, but, when necessary, by resort to prison camps, torture, training and outfitting of secret police and armed forces, military interventions, limited wars. The CIA functions as the consummate creation of thieves and robbers. It is no more an aberration than was the execution of Jesus. It gives undercover expression to the actual nature of the governing elite that controls its being.

In the Old Testament the sheep are the little people of God—so often oppressed, harassed, and exploited. What becomes clearer in the New Testament is that God cares passionately for all mistreated people, whether within or outside Israel and whether they know Him in His caring or not.

Thieves climb over the fence to get at the sheep. In John 10 the sheep are those who are attached to Jesus, the good shepherd; they do not follow the thieves and robbers. But there are others who do. Oligarchies need people—as accessories and as victims. In the United States and in the other rich nations of the Western alliance, the accessories to the wrongs perpetrated far outnumber the obvious victims, for the masses of victims are usually farther away. This is nothing new. In any empire there has been, along with the governing elite, the broader overlord caste or ethnic group. A population can become by and large a nation of thieves. When the seized and scattered are accessories, they do not even realize that they have been co-opted.

Those who covet and steal are idolaters, the slaves of Mammon. When Jesus said, "You cannot serve God and mammon" (Mt. 6:24), he was not giving one example among many, as though he could just as well have pointed to other idolatrous dynamisms. His warning focused on Mammon—the power of money, possessions, acquisitiveness, greed—as the primary dynamism opposed to God. In this book we have been viewing the collectivity as chief idol over against God. So it could be asked, which is more central, Mammon or the absolutized collectivity?

What we discover here are symbiotic idols and idolatries. There is an intermeshing as Mammon and the collectivity mutually support and enhance each other. In any collectivity Mammon's chief adherents and beneficiaries seek more and more wealth, possessions, power. But it is the governmental structures that secure and integrate the arrangements for oligarchic acquisition. Only as Caesar rules, can Mammon hold sway. And that sway shapes Caesar's rule providing it with its motive power. For the elite beneficiaries, Mammon is master as prime motivating dynamism; but the collectivity is the most deeply revered idol, for if it goes down, all else may go down with it. This is precisely the picture that comes though in the lamentations over Babylon in Revelation 18.

It is well understood in great corporations that even with all their advertising they cannot win the allegiance of the populace. But even though that primary allegiance goes to the nation-state, it still comes indirectly to these vested interests because they stand behind and control the nation-state.

Mammon's mastery presses out beyond the leading beneficiaries to take in the wider population. ("For all, least no less than greatest,/all are out for dishonest gain"—Jer. 6:13 JB.) People generally see themselves as lesser beneficiaries of the prevailing societal arrangements; or if not, they set out to get those benefits. Leaders foster the ascendancy of Mammon. Most of all through the mass media, "life" is offered: a technological cornucopia of things to consume and possess, affluent life style, entertainment, sports spectacles. To let one's life be determinatively shaped by the acquisitive desires that mold the lives of the nation-state's chief beneficiaries and providers is to be aligned with them. And fearfully strong is Mammon's lure for nearly every one of us.

Mammon's dynamism parallels and complements the idolizing of the nation-state in the fateful impulsion toward wars and nuclear annihilation. Corporations demand and get more and more military contracts. There is profit in the building of new weapons systems and the endless accumulation of weapons, including nuclear warheads, even when there is no sound military justification for them. There is profit in the selling of weapons to whatever countries can afford them, no matter how much those weapons may augment repression or the danger of international conflict. There is profit in sales of nuclear reactors to dozens of countries, even though this creates the prospect that most of these countries will be armed with nuclear warheads in the near future. There is money in the exploitation and correlative repression of peoples in the poor countries, regardless of the deepening instabilities and explosiveness of conditions in those areas. Big money dominates government and the media. When Mammon provides his benefits (as Baal seemed to dispense his lush blessings to Palestinian peasants), his dominion is collectively accepted and celebrated.

When various contemporary idolatries are scrutinized—"the consumptive mentality; the will to power and domination; the oppressions of race, sex, and class; the arrogance of national destiny; and the efficacy of violence"[3]—they are, in large measure, facets of the two central symbiotic idolatries.

In the John 10 passage the thieves and robbers are persons. "The thief" is a less personal, more general, darker figure. In the wolf there is imaged the nonhuman, the anti-human. When we survey the current national and international scene, there are thieves and robbers—identifiable oligarchs who fit that description. But behind these, far more decisive than these, are the institutional structures that "steal and kill and destroy." Yet still behind and into all this is the dread anti-God, anti-human dynamism, the Power of the Abyss, the Destroyer, Abaddon, Apollyon (Rev. 9:11). Oligarchs and oligarchic structures do their thing, and the wolf comes: There is the desolation of life in ghettoes and technologically less developed countries, the imprisonment and torture of dissenters, the uprooting and slaughter of millions in wars, the approach of thermonuclear annihilation.

Especially with regard to this last, it can be seen that the hireling flees—image for any leaders in their drivenness, failure, their inability in deed to live out the good intentions of their rhetoric. Thus national leaders, whose chief responsibility is for the well-being of the people of a country (not to mention those of other countries), do have some awareness of the nuclear threat, but can bring themselves to no decisive countermoves against it. What they do in their wrongheadedness and bewilderment more and more clears the way for the climactic coming of the wolf. But how many church leaders are putting their lives on the line in a stand against that infernal coming?

Chapter 11

THE DEVIL'S DICTATION

> Very near the path of life which Jesus had received as His task from His Father, only one step removed from it, was the road of political-religious power over the masses which Mohammed chose. The slightest concession in this direction and all the world would have applauded Jesus. His whole life was a journey along the edge of this precipice. All the time they wanted to drag Him over it. They wanted to make him King. They wanted to spread the fame of His miracles. Even His own disciples were in this respect His greatest danger....But the temptation becomes even more serious at Gethsemane and on the Cross. In the terrible hours when the great darkness came down upon Him, He was suspended between heaven and earth. The whole weight of the world was dragging Him down and attempting to break the link which tied His soul to the Father above. If the connexion had broken, if He had rebelled against the Father, then He would have fallen away from God, and we with Him. Then all would have been lost for ever.[1]
>
> *Karl Heim*

One of the three temptations Jesus faced in the wilderness was obviously political: the prospect of ruling over all the kingdoms of the world. A number of biblical scholars have shown that the other two temptations were also essentially political and closely related to the one about seizing political power. But little has been done to show how the temptation narratives provide some of the most important material in the New Testament for understanding political dominion throughout history. The messianic expectations vibrant in the Jewish masses at that time were shaped by the prevailing political actualities: The Messiah was to come and defeat other rulers by using the same power by which they exercised dominion. The power offered to and refused by Jesus is the power accepted by those who rule.

The devil showed Jesus "all the kingdoms of the world in a moment of time" (Lk. 4:5). They were somehow his to show. He then said, "To you I will give all this authority and their glory; for it has been delivered to me, and I give it to whom I will. If you, then, will worship me, it shall all be yours" (Lk. 4:6–7). Satan said that dominion over each and all the nations was *his* to give. Behind and penetrating into any government is the devil's sway. Any who rule do so by taking what is the devil's to give and fulfilling his conditions. If the claim had been a lie, Jesus could certainly have discerned this, and the offer would not really have been a temptation. Jesus later characterized Satan as "the ruler of this world" (Jn. 12:31).

In the words, *"for it has been delivered to me,"* the devil uses the Aramaic passive voice to refer to God—not in reverent avoidance of the holy name, but to have God, though obliquely acknowledged, as rather remote. (The devil is no enthusiast for atheism; God is referred to in each of his three proposals.)

"I give it to whom I will." I *will* is the essence of Satan's rebellion; and he seeks to draw forth in Jesus an *I will* aligned with his.

"If you, then, will worship me." The Greek verb is one that was also regularly used for bowing down in homage to an earthly ruler; and whether the bowing down is to a human being or to a deity, there is in it the recognition of lordship and the acting out of subordination and readiness to obey. Throughout history there has been the tremendous lure of the prospect that limited resort to dark actions will make possible a wide wielding of power for good. It is probable that as Jesus sought to understand what his mission was to be, he felt this Satanic lure: "Jesus, I can show you what to do. I have the strategy, the route to where you need to be. Do what I say—and if that sounds like homage to me, so be it for now. But all will so soon be yours to do with as you will." (The lure of this means-to-the-end offer is a key dimension in most thinking which supports reliance on the military.)

Jesus in his extreme hunger, physical weakness, and vulnerability had submitted to the terrible sway these held over great numbers of people. The extremity of their needs he felt deeply in himself. His own physical need was the context for the first temptation, but its power lay in its relation to the needs of others. One does not break a forty-day fast by eating a loaf of bread. (Better then to change a stone into a jar filled with milk.) As Messiah he could miraculously supply the physical needs of human beings and thus draw ever greater numbers into a new unity within which their needs would be properly cared for.

The promise of material abundance, initially in food, has always played a large part in the rhetoric of ancient and modern collectivities. If a governing elite is to maintain its power base, there must be some fulfillment of that promise. It is so evident how much power that abundance or even the promise of it has for aligning the populace with those who exercise (or who want to exercise) political dominion.

There is in money the power to provide needed bread and desired abundance, power for purchase and for development of the technology. In contemporary nation-states technology has substituted for miracles in providing spectacular abundance. To have turned stones into bread would have been to outdo Mammon. But Mammon, apart from any genie or wonder-working messiah, can provide as satisfactorily as these, if not quite so breathtakingly.

The temptation to jump from the pinnacle of the Temple seems, of the three, the most remote from us. In our common experience only a suicidal impulse, fleeting or obsessive, would lure us toward such a leap. But for Jesus that impulse was clearly not a factor. His temptation was this: the venturesome risking of death to attain a mastery over it. After a successful jump people would rally around him. Death is the supreme threat. Who could better be the Messianic leader of the people than one who would thus demonstrate his mastery over death, a mastery his followers would come to share? That risk-to-mastery leap from the pinnacle of the Temple would presage the risk-to-mastery leap of a Messianic uprising. Such a Messiah would lead in turning back and overcoming the death threat posed by the Roman legions. In the second venture as in the first there would be a petulant expectancy toward God: "You, God, are to bring me/us through." God would be told what He was supposed to do if He was to be duly regarded as God.

If we view this and the other temptations simply under the aspect of their proceeding from the devil, we cannot begin to sense the powerful lure they were for Jesus. The risk-to-mastery route could, from any ordinary human perspective, have been a tremendous, superlatively promising development. Highly relevant here is the place accorded in history to the defenders of Thermopylae, Charles Martel, Joan of Arc, Simon Bolivar, George Washington, (and for hundreds of millions) Lenin, Mao, Fidel Castro. Much good resulted from the course those epochal figures chose—as great good could have come from taking up the seizure-of-power possibilities that presented themselves to Jesus. It was through intense struggle, most probably, that Jesus came to see these possibilities fully under the aspect of their being from Satan.

Through an understanding of the pinnacle temptation Jesus faced, we can discern its main equivalent in human experience generally. There is in the military stance a venturesome risking of death to have mastery over it. The enemy has power to inflict death. In cold or hot war that power is countered with what is hoped can be still greater power of the same kind—armies, tactical brilliance, morale. Most of all, in full scale war there is great risk for many individuals, whether soldiers or civilians, and for the collectivity. Rather than passive vulnerability (such as the Jews experienced under the Romans) there is the daring confrontation with death in its military guise from which can come what seems a greatly expanded mastery over the threat of death. Thus the military victory over Nazism in World War II seemed a risk-to-mastery drama of the most fateful importance. Winston Churchill was a towering exemplar of the leader who defies death, galvanizes a nation into that same defiance, and in dogged confidence presses through a time of extreme risk.

In the Bible "tempting" God means telling Him what He is to do, trying to force His hand. Military preparations or warmaking have regularly involved a sort of "faith." Leaders make the decisions, but God or gods are looked to for bringing the collectivity and its leaders safely through the risks incurred to a triumph over (or at least a warding off of) death and enemies. King after king in Israel and Judah followed this course in rebelling against Assyrian suzerainty, and much of the drama in the book of Jeremiah derived from the same choice made by the last Davidic kings to counter the threat posed by Nebuchadnezzar. Those who entered into such dire risk would typically have felt that they were acting in faith: God must surely bring them through. But this was exactly the sort of "faith" the devil later proposed for Jesus. The success of that risk-to-mastery "faith" as lived out by the Maccabean freedom fighters revived this "faith" as an alluring option for the Jewish masses in the centuries immediately following, so much so that Jesus needed to stand against it. For christendom/post-christendom collectivities this petulant "faith" has undergirded the risk-to-mastery drive in power maneuvers, threats of war, and warmaking. God is expected to intervene in situations brought on by decisions made quite apart from any submission to His Lordship.

This risk-to-mastery motif comes to climactic expression in the nuclear arms race. The two rival alliances with their immense power to inflict death continue to run the risk of mutual annihilation. Their "success" in this brings a sense of mastery over death's imminence, and this sense in turn is what most of all hypnotizes the masses into continued assent: Awesome the risk, but our weapons and our leaders (and God) are bringing us through. In almost any plunge into war's riskiness there is initially at least a headiness, exhilaration, and the deliciousness of danger (perhaps subsidiary elements in Jesus' pinnacle temptation). These could through the centuries be savored just by going to the verge of war. If the current brink is overstepped, and we are plunged into thermonuclear war, that step will be partly infused with that ancient and abiding presumption: We in our daring and high resolve take the plunge and collectively we must surely come through.

Jesus did feed a multitude, but not to win their allegiance, with an abundance of bread that had come from very little bread. Through the centuries he has fed his followers, not with stones turned into bread (for seizure of political power), but with bread hallowed to represent his body broken on a cross (by wielders of that power). Rather than the risk-to-mastery route of a jump and a messianic uprising, Jesus confronted death from another direction. He healed disease, raised the dead, challenged death's institutions and their agents. He let himself be arrested, tortured, nailed to a cross and lifted up; he did not summon the available angelic deliverance but yielded to death's mastery. Jesus took a supreme "risk" strangely comparable to the devil's proposal: Trusting in God to raise him up, he let himself be cast into the abyss. (God's negation of and replacement for a just war stance is found in Jesus who "trusted to him who judges justly"—1 Pet. 2:23.) Jesus refused to give any sign or proof except the sign of the prophet Jonah: letting himself be cast into death's realm and being raised up out of it by God. A jump from the pinnacle could have brought only a brief suspension in death's rule; and the messianic "holy war" could have proceeded only by inflicting death to countermand death—an invalidating contradiction in all resort to arms. When God freed Jesus from death's grip, death was more than temporarily pushed back, it was decisively defeated. "I died, and behold I am alive for evermore, and I have the keys of Death and Hades" (Rev. 1:18). And with this triumph he has been given Lordship over all the nations.

Twice the devil said, "If you are the Son of God": There need not be the hindering lack of certainty; prove this for yourself and others, and that demonstrative proof will bring for you worldwide dominion. Jesus described his inner life as Son like this: "the Son can do nothing of his own accord, but only what he sees the Father doing; for whatever he does, that the Son does likewise" (Jn. 5:19). Through this and this alone the devil was resisted and defeated.

In each temptation the devil came with a possibility ingeniously close to what Jesus was in the process of discovering as God's way for him. God wills that the material needs of human beings be met—through the acting of His Messiah. God wills that through the faith-obedience of His Messiah death and the works of death (such as the oppression of

His people) be challenged and overcome. The Son is to rule over all peoples of the earth. Mammon's power to provide abundance for human beings, the power of rallying spectacle and military daring, the power of centered rule in the collectivity lie most of all in their imitative proximity to the way of the Father for the Son. The effectiveness of that triune power is tangibly, demonstrably there. The signs and proofs continue all around us: affluence for hundreds of millions, mere subsistence for others; continued survival, postponement of nuclear annihilation of peoples; the impressiveness, the enfolding, sustaining character, the unifying benefits of the nation-state. Jesus in the wilderness and in his ministry did not produce the asked-for signs, the demonstrations and proofs. For us who follow him there is only the commonplace bread and wine and his command to share all we have. For us there is the memory of a Roman execution, then a tomb vacated, and his command to face enemies as he did. There is a Sovereign we cannot see, a Sovereignty we cannot incontrovertibly prove, and participation in a corporateness which at its best is least demonstrative. Satan did have a point, and that point infuses the demonstrations of power that dominate our world.

What God had designated as stone Jesus refused to turn into bread. What God had designated as uranium scientists have transmuted into plutonium, strontium-90, cesium-137. The bombing of Hiroshima and Nagasaki and the subsequent nuclear weapons tests came as signs. What Jesus refused to give, Americans and then the Soviets eagerly offered—supreme demonstrations of the power that was theirs. To those who overruled God's designations, to those who achieved the spectacular demonstrations, to those superlatively adept at grasping the necessary means were given authority and dominion over all peoples of the world. This grant has been contingent on the homage paid. Yet the recipient of that homage can delight in the worldwide lack of awareness that it is being paid.

Chapter 12

IMAGES OF REBELLION

> Who dare deny that evil is an organized thing, a universe of greater reality than that which greets the senses, with its sinister landscapes, pale skies, cold sun, and cruel stars? A kingdom both of the spirit and the flesh, of prodigious density, of infinite weight, beside which the kingdoms of the earth are mere figments and symbols. To this kingdom nothing is really opposed save the Kingdom of God.[1]
>
> *Georges Bernanos*

The biblical expose of human presumption in collectivity first comes into sharp focus with the story about the building of the Tower of Babel (Gen. 11:1–9). Human beings soon after history's beginning are pictured as having gathered together to build a city with a tower to show what great things they can achieve. They joined together in order not to be scattered. God took their intent seriously: He saw that this was only a start and that in this collective power nothing they undertook would "be impossible for them." So God confused their language and scattered them, and mercy triumphed in judgment. Disunity was to keep the race from the calamitous successes which would have been attainable otherwise.

Human history moves in the dialectic of that gathering and scattering. Each of the most expansionistic ancient empires repeated the attempt to bring the race together to achieve something great. The king of Assyria boasted, "As men gather eggs that have been forsaken,/so I have gathered all the earth" (Is. 10:14). Those imperial sovereignties worked hard to bring about the political and cultural homogenization of peoples bundled together under their one rule. Though each failed to reach the goal, the illusion of world-embracing empire was maintained by ignoring populations beyond the frontiers, and enough collective might was mustered to show what "great" things human beings, joined together, can do.

Present-day imperialisms continue in that ancient ambition. Economic domination of weaker countries, the support of client governments, the military suppression of independence and liberation movements are prime strategies in the drive to gather humankind together. But it is most of all through the encompassing spread of technology that a wider gathering and more thorough homogenization than was ever achieved before comes about. Through technological developments the dynamics of gathering have quite outstripped the dynamics of scattering. Though the latter is in some ways more extreme than earlier (from "lonely crowd" to the division between West and East), it for the most part feeds back into monolithic gathering. Thus in the United States great numbers of people who are anxious, frustrated, without sustaining ties to others and a nurturing local context seek an end to their isolation in the embracing unity offered by the nation-state, the mass media subservient to it, and its affluent standard of living. In terms of Buber's distinction,[2] the less there is a genuine binding together of persons, the stronger the dynamisms that press them into a massive bundling together.

This consolidating progression is pointed to in the Babylon image of Revelation: What God had scattered has come together again and unifies the whole world. Very significantly, in Revelation 18 the coherence is that of economic domination and coalition rather than of a single all-embracing sovereignty.

Because human beings have now achieved economic and technological structures of unity unparalleled in their spread and cohesiveness, the show of strength that had become impossible after the Genesis dispersion is being actualized. The nation-state that first developed atomic weapons had achieved a more massive linguistic, political, and cultural homogeneity than any other imperial power in all history. Jacques Ellul has written:

> A humanity capable of communicating has in its possession the most terrible weapon of its own death: it is capable of creating a unique truth, believed by all, independent of God. By the confusion of tongues, by noncommunication, God keeps man from forming a truth valid for all men. Henceforth, man's truth will only be partial and contested.[3]

Though no human "truth" presently enjoys universal acceptance, the unprecedented success of current technological means for achieving wide solidarity in such "truth" is plain. The great majority in a country accept the nation-state's dominant myths: its righteous past, its unique goodness and destiny, the prevailing adherence to its high ideals, its peaceful and benevolent intentions internationally. When such a myth system dominates a society, the populace is drawn together in a solidarity which now, as in Babel, finds a climactic material imaging. A tower with its top in the heavens has been raised, a tower created by fire far hotter than that needed to bake bricks or melt bitumen. While representing limitless collective might, it evidences human division, for tower is counterpoised against tower.

In Revelation 18:5 a voice from heaven says of Babylon the great: "Her sins are heaped high as heaven." The intent of Babel's tower-builders results only in that stupendous heap of accumulated sinning. The mushroom towers intimate that greater height, out of the base of which they spring.

Though we can be rightly amazed at the power man has acquired through technology generally and in nuclear weapons specifically, we should remember that the Lord "came down" to get a better look at the diminutive city and tower which the citizens of Babel were building. Nuclear weapons too lie within that smallness. Even an astronomical perspective gives us some sense of this. If the Cold War ends in a near simultaneous exploding of most of the nuclear warheads on this planet, the energy released would be insignificant compared to that given off by the sun during the same minutes. This God who comes down to scrutinize man's mightiest devices is Lord of sun, galaxies, and quasars.

* * *

Much of the attention given in the United States within the past few years to the "principalities and powers" motif in Paul's letters has resulted from Hendrik Berkhof's masterful study, *Christ and the Powers*,[4] and John Howard Yoder's treatment of the theme, drawing heavily on Berkhof, in *The Politics of Jesus*.[5] Three passages from Paul and some quotations from Berkhof can give background for futher reflection on contemporary nation-states in their holding of nuclear weapons.

> For in him all things were created, in heaven and on earth, visible and invisible, whether thrones or dominions or principalities or authorities—all things were created through him and for him. (Col. 1:16)

> ...he raised him from the dead and made him sit at his right hand in the heavenly places, far above all rule and authority and power and dominion, and above every name that is named, not only in this age but also in that which is to come. (Eph. 1:20–21)

> Put on the whole armor of God, that you may be able to stand

against the wiles of the devil. For we are not contending against flesh and blood, but against the principalities, against the powers, against the world rulers of this present darkness, against the spiritual hosts of wickedness in the heavenly places. (Eph. 6:11–12)

In the light of God's action Paul perceived that mankind is not composed of loose individuals, but that structures, orders, forms of existence, or whatever they be called, are given us as a part of creaturely life and that these are involved, as much as men themselves, in the history of creation, fall, preservation, reconciliation, and consummation. This insight he expressed in the terms and concepts of his time. The insight which is embodied in these terms keeps for us its meaning and validity. We find it expressed all through the Bible.

Divers human traditions, the course of earthly life as conditioned by the heavenly bodies, morality, fixed religious and ethical rules, the administration of justice and the ordering of the state—all these can be tyrants over our life, but in *themselves* they are not. These fixed points are not the devil's invention; they are the dikes with which God encircles His good creation, to keep it in His fellowship and protect it from chaos.

The Powers continue to fulfill one half of their function. They still undergird human life and society and preserve them from chaos. But by holding the world together, they hold it away from God, not close to Him.

Where all Powers are seen to be subjected to Jesus Christ, who is made Head over all things for the church (Ephesians 1:22), something quite different has happened. It is then inevitable that the Powers should resort to oppression and persecution. But in this very act of desperation (which also distinguishes our age from that before Christ) their unmasking is repeated and confirmed. They can no longer exist without being forced to uncover their true nature and thereby to abandon their role as gods and saviors.[6]

These quotations from Berkhof can stand as representative of his brief treatise on this Pauline teaching, which is so important for understanding the structures and dynamisms that encompass our living. Rather than reiterating or elaborating on what Berkhof, Yoder, and others have well and convincingly analyzed, I seek to complement Berkhof's study, particularly at several points I find questionable, and to do this with primary reference to nuclear weapons.

"The Powers...still undergird human life and society and preserve them from chaos. But by holding the world together, they hold it away from God, not close to Him." What Berkhof seems hardly to recognize is that any such ordering, because it is away from God—and to the extent that it is away from God—is a disordering, a pseudo-order. Acts "of desperation" by the Powers bring on chaos, the opposite of the *shalom,* the harmony-wholeness-unity, God brings about. But there can be chaos apart from such acts. To whatever degree an apparent ordering is away from God, it is in actuality congealed chaos (which, to be sure, is generally more bearable than the uncongealed). This is not to say that in a stable isolated tribal society, for example, the customs, moral code, leadership arrangements (as principalities and powers) are totally bad. Aspects in them may incline toward God's intention for human life and thus toward ordering which is open to God. But in biblical thought, even these aspects for groups outside the people of God are caught within the overall movement away from God.

The complex array of principalities and powers which cohere as components of the United States have their positive, life-supporting dimensions which we are to recognize and thank God for. But embracing the latter, too, is the over-all fallenness of the powers, their rebellion and movement away from God, which finds especially cogent expression in and through the nation-state as prime power.

In this biblical perspective the Bomb can be seen as a transmutation of the cross. What the cross was in the Roman Empire, the Bomb is now.

Rome spoke of justice, law, peace, order. The Empire relied on various ordering factors such as roads, coinage, commerce, homogeneity of language. But the unifying factor behind all others, even behind the presence of the occupying legions, was the cross: thus those two thousand crosses, each exposing a Jewish rebel, on the hills around Sepphoris, so near to Nazareth. The cross as the chief instrument of torture and execution functioned most formidably to maintain "order."

An important part of what happened when Romans crucified Jesus was an unmasking of Roman imperial power: This, the cross (for the very best person), is the central factor in Roman rule, this behind the facade of the rhetoric and the homogenizing cultural achievements. For those with eyes to see, the peace and order achieved by the cross were now fully exposed as appalling disorder. But it was the pious Jewish oligarchy that turned to the Romans; and the cross was shown to be the chief factor behind their power—if they could not have the traditional stoning. Jewish zealots, among others, had seen behind the Roman facade; but because their reaction was basically an attempt to defeat the Romans within the Roman modes of exercising dominion, they could, in either success or failure, do no more than confirm the potency of violence—a demonstration the very opposite of what God accomplished in Jesus.

In West and East there is the rhetoric of freedom, socialism, democracy, peace, human rights, abundance; there are the unifying technologies. Weapons, though regarded as absolutely necessary, are viewed more as an outer protecting shield set around the vaunted essence of the nation. Because of that Roman cross on which Jesus died, Christians should be able to see more readily than others that the Bomb, like the cross, is really the central ordering factor behind everything else. It is not an exterior shield but the main convergence of all that is dominant in the society. Under everything that has the welcome appearance of order is the abysmal disorder centered in the Bomb. And here we need to keep in mind that we have each had our part in the dynamisms that brought on the cross and the Bomb.

We learn from Scripture that demonic spirits seek a habitation (thus in Matthew 12:43 of the unclean spirit that went out of a man). If pagan idols provided such habitation (Ps. 106:36–38; 1 Cor. 10:19–21), shouldn't the missiles, the warheads, the command centers, plutonium itself be seen as affording the same? Infernal spirits can seize persons, but they prefer to seize social structures through which they can impinge on wide ranges of people. The dominion of darkness in this hemisphere is centered in that vast complex for the manufacture and management of infernal weapons.

It is most regrettable that many Christians who are concerned with disarmament nearly always remain within the prevailing secular perspective. They see disarmament as highly desirable but very difficult and try to hope that the nations may even yet find a way to achieve it. At the one point in the New Testament where disarmament is spoken of (Col. 2:15—"He disarmed the principalities and powers and made a public example of them, triumphing over them in him"), a very different perspective is given within which the usual disarmament concerns and efforts should be understood: Disarmament is what God has imposed on the principalities and powers through the Death and Rising of Jesus Christ.

The meaning of nearly every word in the Greek text of Colossians 2:15 has been disputed by scholars. The initial participle indicates some sort of stripping away, despoiling—of weapons or of dignity and authority. But weaponry, if implied, is spiritual—is, as Berkhof puts it, "the power of illusion, their ability to convince men that they were the divine regents of the world, ultimate certainty and ultimate direction, ultimate happiness and the ultimate duty for small, dependent humanity."[7] The further images of public exhibit of the principalities and powers, likely in triumphal procession, express God's having overcome them and put them in their place—which is properly that of exposure in their defeat.

Looming into view in Colossians 2:15 are not only the vanquished but even more the Victor; and allegiance to the Victor determines the relation to the vanquished. Paul's attention in the passage is directed to the sway of legalisms, customs, human regulations. But included among the principalities and powers are the structures we have been dealing with here. It is significant to note that the portrayal of the Suffering Servant in Isaiah 52:13–53:12 has, near the end, a similar victory image: "he will divide the spoil with the strong."

What prevents disarmament as something which nations are urged to carry out is the enthralling illusion with which any population views the encompassing nation-state. Only when persons understand that this power has already been stripped, exposed, put down by God (or when persons, apart from Christian faith, come to a demythologizing of the nation-state and its power) can there be adequate readiness for disarmament in the common reflexive sense. Otherwise people refuse to enter into the risk that disarmament might result in the collapse of their nation-state, leaving them woefully exposed to the depredations of the enemy.

Biblically and quite practically, Christians best witness for disarmament when they live out the truth pointed to in Colossians 2:15.

* * *

For humankind generally, giants, dragons, monsters have been images of immense threats dimly perceived. In the book of Daniel successive empires are pictured as huge savage beasts (Dan. 7). One ethnic group, then another, becomes through rampaging expansion a monstrous coherence of power and peoples. Such rampaging, with oppression and persecutions, was very much a part of history before Christ's triumph over the powers. A beast proceeds by perverse mimicry of God's intention that all life on earth be drawn into a shalom unity under one rule. In Revelation 13 the succession is seen as one beast, which, as has been well put, "represents the combined forces of all political rule opposed to God in the world."[8]

At present those forces are more interlocked globally than ever before. They have brought about a worldwide uniformity, in terms of the primacy of the nation-state, of technology, of propaganda (which, as Jacques Ellul shows, corresponds so strikingly to the picture given in Revelation 13 of the second beast that draws all the earth into worshipping the first beast).[9] This unitary dominion of the beast, in spite of the friend-enemy divisions that demarcate the planet, is most fatefully mediated by the Bomb. The vast farflung systems of counterpoised weapons together constitute a single actuality, menacing all humanity and the whole of God's earthly creation. Of the beast it is written, "authority was given it over every tribe and people and tongue and nation, and all who dwell on earth will worship it, every one whose name has not been written before the foundation of the world in the book of life of the Lamb that was slain" (Rev. 13:7–8).

In Daniel 7 and Revelation 13 the beasts rise out of the sea—out of the chaos, the abyssal waste over against God, which imperils all ordered creation. "Behold, the four winds of heaven were stirring up the great sea" (Dan. 7:2), and one beast after another comes up out of the sea. Each is *of* the sea. The shape and movements of each express that chaotic raging opposed to God.

In Hebrew thought God had raised His creation out of the formless chaos, and only His holding it up kept it from collapse into that chaos. The story of the Flood indicates how ominous is the threat and how extensive the sinking into formless desolation can be. In the Exodus God caused the deeps of the Red Sea to congeal into towering walls (15:8) for the rescue of some and the ruin of others. Old Testament prophecies were filled with premonitions of the inundations of chaos that come upon the collective amassing of human sin.

In biblical times after the Flood and during the centuries since, war has been the most notable and decisive way by which these desolating inundations come. Nuclear weapons, still more grimly than earlier armaments and armies in their readied state, represent the imminence of chaos as it impinges on us. In the Old Testament imagery, chaos was a magnitude lurking within creation, as evidenced by awesome storm or tempestuous sea. Twentieth-century scientists hit upon a discovery in line with that Hebrew understanding: the potential for immense chaos lurking in the atomic nuclei of certain elements. The nuclear weapons systems are the most complex technological constructs of the human mind, fantastically ingenious orderings of millions of component parts. But contained within that pseudo-order as its very essence is ultimate disorder. The desolating cataclysm, the void, is there already in these weapons that are so near to us, so much in our midst.

That chaos is present within us in our repressed fear of the cataclysm and in the deeply hidden personal disorder and desolation from which these weapons have emerged. The readiness to have those engines of chaos is surest evidence of a chaos usually as well hidden within people as those engines are hidden in the depths of earth and sea. The fusion of human beings with the weapons complexes they have constructed comes most of all, not in the control systems, but in the intermeshing oneness of the chaos within the people and the chaos leashed within those weapons.

Hell sets the tongue on fire (Jas. 3:6). The tongue by its devastating words brings the speaker toward hell (Mt. 5:22). With nuclear weapons, *raising hell* has become, still more than before, an awesome possibility. Damning thoughts, deadly words, weapons of annihilation veer toward a terrestrial imaging of their origin. Hell can be thought of theologically as the destroyed destroying (Rev. 11:18)—which is what nuclear war and its aftermath would be.

Chapter 13

HERODIANS

Free us from fear, we cry. Our sleep is fretted,
Anxious we wake, in our terrestrial room.
What wastes the flesh, what ticks below the floor would
Abort all futures, desecrate the tomb.

Free us from fear. The shapes that loom around us
Darkening judgment, freezing all that's dear
Into a pose of departure—these are shadows
Born of man's will and bodied by his fear.[1]

C. Day Lewis

The state first comes into view in the New Testament in Matthew 2 with the story of Herod and the slaying of the innocents. This story, set at the beginning of the gospel narrative, should be understood not as exceptional, but as characteristic of the behavior of governments.

Herod ruled in Jerusalem, "the city of the great King," God, who intended that it be the capital of the human race. Herod, far from being subservient to that great King, was an Edomite pretender, an unworthy, crafty tyrant. His domain was small, but within it he wielded power with a capricious absolutism.

There was much that threatened and jeopardized Herod's waning power. But, when from the lips of alien believers he heard about the infant "king of the Jews," he sensed rightly that this infant constituted the threat behind all threats. "He was troubled, and all Jerusalem with him." He called together his think tank, the court theologians, to ascertain where this incognito king could be found. They answered, quoting the prophet Micah, that he would be born in Bethlehem. With expressions of eagerness to go himself and do homage to the new king, he sent the believers ahead to find the exact location. Warned by God, however, they did not fulfil that role. And Joseph, also warned by God, fled with mother and child away from Herod's tyranny into Egypt.

Herod, waiting on and on in anxious suspense, had to conclude at last that the believers had disobeyed his command (civil disobedience right at the beginning of the gospel story!). But he did have general information on the locale and time of the infant king's advent. In his fury he dispatched soldiers, who, in dutiful soldierly fashion, carried out his ghastly orders to kill all male children, two years old and under, in the Bethlehem area. Herod's murderous intentions were aimed toward the coming messianic King but struck instead the least of his brethren.

Death, not the feared infant King, took from Herod all his imperiled power. But, Herodian rule with its apprehensive determination to do away with the rival King continued. What Herod "the Great" was pre-eminently, his dynastic successors, as they come into view on the margins of the New Testament narratives, were in their lesser ways. His son, Herod Antipas, played out the dynastic style as the lethal thrust finally reached its mark (Lk. 23:6–12). A grandson, Herod Agrippa I, "laid violent hands" on ministers of that King, killing James and imprisoning Peter (Acts 12:1–3). When he welcomed adulation as a god, "the angel of the Lord struck him down.... He was eaten away with worms and died. The word of God continued to spread and to gain followers" (Acts 12:23–24 JB).

Behind the "great" Herod and his lesser successors loomed Rome and the Caesars. The Herodian reaction to the coming King found its complement in the Roman response. Jesus' designation as King, which had so agitated the first Herod, reappeared as the words stating his criminal offense, written on a board and placed on a Roman cross above the Agitator's head. Sensing their common jeopardy, "Herod and Pilate became friends with each other that very day" (Lk. 23:12).

Later when the wider Roman imperial apparatus became more and more troubled by reports about the new King, it had the same problems that had thwarted the first Herod—inability to locate him and the refusal of believers to collaborate. During successive persecutions the Romans slaughtered far greater numbers than Herod had, in the same desperate hope that in the midst of their suffering and death the elusive King would meet his end.

Later still, Constantine and his successors reverted to Herod's unfulfilled strategy: going and paying homage to the infant King. They did this, though, not as prelude to an execution, but as a tactic to retain power. For an infant (unspeaking) king does not need to be taken into account as King over kings and Lord over lords. Christendom rulers from the fourth century A.D. onward wanted an ethereal savior and a lord who would be without claims or commands opposed to their own. They easily found court theologians and religionists to aid in the matter. The emergence of the Madonna-and-child motif and the Christmas preoccupation with a babe in a manger helped to provide a "christ" conveniently remote from the tumultuous arena of competing political configurations. Church hierarchs in that arena needed the same sort of "christ." Around the world those traditions continue wherever there is worship of one whose lordship has no decisive political relevance or weight.

Contemporary nation-states in their centralized rule stand, to a greater or lesser degree, in the Herodian-Roman continuum. The first Herod discerned dangers from many sides and with infernal shrewdness recognized in the report about an unidentified child the Danger which other dangers only intimate. Under the impulsion of absolutist power, Herod acted not only for himself but for all absolutized sovereignties. His varied strategies for eliminating the rival King have persisted on into the efforts of current nation-states. Governments enlist believers to do their bidding in assignments covertly contrary to the dominion of the messianic King. Homage, most of all at Christmas, is paid to an infant "king" who is quite without any lordship that would call into question what a populace and its leaders are bent on doing. To counter grave threats to their power (and the dimly sensed One who is chief Threat), governments slaughter multitudes of innocents in wars and repressions.

Chapter 14

NAZISM'S CULMINATION

Even if we lose, we shall win, for our ideals will have penetrated
the hearts of our enemies.[1]

Josef Goebbels

Every German had a calling when Hitler gassed the Jews, but the
calling concerned not only resistance to the overt crimes but to the
situations that brought Hitler to power and made his reasoning
seem eminently patriotic. Every American has a calling with respect
to nuclear weapons, but the calling concerns not only the crime of
their use but also the ways of thought and conduct which persuade
us that preparation for indiscriminate murder upholds freedom and
justice. Our calling reaches through the whole of life. It may not
occur to individual Germans that the way they lived thirty or forty
years ago made it either a little harder or a little easier for the Jews
to be gassed. But that was exactly the case. It may not occur to
individual Americans that the way we live today makes it either a
little harder or a little easier for someone to start a nuclear war. But
that too is exactly the case.[2]

Norman K. Gottwald

To a large degree, the power of evil resides in the lie—in disguise,
deception, and hiddenness. The disguise, though, may wear thin or be
torn away, the deception may collapse, and the lie come into the open.
Often when this happens, evil seems to have become still more
powerful than before, as when a dictatorship ceases to give much
attention to manipulation of the public through propaganda and rules
with utterly brazen ruthlessness. But when evil has to proceed
without the camouflaging lie, it is rushing to its own demise.

The Word and Spirit of God work in human beings to rend the
disguise and unveil wickedness so that discernment can come. But
helping to prepare for this there is also God's work of rending and
unveiling in world events: When evil is drawn into a risk-all showing
of its hand, it can more readily be seen for what it is.

In Nazism there was much disguise and deception, without which it
could not have come to power. But the unmasking that came in the

terminal exertions and collapse of the Nazi movement was on a larger scale than anything comparable in history. The way evil hid itself in Nazism and what was ultimately exposed can help us identify similar elements that remain disguised in the nuclear arms buildup.

In Nazism power almost without limit was centered in one man and those around him. In the pyramid virtually all exercise of power moved from the top down. It was left only to Hitler and his top advisors to limit their power of life or death over the many, and they did not.

In the arsenals of nuclear weapons far more life-or-death power than Hitler ever had is at the disposal of the American or the Soviet leader and those around him. The masses find themselves, but also put themselves, under the absolute power of the leader; they must trust him to responsibly limit that power from the top. He has the final word as to whether they live or die; and his is the decision whether hundreds of millions are spared or sent into the nuclear ovens. Unlike the Germans under Hitler or the Russians, the American people have again and again ratified this arrangement in what were experienced as *free* elections.

The limit put on the power of the sovereign to inflict punishment and death is one of the most significant aspects in the development of democratic institutions: a guarding of human rights (most notably the right to live) over against the arbitrary will or whim of the ruler(s). Warfare has always come as a movement directly counter to that development: The lives of a great many people (soldiers and also civilians) are put fully and without any clear limit under that will. Now the entire citizenry of each nuclear power is under the same subjection.

The framers of the Constitution of the United States recognized human fallenness and the dangers that go with the exercise of power by governmental leaders. They set up elaborate checks and balances to prevent undue concentration of power in the executive branch of government. But now the only real checks and balances over against the monstrous thermonuclear power held by the President and other top national security managers in the executive branch are those provided by rival governments. Such checks and balances were for Hitler too the only decisive ones.

In a thermonuclear confrontation, my survival, that of the persons dearest to me, that of the entire human race will depend on the common sense, the rationality, the restraint of the American President. Decisions by him and those around him could deprive us of life quite apart from any "due process of law." This awesome dependence on the American President has, for more than three decades, been a central factor in the human situation. Whether or not nuclear war devastates the earth is already being largely determined by the cumulative military and foreign policy decisions of each successive American administration. But the folly of accepting that dependence would be demonstrated only by the outbreak of nuclear war.

Hitler created a bond between most Germans and himself as the *Führer*. But also for Germans who resisted Nazism and for hundreds of millions of people in other countries the bond with Hitler was there in terms of the onrush of results of his leadership. We can feel now what Germans of good will felt in the 1930s—if we discern in our leaders a worsening madness far more fateful than Hitler's. No matter how much we may live out an opposition to nuclear militarism, there is for each of us a terrible bond with the American President and his advisors, with the Soviet leaders, and increasingly with less prominent persons who are in a position to seize the levers of thermonuclear destruction. Whether affirmed or resisted, the bond is there for people of all countries.

In Nazism there was the chain of command from top to bottom. Superiors issued inhuman orders and subordinates dutifully carried them out—Hitler to Eichmann, Eichmann to Hoess and on down even to the Jewish special detachments in Auschwitz. Rule in any collectivity is possible only because subordinates remain obedient. What stood out in Nazism was the rigor of the subordination and the ghastliness of so many of the commands.

Any military establishment operates with comparable top-to-bottom rigor and, in war at least, with ghastly orders. But now, because of the destructiveness of nuclear weapons, the prospective commands would bring much greater slaughter than did those that moved down the Nazi pyramid. Concentration camp guards obeyed and murdered six million. Now several clean-cut, good-natured lads at the firing controls of a Poseidon or Trident submarine or of a Soviet missile command post could annihilate far more human beings than the guards at the concentration camps—simply by obeying the command. It was seen as appalling that lower-level Nazis carried out orders and annihilated millions. That lower-level Americans (and Russians) wait in readiness to annihilate hundreds of millions is generally and almost casually accepted as a necessity of the Cold War.

Hitler as Chancellor did not (so far as is known) personally kill a single human being; nor has any American President. The deed is delegated. But the missileman at the bottom of the chain of command is, so to speak, at the executive top of another pyramid. He, too, delegates the remote deed, now to subordinate weapons.

In Nazism children and youth were molded into marionettes of the state. Great effort went into this, and general success was achieved.

People, looking at communist (or capitalist or other) regimes, frequently say, "If they were allowed to overrun us, they would take our children and bring them up in that evil system." There is poignancy in this deeply motivating fear of ideological kidnapping. Such kidnapping has all too often been carried out. And the means for doing it have become more and more refined. The danger is very real behind a number of frontiers.

But how ironical it is that people generally accept a state of affairs quite similar to the kidnapping they so much fear. The great majority of parents, themselves already taken over by the nation-state and its ideology, hand over their children to television violence, war toys, schoolbook patriotism, nationalist liturgies; to Cold War concepts, anxieties, hostilities; and to the military when this is asked of them.

Probably the worst example of ideological kidnapping before the twentieth century was that of the janissaries under the Turkish sultans. Christian parents were forced to hand over children who were taken away and reared to become elite Turkish soldiers of Moslem faith. Horrible as that practice was, is it not in some ways worse when parents who see themselves as Christian allow their children to grow up as non-Moslem janissaries? The latter practice was common in European christendom and is prevalent around the world today. Rejection of Christ's way is not imposed by outsiders, but is unwittingly passed on from parent to child. Any nation-state, whether Nazi, communist, or capitalist, tries to mold children into its instruments. ("The king . . . will take your sons and appoint them to his chariots and to be his horsemen, and to run before his chariots. . . . He will take your daughters to be perfumers and cooks and bakers"—1 Sam. 8:11,13.) But how deplorable it is when church-going parents serve as prime intermediaries in this process.

Guards in the concentration camps were the product of Nazi indoctrination. A great many men on Poseidon or Trident submarines, in the Strategic Air Command, in the sanctums of the Pentagon are to a very substantial degree the product of an indoctrination by church and churchly home which is aligned with the indoctrination by the nation-state. Though there was a comparable alignment in Germany, concentration camp obedience as actually carried out was not generally held to be compatible with Christian faith. An indication of what we have come to lies in the fact that there is within the churches no such general clarity with regard to obedience in thermonuclear command post or its affiliates.

There was in Nazism the rousing cry against the threatening adversary—mainly communism and the communists. (The Jews were an accessible scapegoat, not so much an ominous adversary.) Relatively few Americans realize that without widespread and drummed-up fear of a communist take-over Hitler could hardly have come to power, overrun most of Europe, and wrung the last measure of despairing resistance out of the German people in the final months of the war.

Without that same fear and outcry (and its counterpart in the Soviet Union) there would very probably not be the fantastically expensive buildup of nuclear weapons. Leaders would not be entrusted with the totalitarian power to destroy the earth, and there would not be, in each of the major powers, the big majority ready to give the last full measure of devotion in nuclear fires. The clamorous fear and fearful clamor that brought in and energized the Nazi regime has done the same for the much greater nuclear despotism.

Anti-communist crusader Billy James Hargis described his approach to the people who came to his meetings and stayed late afterward to ask questions:

> They wanted to join something. They wanted to belong to some united group. They loved Jesus, but they also had a great fear. When I told them that this fear was Communism, it was like a revelation. They knew I was right, but they had never known before what that fear was. They felt better, stronger, more secure in the knowledge that at last they knew the real enemy that was threatening their homes and their lives. They came to me and I told them. That is why they are loyal followers and that is why they will always be with me to praise Christ and destroy Communism in the United States.[3]

In his own way and in spite of the perverse admixture of Christian words, Hargis with this explanation penetrated deeply into the psychopathology of the Cold War and the Nazism that preceded it. People are bedeviled by fears and insecurities. Threat seems so encompassing, yet, for the most part, hard to identify. When a particular group or entity has been identified as the center of all that is threatening, the world seems simpler. People feel better able to face and combat such a threat. Individual impotence and vulnerability are replaced by the strength, security, and purposefulness of the group that has supposedly identified the real threat.

Such movements of the Far Right have come to loom larger and larger in the United States, also in church circles. Those movements, though, are like cartoon exaggerations of the basic Cold War mentality that has shaped the main ranges of American society from Truman through Kennedy to the present. Similarly, the pseudo-Christian Far Right with its old time religion and flag-waving Americanism proceeds with a merger which has infused much of American church history.

A close parallel to the "Christian" Far Right is to be found in the "German Christians" and their merger of religion with Nazi ideology. The Confessing Church as it came together in the 1930s took the emphatic position that such a merger was a negation of the Gospel, a denial of the faith. To give oneself to that merger was to be in mortal danger spiritually. That same warning needs to ring out from a confessing church now to those lured by the Far Right.

Nazism had a Molech visage: the readiness to sacrifice human beings, any number of them, on the altar of the national myth. ("They have built the high places of Baal in the Valley of Ben-hinnom, there to make their sons and daughters pass through fire in honor of Molech" [Jer. 32:35 JB]. Molech means "the king"—title of the chief god of the Ammonites.) The monstrosity of Nazism lay most of all in the massive extent to which the Nazis carried through on this inherent feature, though usually restrained, present in any collectivity. The Russian Civil War, the American war in Indochina, the massacres in Indonesia, East Pakistan/Bangladesh, Uganda, South Africa show that the Molech visage at its worst may emerge in any country.

But the Molech potential of the nuclear powers far surpasses the worst horrors perpetrated by the Nazis. When deputy Gestapo chief Reinhard Heydrich was assassinated near Prague in 1942, the Nazis in reprisal surrounded the village of Lidice, executed the 172 men and boys found there, imprisoned all the others, and leveled the village to the ground. The name and event were taken as epitome of Nazi ruthlessness. But the massacre which each superpower is prepared to carry out is unspeakably bigger than all the Nazi Lidices put together. Auschwitz functionaries dropped crystals of hydrogen cyanide through perforated vents in a chamber packed each time with 2000 human beings. Current functionaries preside over cylindrical concentrations of death all ready to be dropped simultaneously onto hundreds of teeming cities.

Hitler sought to bind the fate of humanity to the fortunes of his blood myth. He would probably have dragged the whole world down in his and the myth's collapse, if he could have. Without the technological limit Hitler had, the American people and the Soviet people have bound the fate of humanity to the fortunes of their competing myths.[4] All peoples are bound to the altars. The sacrificial fire is kindled and ready.

The word Molech evolved when faithful Hebrews combined the consonants for "king" (as the Ammonites titled their national god) with the vowels of *bosheth,* a word meaning shame, in the sense of the ignominy, the consternation, when people are plunged into ruin. ("The sword is without, pestilence and famine are within.... Horror covers them; shame is upon all faces"—Ezek. 7:15,18.) Any idol was seen as bringing this on, and thus itself as *bosheth.*

The exalted self-image of the collectivity ("king") demands human sacrifice. It is crucial that God's people refuse to speak the vaunted words of a nation-state as others mean them, but that they speak them in such a way as to express the approaching ignominy and ruin. "National security," for example, must be vocalized as the utter jeopardy and impending desolation of all. *Bosheth* is the human condition that comes when God tears away evil's disguise. For Nazism this has already occurred. For the present dominant political structures it is close ahead. The preventive or preparatory task for Christians is to express that unmasking now.

Chapter 15

ROMANS 13:1–7

No other verses in Scripture have had, *through wrong interpretation,* such immense influence on world history. The passage is given here in its immediate context. The translation departs at points from the Revised Standard Version of the Bible in an effort to get behind the overlay of traditional interpretations and closer to the original Greek.

> Repay no one evil for evil, but take thought for what is noble in the sight of all. If possible, so far as it depends upon you, live peaceably with all. Beloved, never avenge yourselves, but leave it to the wrath of God; for it is written, "Vengeance is mine, I will repay, says the Lord." No, "if your enemy is hungry, feed him; if he is thirsty, give him drink; for by so doing you will heap burning coals upon his head." Do not be overcome by evil, but overcome evil with good.
>
> Let every person be subject to the governing authorities. For there is no authority except by God, and those that exist have been assigned a place by God. Therefore he who counters the authorities sets himself against God's ordering, and those who set themselves in that opposition will incur judgment. For rulers are not a terror to good conduct, but to bad. Would you have no fear of the governing authority? Then do what is good, and you will receive its approval, for it is God's servant for your good. But if you do wrong, be afraid, for he does not bear the sword in vain; he is the servant of God to execute wrath on the wrongdoer. Therefore one must be subject, not only to avoid wrath, but also for the sake of conscience. For the same reason you also pay taxes, for the authorities are ministers of God when they attend to this very thing. Pay all of them what is properly due[1] them, taxes to whom taxes are properly due, revenue to whom revenue, respect to whom respect, honor to whom honor is properly due.
>
> Owe no one anything, except to love one another; for he who loves the other person has fulfilled the law. The commandments, "You shall not commit adultery, You shall not kill, You shall not steal, You shall not covet," and any other commandment, are summed up in this sentence, "You shall love your neighbor as

yourself." Love does no wrong to a neighbor; therefore love is the fulfilling of the law.

As a background analogy for understanding Romans 13:1–7 we can take the situation in a collapsing marrige as a husband and wife sink in a vicious circle of reciprocal prosecution. This fighting of theirs is not away from all relation to God. There is a realm of dark sowing and reaping: "God is not mocked, for whatever a man sows, that he will also reap" (Gal. 6:7). When a husband and wife sow bitterness and accusations, they reap from each other more of the same. Each is for the other God's agent of retribution. God does not want this destructive reciprocity from them or for them. He is not author of what they inflict on each other; it is not the stirring of His Spirit that leads them in it. Their behavior is the opposite of the love He requires of them. But by His judgment persons who set themselves against each other are caught in an escalation of hostility.

Both husband and wife may be reaping the deserved punishment, but this is not God's central intention as He rules in the process. By letting things get worse, He wants them to see the folly of the course they have taken. They are caught in a dreadful dynamic, but He wants to make of that the context for their recognizing that there must be a way out. A broken marital relationship, precisely because it is so unbearable, can help toward a readiness to recognize that God is offering a breakthrough to reconciliation and a new beginning. The relationship had been beautiful. There were the breakthroughs and new beginnings earlier. The dynamic of grace, already experienced in such times, is stronger, if they turn to it, than what they are trapped in now. So it is that the husband and wife as God's agents of retribution are, without knowing it, serving His central intention.

The role of the Assyrian Empire as presented in Isaiah 10:5–19 and that of Nebuchadnezzar as seen again and again in Jeremiah are comparable, on the international scene, to the role of this husband and wife. The imperial invader is God's agent in His dealing with His apostate people. They reap what they have sown. But in letting this come upon them, God is striving to show them the folly of their ways. In the midst of national collapse He is calling for a return into covenantal relationship with Him. God is not the source of the arrogance of the invaders or their ruthless slaughtering. His punishment is about to come upon the Assyrians or the Babylonians for that. But in the realm of dark sowing and reaping, of wrath, God rules through the sin of imperial leaders who do not know Him. As His agents of retribution they serve His central intention of bringing His people back into faithful loyalty to Him. It can, for example, be seen historically that Nebuchadnezzar did serve this purpose of God.

In many Old Testament passages God is seen as raising up and acting directly through the invader: He becomes the One who destroys and kills. God's aversion to Israel's sin and His rule over what happens are so intensely perceived that His role as chief Actor can overshadow a sense of the desperate autonomy of human actors under and yet apart from Him. In the marital analogy a wife may discern, even in the smouldering rage of the husband and the agony of the collapse of their relationship, God's judgment—His aversion to her sinning, His warning and call to turn back.

What Paul writes in Romans 13:1–7 needs to be seen as basically a restatement of the perspective revealed earlier in the Old Testament prophets. The starkest words in the passage are in verse 5: The governmental authority "is the servant of God to execute . . . wrath on the wrongdoer." (The Greek text has no "his" with "wrath.") The sinning wife is God's agent over against the sinning husband; ruthless Assyria is God's agent over against faithless Israel; the Roman authorities or any civil authorities are, by and large, God's agent over against persons who commit crimes. Governments are not outside God's rule. They *are assigned* by God *a place* (the plain meaning of *tetagmenai eisin* in verse 1), a role in the realm of wrath. They are His agents like arrogant Assyria or the quarreling husband, but God is not the author or source of their behavior. Only in the domain of grace is God the Source: "not I, but the grace of God which is with me" (1 Cor. 15:10). Civil authorities in bearing the sword, which represents rule within the society by threatened or inflicted violence, are sinning, going contrary to God's way of love described in the verses immediately before and after the Romans 13:1–7 parenthesis: "Never take vengeance into your own hands. . . . Love hurts nobody" (Rom. 12:19; 13:10 Phillips). But in the retributive dynamisms that emerge under God as He sets Himself against sin, civil authorities do have their place along with Assyria and the nagging wife. A person who has been arrested, tried, and imprisoned for a crime may sense in all this God's merciful dealing with him. He may learn that this punishment is better for him than the illusion of success in evil. He thus comes to see the authorities as an agent of God, even though he may find that they, in their actual treatment of him, have again and again acted contrary to God's love.

Paul states the converse side as well. If a person does what is right rather than what deserves punishment, he receives, not wrath, but approval, from the governing authority, which, through this, "is God's servant for" his good. "Approval," though it may take more explicit form, comes primarily as a governing authority gives to good behavior the proper response of no "wrath." Under God that response contributes to the well-being of the person (and the society).

Forms from the Greek root meaning *to put in order* occur four times in Romans 13:1–2. Because of the *ordino, ordinatio* of Jerome's Vulgate, the English-speaking countries received *ordain, ordinance* in the Authorized Version, and there were comparable renderings in other modern languages. *Ordino, ordinatio* in classical Latin refer, as do the Greek words used by Paul, to simple ordering, setting in order, as of rows of trees, military formations, parts of a manuscript. But the words drew to themselves in the christendom context such an overlay of ecclesiastical and theological sanctity as to quite block any understanding of what Paul had actually written. God does not consecrate and hallow the civil authorities; such hallowing is reserved for the Messianic community. But He does allot to the civil authorities a place, a role; they too, even in their covert violence or their raging, are not outside his ordering of all things in this fallen world.

Romans 13 and Revelation 13 have of course often been considered side by side. This juxtaposition can help prevent the traditional misconceptions that have gone with the isolation of Romans 13:1–7 as sole basis for a Christian view of the state. In studies comparing the two passages a most significant point where the teaching of the seemingly very different chapters coincide has seldom been noticed. The key uniting word is *exousia,* usually translated as authority or power. In Romans 13:1 Paul, after asking his readers to subordinate themselves to the governing authorities *(exousiai),* writes, "For there is no authority *(exousia)* except by God." The *exousia* remains the focus of discussion in the next several verses. In the account of the first beast found in Revelation 13:1–10 *exousia* occurs four times. In the first two the dragon has given his *exousia* to the beast. In the second two an *exousia* to proceed for forty-two months and an *exousia* over all the inhabitants of the earth were given to the beast. In verses 5–7 *"were given to him"* is repeated four times like a refrain. There is in this Semitic passive, clear reference to God as the One who gives. Also to be seen in relation to these passages is the devil's statement that "all this *exousia* ... has been delivered to me" (Lk. 4:6) and Jesus' words to Pilate, "You would have no *exousia* over me unless it had been given you from above" (Jn. 19:11).

Exousia comes from the verb *exestin,* "it is free," meaning "that an action is possible in the sense that there are no hindrances or that the opportunity for it occurs, i.e. 'to have the possibility,' 'to be able'... that an action is not prevented by a higher norm or court, that 'it may be done or is not forbidden.'"[2] The most basic meaning of *exousia* is the possibility of action. That possibility is not inherent in the actor; an overarching context confers it as permission, freedom, right, or authority. In one instance the possibility for action can be understood as permission—what is not forbidden—in another as delegated authority.

The connotations of the Greek word *exousia* are very important for understanding Romans 13:1-7 and the other passages. Unlike the English words *authority,* in some of its uses, or *power,* which tend to focus only on exercising sway *over* some sphere, *exousia* points to its own derivative character, its aspect of being *under. Exousia* is used a number of times to express Jesus' God-given power and authority to act. "All *exousia*...has been given to me" (Mt. 28:18—with the same noun and verb as in Rev. 13:5-7). God confers His *exousia* (which, while not derivative, has its determining context in who He is), His authority, power, freedom, on His Messiah and on His Messianic people. But to the beast God *allows* the possibility, the space, the delimited time to act—over against Him. The latter *exousia* is "authority" only because the allowed scope for acting involves a *de facto* sway over others. It does not involve God's conferring His authority or anything else that is distinctively His. It is not a "right," an authorization, but rather the bare, unsupported, unhallowed possibility of acting which is simply allowed.

Exousia was a favorite word in the self-characterizations of rulers in the ancient Mediterranean world; attention was focused on the impressiveness of dominion *over.* The inflatedness of this usage can be sensed in the devil's boast, even while he was acknowledging the derivative character of that *exousia,* or in Pilate's irritated words to Jesus, "I have *exousia* to release you, and *exousia* to crucify you" (Jn. 19:10). Pilate's *exousia* to crucify, as Jesus located it in the context of God's rule, was only God's permitting him a bare, bleak possibility of acting over Jesus—*under* God; God did not authorize Pilate's power or his deed. Jesus' reply was intended to deflate Pilate's self-image.

The *exousia* pointed to in John 19:11 and in Revelation 13:5-7 is a mystery which believers through the ages have been faced with: that evil is perpetrated only as God allows this. The permissive meaning of *exousia,* which we have just considered, is in line with that biblical view.

Revelation 13:5–7 can help us understand that God's permitting evil is the ground, not for mute perplexity, but for resilient hope: evil dominion is *under* God; He it is who allows its limited and soon-to-be-terminated scope.

In Romans 13 Paul uses *exousia* in the sense of governing authority, government. But that specific meaning still retains something of the connotations we have been scrutinizing. Paul, in a deflation of the governmental claim, emphasizes the *under* aspect: There is no government except by God; He allows the scope, the possibility to act; all is within His overruling sway (just as is the case with the beast in Revelation 13).

As we have seen, *exousia* can refer to a delegating of power and authority which brings with it full backing by whoever has done the delegating. For the New Testament writers this has come preeminently to Jesus. But *exousia* can refer simply to the possibility of action as something permitted. Within the christendom tradition the *exousia* sentences in Romans 13 have been seen in terms of the first meaning—and thus in analogy to the *exousia* of Jesus Christ. But the sentence that immediately precedes mention of the "authorities"—"Do not be overcome by evil, but overcome evil with good"—points toward the second, permissive meaning. After that sentence Paul proceeds to consider what would come to mind as the most notable source of evil inflicted on Christians—"the governing authorities." Believers were to face and overcome that evil, too, with good. Relevant also is the fact that Nero was Emperor when this letter was written. It is not said that God bestows on the *exousia* a divine consecration, but rather that He assigns it a place, a role.

There is in the passage nothing that would give basis for *not* seeing those sentences in terms of the second, permissive meaning of *exousia*—if the characterizations, "servant of God" and "ministers of God," are understood to center in a role as agents of wrath, that, like Assyria or the sullen husband, do not have God as author and source of their behavior. God does not consecrate anyone to be a sullen husband. He did not command (and surely would never have commanded) faithful Israelites to join an Assyrian invasion. The execution of wrath, though under His permissive rule, is separated from Him; and those who have given themselves to Him as source of their living are to keep that distance too ("Never take vengeance into your own hands.... Love hurts nobody"). Romans 13:1–7, if understood in terms of God's permissive ordering, is in harmony with the over-all New Testament perspective on government as we have seen it in other passages.[3] Governmental dominion is possible only as God allows it scope. God permits that dominion but does not confer on it His authority or direct authorization. He orders and overrules it so that even in its opposition to Him it is made to serve His purposes. Christians can face even the most malevolent authorities with a confidence in God's overruling sovereignty.

The most difficult element in the passage is not any injunction to unconditional obedience, for there isn't that. What is called for is submission, recognition and acceptance of the sway held under God by those wielding political power.[4] The most perplexing part, not only for pacifist Christians, but for any who have some real sense of the innumerable injustices, persecutions, repressions perpetrated by governments throughout history, is the seemingly bland assertion that "rulers are not a terror to good conduct, but to bad"—live right and you will have nothing to fear from the authorities. The statement may be correct for what has been the preponderant behavior of civil authorities within most societies. But millions of people throughout history have become victims of governmental terror precisely because what they were doing was good and right. This was the experience of the Hebrews in Egypt, of David, Elijah, Naboth, Jeremiah, and of many, many others in the Old Testament. Before Romans 13:1–7 was written, Christians, among them Paul himself, had often received bad treatment for good conduct. Had Paul quite forgotten, among other things, the basket escape from Damascus and the official whipping at Philippi? The execution of Jesus would seem to constitute the supreme refutation of Paul's seeming optimism about governmental authorities. Indeed the past and current history of God's people was so filled with incidents in which rulers were "a terror to good conduct" that Paul could hardly have reckoned with the prospect that these statements of his would be taken as simple, dependable generalization about how governments do act.

There were factors impinging on Pilate that pointed him toward the right decision: his own diminished humanness, the norms of Roman justice, the pleas of his wife, and some inkling of who this Jesus in front of him was. These were pointing him toward the right decision. Something comparable is found in Romans 13:3–6; Paul sets down for Christians what they should expect from governing authorities. Through the criteria given, persons in government are indirectly confronted with what God wants of them.

In the United States during the sixties, those within the shriller circles of the anti-war movement typically expected the worst and nothing but the worst from the government; police were counted on to act like "pigs"; and such expectations were often fulfilled. In contrast, Christians who enter into nonviolent witness strive to reach the humanness of those who wield power; they can appeal to the recognized norms for justice in the society; they plead, hoping for the right act; they seek to mediate some sense of the hidden Lordship of Jesus. This stance and spirit can help us make sense of those puzzling statements in Romans 13. Instead of being a simple description of the way governments always or nearly always function, the verses delineate the expectancy with which Christians are to face political authorities. No government as such has God's backing, but Christians in their relations to the governing authorities have the backing of His norms for government. This stance toward authorities is a main aspect of the endeavor to "overcome evil with good." The book of Acts records various instances in which Christians with forthright expectancy and an appeal to recognized norms won authorities over to a right decision. When they are not won over, and Pilate himself was not, even their abject drivenness or their raging is still made to subserve God's purposes.

There is in the passage another implication that has relevance to the issues of violence and nonviolence. Though Paul was writing within the Roman imperial context to Christians in Rome for whom independent non-Roman governments were hardly in the picture, he was pointing, at least obliquely, to any and all governing authorities. If the passage is studied in relation to the multiplicity of modern nation-states, there is in it no basis for concluding that any government is outside God's ordering or a role as His agent. (The usual practice has been to take the passage as hallowing description of one's own government—but as a norm which rival governments go against.) "For there is no authority except by God, and those that exist have been assigned a place by God." The focus is naturally on subordination to, or stated negatively, not setting oneself against, the authorities one lives under. But the reasons given for this, point by implication toward not setting oneself against other governments, also any that come to be officially designated as enemy governments; for God assigns to them a place as well and uses them as His agents, and to set oneself (as in war) against some other government is to set oneself against God's ordering.

PART III

ECHOES OF GOD'S LAUGHTER

Chapter 16

GOD'S LAUGHTER

Why this uproar among the nations?
Why this impotent muttering of pagans—
kings on earth rising in revolt,
princes plotting against Yahweh and his Anointed,
"Now let us break their fetters!
Now let us throw off their yoke!"

The One whose throne is in heaven sits laughing,
Yahweh derides them.
Then angrily he addresses them,
in a rage he strikes them with panic,
"This is my king, installed by me
on Zion, my holy mountain."

Psalm 2:1–6 (JB)

God, scrutinizing the nations, laughs! The image jars us. This is not a divine laughter we would choose to hear. We may find it un-Godlike that the Father of Jesus Christ would laugh in derision at anybody or anything. Yet the crucial importance of listening for that laughter is pointed to by the fact that Psalm 2, with its stark and rousing political images, was for the first followers of Jesus Christ one of the several most quoted passages in the Hebrew scriptures.

The nations continue to rage. What is over against each most of all is not the threatening might of rivals but the nearly inaudible laughter of God.

Arthur Koestler has written:

> Thus irony consists in defeating an opponent on his own ground, that is, by accepting his premises, his values, his prejudices, his methods of reasoning, for the purpose of unmasking their implicit absurdity. It pretends to take seriously what it doesn't; it enters into the spirit of the other's game to demonstrate that the game is absurd.[1]

Irony thus understood is a prime element in a great many Old Testament passages having to do with the unfolding events of the time. The prophets so vividly saw that God's opponents are defeated on their own ground. It is not that God, acting openly as God, defeats them. They defeat themselves; they parade their own ridiculousness; they bring on their own ruin.

> *The nations have sunk into a pit of their own making,*
> *they are caught by the feet in the snare they set themselves.*
> *Yahweh has made himself known, has given judgment,*
> *he has trapped the wicked in the work of their own hands.*
> (Ps. 9:15–16 JB)

There is in evil such titanic power, turned not only outward centrifugally against what is round about but also inward centripetally upon itself. Evil brings on its own ruin, but this does not happen apart from God. Evil's rebellion against God is very much in relation to Him. He is there at the hurling of the No against Him. As evil moves to its own undoing, God is very much involved; in evil's destroying itself God triumphs over it.

In general, this process moves slowly enough that we hardly notice it. When a fallen tree decays through many years, the dissolution can hardly be perceived. Yet the dissolution of the same tree, if it was destroyed in a forest fire, would be vividly seen. In human affairs it is as if evil's slow rot becomes, at certain points, a spontaneous combustion that brings on the engulfing fire. In biblical thought evil's dissolution at the close of history and beyond (hell) is represented as conflagration—with the terrible danger for human beings of getting inextricably drawn into it.

What we find again and again in the writings of the Hebrew prophets is the depiction of some march of events in process of unmasking the absurdity of human rebellion against God. A prophet's cry caught up the unheeded warning resonant in the events and called for a turning back before the terminal event toward which a rebel people was rushing.

As prophet and more-than-prophet Jesus cried out to the unholy city: "O Jerusalem, Jerusalem, killing the prophets and stoning those who are sent to you! How often would I have gathered your children together as a hen gathers her brood under her wings, and you would not! Behold, your house is forsaken" (Lk. 13:34). But their *would not* held firm against his *would,* and the city was destroyed. When eyes do not take in the march of events, nor ears hear the prophetic cry and that ominous laughter, irony reaches its final expression in catastrophe.

The current world nuclear situation is bursting with irony. Since the nations have not capitulated to the Advent of the Lord's Anointed, they find themselves encompassed by a contrary advent much within the context of their premises, values, methods of reasoning—the advent of nuclear weapons. It is on their own chosen ground, not by some intervention from on high, that total defeat is pressed upon the nations, and the absurdity of their illusions is unmasked. (To the extent that churches have taken for themselves that same ground, as is still all too much the case around the world, the same defeat comes upon them.) God's laughter echoes through the imperial urban canyons and down into the underworld of nuclear weaponry, then back toward any ears that are open to hear. "This aeon is at an end. The world...can have a future only in the new aeon determined by...the lordship of God."[2]

The intent of God's taunting laughter is to impress upon rebels this awareness, to make them see what they have refused to see. The discovery that one is being laughed at can be acutely unsettling—most of all, surely, when it is God who laughs. God's irony is directed not toward the defeat of those who oppose him—they are already defeated—but toward their capitulation: the acceptance of defeat and disillusionment and their submission to God's gracious sovereignty:

> So now, you kings, learn wisdom,
> earthly rulers, be warned:
> serve Yahweh, fear him,
> tremble and kiss his feet,
> or he will be angry and you will perish,
> for his anger is very quick to blaze.
>
> Happy all who take shelter in him.
>
> (Ps. 2:10–12 JB)

Submission to Yahweh must come as homage to His Messiah, to whom He has said,

> You are my son,
> today I have become your father.
> Ask and I will give you the nations for your heritage,

the ends of the earth for your domain.
With iron scepter you will break them,
shatter them like potter's ware.

(Ps. 2:7–9 JB)

The raging of the nations has not erupted outside of the rule of Yahweh and His Messiah. It has broken out against that rule: "Now let us throw off their yoke!" As with man's personal rebellion and fall, so with collective rebellion and fall. Already in this Old Testament scripture, the rule of the Messiah is not a late remedial move by God but a given since the very beginning. As the Word-become-flesh/Jesus was with the Father in the beginning, so the sovereignty of that executed Galilean peasant over the nations surges toward a fulfilment of the power that was His before any attempt to negate it. Decisive for the fulfilment was the convergence of all that rebelling as imaged in Psalm 2 into the crucifixion of Jesus of Nazareth (Acts 4:25–28).

What is most obvious in history, past and present, is the commotion and clash of nations set against each other. But in Psalm 2, in the Gog/Magog prophecy of Ezekiel 38 and 39, in the apostolic prayer of Acts 4:24–30, in the battle images of Revelation 19 and 20, the nations are in alliance, acting in concert, set not against each other but against God and His Anointed: "in this very city Herod and Pontius Pilate made an alliance with the pagan nations and the peoples of Israel, against your holy servant Jesus whom you anointed" (Acts 4:27 JB).

This biblical perspective, if held by God's people, holds them back from participation in any raging (even "defensive") of the particular nation in which they reside, against another. For they understand that the crucial confrontation is not between one nation or alliance and its counterpart, but between God and all nations in their concerted raging.

If *détente* between the United States and the Soviet Union "has been nine tenths rhetoric and one tenth policy,"[3] *détente* in both these components has exemplified the plotting and revolt pictured in Psalm 2:1–3. The rhetoric has camouflaged the continued frenzy of military buildup; and to the extent that the superpowers do stand together, as in the SALT treaties, even their common stand is set against God, His Rule, and His creation. It is so evident, also apart from biblical faith, that the immeasurably critical issue is not success or failure in the rivalry between West and East. The issue is whether or not this and other rivalries bring on an irreversible devastation of this planet.

The deepest fear in any nation is that of an overwhelming thrust by some adversary: impotence, demolition, an end of all. Yahweh strikes the nations with panic as He points to the One from whom that irresistible thrust is about to come.

Yet it is difficult for us to see this latter dimension in human events. What seems to dominate the world is the fear in Eastern countries of the West and the fear in Western countries of the East—and the anxiety about what is ahead because of the nuclear arms buildup. That fear has a certain appropriateness. There is the very real possibility of a demolishing strike by the other side. But in Psalm 2:5 the nations are driven beyond fear into panic—like that of the Egyptian army mired between those walls of water (Ex. 14:24–25), like that of the Midianites before Gideon (Jg. 7:21–22), like the panic in the Philistine camp after the raid by Jonathan and his armorbearer (1 Sam. 14:15). Panic is "a sudden and excessive feeling of alarm or fear, usually affecting a body of persons, and leading to extravagant or injudicious efforts to secure safety."[4] There is something so uncanny about such a mass frenzy that the ancient Greeks saw it as brought on by the god Pan, the name from which the word is derived. The Hebrews discerned God behind it. The most notable example of panic is that of an army fleeing in wild confusion. Panic impels people to such extreme efforts to save their lives that it provides the most dramatic confirmation of Jesus' warning, "Whoever would save his life will lose it" (Mk. 8:35).

The East-West struggle has been much analyzed in terms of fear. But it can be better understood in terms of panic. If the frenzied commotion in the midst of a calamity were filmed and then projected in very slow motion, the behavior would still be panic. During the years when the black death ravaged Europe, there were the periods of slow-motion anticipatory panic which would then erupt in surges of racing panic. The panic of nations pictured in Psalm 2 is generally the slow-motion kind, punctuated by intense accelerations.

In panic people are overwhelmed and confounded by an immense threat. For both the ancient Greeks and the Hebrews the deepest impulsion to panic came when a group of people felt themselves to be in a confrontation with the supernatural, the divine. In our time this motif is played upon in a great many science fiction and horror movies. These in turn show that the unnerving sense of being up against the more than human is very widespread.

It is hard for us, even within biblical faith, to enter into the perspective of Psalm 2, partly because we are so encompassed by the dynamisms of one nation fearing another. We can, though, see in the

Soviet Union a superpower engaged in titanic social, economic, and military endeavor, given impetus by an orchestrating rhetoric. The imperialistic, warmongering West, the United States in particular, is pointed to as the supreme threat to all that they are working for. And in terms of the destructive potential of the Western nuclear delivery systems, that identification would seem grimly accurate. But Christians can recognize a still more ominous threat: the immense, impending weight of God's No to and His judgment upon so much of that Soviet endeavor and rhetoric. In Jesus' parable of the enterprising rich man who wanted to eat, drink, and be merry, (Lk. 12:16–21), the terror lies not in the man's unplanned-for death but in God's pronouncement, "Fool!" Even within history that word can reverberate over entire nation-states, apart from awareness of its source.

Nazi Germany's going down in colossal discredit (something quite different from complete defeat without such an utter discrediting) is an intimation of what we are pointing to here, that God's judgment is a far more awesome threat than the menace or even the overwhelming victory of an enemy coalition. The illusion that the enemy coalition is *the* threat becomes the chief factor in promoting the behavior that brings on the immensity of God's negating judgment. The worst that could come upon the Russian people would not be nuclear obliteration in itself or even the slower ravages of radiation sickness, but the abrupt discrediting of the collective illusions by which they had lived. The worst that could come would be summarized in that pronouncement "Fool!," whether recognized as God's summing up or not— though that word, if not heard too late, is meant to stop and turn those so characterized to Him who in anguish speaks it.

All this, perhaps more readily seen with regard to the Soviet Union, applies just as much, and probably even more, to the United States and its major allies. *Here* is titanic endeavor, a subtler rhetoric, a far wider achievement of the fool's style described in the parable ("My soul ... take things easy, eat, drink, have a good time"—Lk. 12:19 JB), a more callous repression and exploitation of the world's poor, and, complementing the illusion of the other side as chief threat, an illusion more pernicious than that of socialist righteousness—the myth that a Christian righteousness and moral idealism determine the Cold War stance of the United States and its West European allies. One is reminded of the tough pragmatism of Pilate and the calculating piety of Caiaphas. And more terrible it is for a Caiaphas to hear at last the final characterization "Fool!" than even for a Pilate. Disciples should be able to sense that the supremely ominous threat to American (and

Western) society is not Soviet nuclear weapons but God's impinging judgment as it moves toward a more drastically negating demolition than any that Soviet weaponry could bring about. We are thinking here about a judgment within history.

Nation-states generally, also in the East, seek support and corroboration from the churches. This is to be understood, most of all, as a countering of a dim, repressed sense of being up against God. The opposite of that alignment with the churches too much intimates the threat.

God has installed His Messiah on Zion; He has exalted Jesus at His right hand. This Lordship of Jesus constitutes the supreme (though still uncompleted) discrediting—beyond anything else that could be conceived—of what the nations and their leaders have chosen to be; for in their economic, foreign, and military policies they move, madly and grotesquely, counter to Jesus and his way.

Jesus stands as the rejection, the utter discrediting and ultimate demolition of the policies and values to which the nations are committed. "None of the rulers of this age understood this [the wisdom of God superseding their own wisdom]; for if they had, they would not have crucified the Lord of glory" (1 Cor. 2:8). Yet even in their delusion, they have some sense of the power that is overwhelming them, and this throws them into the panic depicted in Psalm 2. So it is that nation is set against nation in what is comparable to the battlefield panic of certain Old Testament stories: "Yahweh made every man in the camp turn his sword against his comrade" (Judg. 7:22 JB).

On closer examination it can be seen that Nazi Germany went down in only partial discredit. Its victorious discreditors had proceeded and still proceed within perspectives jointly held by victors and vanquished. A collective ignominy can be fully recognized for what it is only through an understanding of God's No proclaimed by the Hebrew prophets and lived out by Jesus.

The iron nails that tore through Jesus' flesh can be thought of symbolically as transmuted into the iron scepter with which he smites the nations. In his encounter with the rulers of this age resulting in his submission to the Cross, he has turned their modes of exercising power into the cause of their total collapse. In the remarkable promise of Revelation 2:26–27 Jesus shares with his faithful disciples this scepter, this sweeping advance of his dominion over the nations. We can take part in his shattering of the nations if we are willing to share in the death he suffered under their rule.

Chapter 17

RULERS SO-CALLED

Such contradictions raise grave doubts, not so much about the integrity of leaders who say they want to avoid Doomsday, as about whether they are still masters of unfolding events, or impersonal vehicles for a self-fulfilling lunacy.[1]

Sidney Lens

God narrowed Himself down into Jesus Christ. The Incomprehensible, the Inscrutable became a human person in our midst. Because collectivities are too spread out to be seen in full, they strive, in their competition with God, toward a comparable focusing. Kings, emperors, presidents are needed primarily as the identifiable focus for the collectivity (and for the ruling elite). Children usually see the President or his equivalent as the government. To some extent that convenient oversimplification remains in us all. The impulsion toward having graven images takes this form too. And in mutual reinforcement "Presidents quickly come to see themselves as personifications of the nation."[2] To be part of a selected group favored with a personal appearance by the President is to be enveloped in a mesmerism that must be rooted in an awe before the royal presence as experienced through thousands of years.

Because the collectivity is cornucopia, it must, in the image of biblical apocalyptic, be horn as thrusting might; and both cornucopia and horn have a tip—the ruler, who is the most comprehensible representation of all that extends out below him. Toward him are directed the unfulfilled but hardly ever abandoned hopes for a better future. His is the power, and to him, people desperately want to believe, belongs a wisdom commensurate with that power.

The Hebrews insisted on having a king so that they too might have a visible, identifiable head "like all the nations" to govern and to lead them in war (1 Sam. 8:20). The culmination of their insistence on being like the other nations came when the Jewish oligarchs told Pilate, "We have no king but Caesar" (Jn. 19:15); they pushed aside not only Jesus but their entire Hebrew past as it centered in God's Kingship.

The early church saw Jesus Christ as the Head, the One in whom all persons, all things, cohere or are to cohere (Col. 1:15–20). Any cohesions apart from his are makeshift substitutes, made necessary by the rejection of the one coherence for which everything was created. These substitutes must have their mimic heads.

The absurdities of the standard collective arrangement are manifold. How can anything so vast and variegated as an empire (or even a lesser nation-state) be comprehended in a single frail human being? How can *one* be rightly over great multitudes of people? How can one·person begin to be great enough, wise enough, for the position? How can all the needed vision, understanding, initiatives, and action have their center in him? If the continuing existence of the collectivity is seen as the supreme imperative, how can a vulnerable mortal who is to die so soon effectively represent that existence?

Such dilemmas and the efforts at resolving them shaped the political history of Israel. The people being who they were, the arrangement with God as their ruler did not seem very workable politically. God condescended to choose, anoint, and deal with kings, most notably David, with whom He established a covenantal relationship which those who succeeded David were also to have.

In Revelation 5 John sees a scroll in the right hand of God enthroned in majesty. An angel calls out, "Who is worthy to open the scroll and break its seals?"—worthy to resolve the enigma of human history and to lead in the break-through into the New Age. The yearning and expectancy which fills that question permeated the ancient world and came to most notable expression in the ceremonials at the accession of kings. The wistful affirmations that have come down to us in the prophecy of Nathan (2 Sam. 7:1–17) and the royal psalms had their antecedents in Egyptian court usage and their parallels in other countries. As Gerhard von Rad explains, "Unquestionably every accession, in Jerusalem as elsewhere, was understood as the announcement of a new divine order for the conditions of human life, and even of those in nature."[3] (The contemporary world is filled with faded analogues to this.)

But King Saul was a disaster for Israel. Even David, the idealized model king, was, as the bibical accounts show in stark honesty, an erring, buffeted, and (toward the end) embittered man, whose last recorded words had to do with instructions for killing some personal enemies (1 Kg. 2:5–9). Solomon was at his wisest when he confessed:

"I am but a little child; I do not know how to go out or come in. . . . Who is able to govern this thy great people?" (1 Kg. 3:7,9). The historical narratives make plain that even an infusion of divinely given wisdom was not enough to overcome his pathetic inadequacy. And each successive son of David proved to be inferior to the very imperfect dynastic father rather than one whom that father could call Lord (Mk. 12:35–37). The chief significance of the whole sequence of Hebrew and Jewish kingship was to demonstrate the conclusion that drove John on Patmos to weep: "no one was found worthy" (Rev. 5:4).

And thus it was that long before the birth of Jesus, royal psalms and similar passages were reinterpreted as pointing to a Messianic advent still to come. Throughout the New Testament these passages are seen as fulfilled in Jesus. "Weep not; lo, the Lion of the tribe of Judah, the Root of David, has conquered, so that he can open the scroll and its seven seals" (Rev. 5:5). He alone, and no other, has "divine right." Nothing in the New Testament intimates for later non-Hebrew rulers any sort of Davidic status (as in the christendom heresy).

From Saul to Zedekiah the Old Testament record gives great importance to whether God's people had a good or a wicked king. All that pendulating found its conclusion in Jesus: God's people have a Sovereign who is incomparably good. And the question of the relative goodness or badness of other rulers becomes marginal except as the wickedness of heads of state veers into persecution of the church. An implication of this perspective in the present American context is that the crucial factor for the increase of human well-being lies not with having a good President (if indeed there could be such) but with the loyalty of God's people to *their* Sovereign—a loyalty that can be woefully diminished by giving any sort of Old Testament centrality (itself an interim concession) to the President or the government.

Converging toward the one political head of any collectivity are the ruling directorate, the advisors, the proliferating bureaucracies. From the central few come the words of command and various modes of mediated presence. The Romans had coins, statues, inscriptions, monumental buildings, incense rites, and most of all the presence of their occupying legions. Contemporary means are even more effective. While radio was the most advanced medium, Gabriel Marcel pointed out:

> A Hitler or a Mussolini, speaking into the microphone, could really seem invested with the divine privilege of being everywhere at once. . . . How can we allow that it is quite safe for any individual,

whoever he is, to be granted the gift of being everywhere at once ...?"[4]

Now after the spread of television that question has become even more urgent—with regard to any television personalities but especially with regard to the focal leader. In a time of dramatized crisis he can arrange a personal epiphany before the eyes of a large segment of the population. The Head of the church stands behind the curtain of the seen. The head of state can be there in a mimic advent for all to see. The nation-state, over against God, would seem to be at its strongest in this vivid, undeniable incarnation. Television and the other media constitute the nation-state's remarkable substitute for the Holy Spirit.

In ancient empires rulers consulted sages, diviners, and augurers to penetrate into the future and determine what would be the best course of action. Many Old Testament stories attest the key role given these court specialists. The Babylonians and Assyrians had an exalted class of priests who were expert in examining the livers of sacrificial sheep to divine the intentions of the gods. In this "science" each part of a sheep's liver had a name and numerous characteristics to watch for. So important was this mode of divination that every army contingent had such a priest assigned to it.

It is important that we see government-financed think tanks, military gamesmen, warrior intellectuals as a contemporary continuation of that ancient and enduring arrangement. The innards of computers have replaced sheep livers. Babylonian rulers and populace relied on what was regarded as the most advanced and brilliant rationality of the time; Americans and Russians do the same. What priests discovered in sheep livers or augurers found in bird entrails depended mainly on the inclinations of rulers and consultants. So too with computers. We know that Roman augury was consistently used to manipulate public opinion.

Ron Rosenbaum has given a glimpse of the most imposing current divination.

> The SIOP [Single Integrated Operating Plan] machine is a vast computer complex in a subbasement of the Underground Command Post that generates the Emergency War Orders for transmittal to each element of the SIOP attack. In addition, the SIOP machine is constantly war-gaming its own war plan against its own estimate of the Russian war plan, which SIOP calls RISOP, and updating itself after it counts the computerized death score.

He adds a most revealing comment: "Even in sophisticated strategic literature the SIOP is spoken of with reverential, almost Delphic, awe, and its pronouncements are surrounded with Delphic mystery."[5]

In 1 Kings 22 Ahab and Jehoshaphat, the kings of Israel and Judah, decide to inquire of the Lord before going to Ramoth-gilead to attack the Syrians and recapture the town. The four hundred court prophets predict victory with such facile unanimity that Jehoshaphat asks whether there is another prophet who might be consulted. Ahab summons Micaiah son of Imlah, but only reluctantly because of his record of prophesying woe instead of weal. Micaiah tells of two visions, one of "all Israel scattered upon the mountains, as sheep that have no shepherd" and the other a scene in heaven's throneroom in which a spirit stood before the Lord and offered to bring Ahab to his downfall by being "a lying spirit in the mouth of all his prophets." The lie that Ahab longed for and wanted to live out was given him as prestigious pronouncement by the court prophets, who in the subtlety of the text are designated as *his* (not the Lord's).[6] Contemporary establishment prophets join in fabricating a comparable lie; the church comes forward too infrequently as successor to Micaiah son of Imlah; and long ago warnings ring out also toward current advisers and those who engage them:

> *Monstrous, horrible things*
> *are happening in the land:*
> *the prophets prophesy falsely,*
> *the priests teach whatever they please.*
> *And my people love it!*
> *But when the end comes, what will you do?*
>
> (Jer. 5:30–31 JB)

> *Oh, they [the advisors] will be like wisps of straw*
> *and the fire will burn them.*
> *They will not save their lives*
> *from the power of the flame.*
> *No embers these, for baking,*
> *no fireside to sit by.*
>
> (Is. 47:14 JB)

* * *

Jesus' plainest statement about those who wield political power (and thus about governments) has been generally overlooked by the churches. The history of the last two millennia would have been far different if this passage, rather than Romans 13:1–7, had been given its rightfully central place in determining a Christian view of the state.

The disciples were quarreling about which of them would have the chief positions. Jesus introduced his command to them with a totally contrary example and made his point twice: "You know that the so-called rulers in the heathen world lord it over them, and their great men have absolute power. But it must not be so among you" (Mk. 10:42–43 Phillips).

"So called rulers": Men seize the role but do not fill it. They try to rule, they seem to rule; but from the perspective of what true rule should be, they are only pretenders, usurpers. Though heathen populations take the appearance for reality, Jesus' disciples should not.

"Lord it over": This, according to Jesus, is the essence of what those who wield political power do; certain persons lord it over others. The drive for the power to lord it over others had just shown itself among the disciples. This perverted alternative for human relationships can emerge at any level, but is most striking and obvious at the political top.

"Their great men": Jesus alludes to the exalted claims which apparent rulers make and promote with all the power and media at their disposal. Augustus, emperor during the first half of Jesus' earthly life, had taken that name which means worthy of reverence or worship. He was celebrated as father of the fatherland, father of the earth, Liberator, heavenly Savior. The world in which Jesus lived out his ministry continued to reverberate with such claims.

"Have absolute power": They lord it over, tyrannize, dominate others. Such power as they have, rather than being directed to serve the good of others, is used primarily to reinforce their power, to make it more complete and secure. Ordinarily, heathen populations yield subserviently to such absolute power and to the self-characterizations of those who seem to rule. If the deep human need to be subordinate does not, as the Creator intended, find its fulfilment under His Lordship, it gravitates toward the encompassing political dominion.

When Jesus said these words, he and his bewildered, fearful disciples were on the road going up to Jerusalem. Soon he would be face to face with a Gentile ruler, so-called, and with the collaborating Jewish authorities, who lived out much of the heathen style. Jesus experienced in his own person the accuracy of his characterization of government. The pretender, Pilate, faced the true King, Jesus. A ruler who had authority over others mainly because he had soldiers under his command met One whose authority lay in the attracting, impelling power of the Truth he incarnated (Jn. 18:36–37). Pilate could and did exercise his "absolute" power over Jesus, power conceded to him by God. But the real power, as the narrative in John 18:28–19:16 discloses (and history since then confirms), belongs to the King of Truth, who in total contrast to any "so-called rulers" came "to serve, and to give his life as a ransom for many" (Mk. 10:45).

When we survey the politics of the contemporary world, Jesus' characterization of Gentile rulers remains sadly accurate. That is the way things are around the world. Jesus was describing totalitarianism, without benefit of the term.

There is in Pascal's *Penseés* a remarkable echo of Jesus' statement about those who seem to rule:

> If they [Plato and Aristotle] wrote on politics, it was as if laying down rules for a lunatic asylum; and if they presented the appearance of speaking of a great matter, it was because they knew that the madmen, to whom they spoke, thought they were kings and emperors. They entered into their principles in order to make their madness as little harmful as possible.[7]

There could hardly be a better formulation than this for one aspect of the perspective Christians should have toward rulers. Disciples are to be graced with a smile of detachment, a sense of humor derivative from that which Jesus gave indication of in his designation "so-called." Only so can Christians, with a measure of spiritual safety, move over into an alien perspective in the hope of rendering the "absolute power" of rulers "as little harmful as possible."

Jesus and Pascal tell us that the "great men" of politics do not deserve that characterization; theirs is not a great matter. But both point to a somber analogue of that pretended greatness, the "absolute power" and the madness that brings on enormous harm. With true greatness so hard to approach, there comes the frantic shift toward reliance on its dark analogue. For Lyndon Johnson a pursuit of greatness veered away from the war on poverty to war in Indochina. Such "greatness" as the heads of state of the nuclear superpowers have lies in their absolute power to annihilate. Theirs is hardly "a great matter" in any humane, positive meaning of greatness, but great only in terms of the irreversible disaster for humanity which they move ever closer to.

If nuclear war comes, the benign achievements and attributes of recent American Presidents and their administrations will be very literally overshadowed by the results of their ever escalating militarism and their specific contributions to that global catastrophe. With Franklin Roosevelt came the enormous growth of the U.S. military in World War II and the development of the atomic bomb. With Truman came the dropping of two atomic bombs on cities and a doughty readiness to enter into the East-West struggle. The Eisenhower administration rejected Soviet initiatives that could have opened the way to general disarmament.[8] John Kennedy accelerated the nuclear arms race and provided in the Cuban Missile Crisis a model of "courage" which may reappear as the determining factor in the outbreak of World War III. Johnson and Nixon prosecuted the Indochina War, whose worst result may have been the diversion of attention, even in peace movement circles, away from the urgency of disarmament. With Ford came the acknowledged shift to a first-strike posture. Carter so openly juxtaposed a professed Christian faith and preparedness to incinerate many hundreds of millions of human beings.

Jesus, in calling his disciples to live the opposite of the style of Gentile rulers, said, "For the Son of man also came not to be served but to serve, and to give his life as a ransom for many" (Mk. 10:45). A head of state has always had considerable life-or-death power over people. Power for death has ordinarily found narrow or wide expression. But now a single human being, the head of each thermonuclear alliance, has potential life-or-death power over all human beings. The one man Jesus died for all. Now one person can very possibly and quite soon initiate the killing of all. Gentile "absolute power" has now reached this supreme contrast to the servanthood and death of Jesus.

There has always been a certain Adamic dimension to political headship. A multiplicity of human beings is narrowed into the one representative head. The many sin in the one; the sin of the one spreads into the few and the many. In the present Adamic headship one man could recapitulate the Fall and horribly intensify its consequences for all humanity. "Sin came into the world through one man and death through sin, and so death spread to all men because all men sinned. . . . Because of one man's trespass, death reigned through that one man" (Rom. 5:12,17). Vast technological arrangements are such that the trespass of one representative person can suddenly make death's dominion complete or nearly so.[9] The sin of one spreads electronically to become the sin of others, and death, with perhaps total sway, spreads over all—because all have sinned and, with varying degrees of contributory involvement, have entered into those arrangements. The only thing really that is counterpoised over against this immensity is "one man's obedience" (Rom. 5:19), God's abounding grace through him, and the obedience of those who have been drawn together to him as Head.

But there is irony in the current uncertainty of political headship. The decision to bomb might be made by an insubordinate subordinate. The commander of a Trident submarine could, just with the nuclear weapons at his disposal, completely devastate the Soviet Union. Two uniformed conspiring functionaries at a missile command post could seize that initiating power. A lower-level officer, who in the aftermath of thermonuclear exchanges might remain unidentifiable, could grasp that fateful headship. Or it could be the leader or military insubordinates in a lesser nation-state—or even a group of terrorists. The President of the United States and the Soviet Premier have that awesome but declining headship. Those who might displace them in it are many indeed and constantly increasing as horizontal nuclear proliferation brings more and more loss of control by the superpowers.

In the American political system the President and his managing directorate need to put up with a great deal of criticism and disparagement. At any one time there are millions of citizens who in coffee-time grumbling label the incumbent President as unfit for his office. Some of this enters the mass media. But in the context of such partisan attack, one point is very seldom made: that the President is unfit to have the final say about the use of nuclear weapons. A negative estimate there would come too close to a questioning of the basic political system (as structure of salvation). And not to trust the nuclear overlord would impel the nation toward facing its peril.

But an amazing irony is that this trust, to maintain itself, must receive extrapolation to include the Soviet rulers. "Deterrence itself seems to be based on the ultimate irrationality. It must rely on the common sense and rationality, and ultimately on the humanity, of those we distrust the most."[10]

The pathetic littleness of heads of state comes very clearly into view in the contrast between peace rhetoric and actual foreign and military policy. President Dwight D. Eisenhower in his State of the Union message, January 9, 1958, said,

> There is only one solution to the grim problems that lie ahead. The world must stop the present plunge toward more and more destructive weapons of war and turn the corner that will start our

steps firmly on the path toward lasting peace.... This will require more than words of peace. It requires works of peace.

One would have supposed that Eisenhower, as holder of the most powerful political office in the world, could have provided the needed leadership for turning the corner—a process that could have been carried through with much less difficulty in the fifties than later. But the step from such hope-arousing words to decisive changes in American military and foreign policy was not taken. Similar statements could be given for each of the Cold War leaders. The magnetism and pathos of John F. Kennedy came in considerable measure from his expressing so memorably what had to be done while in his foreign and military policies doing mostly the opposite.

Though duplicity is a partial explanation for such statements, we can concede that there has been also in these heads of state some honest yearning for an end to the whole bloody business and a breakthrough into a new era for the human family. An exalted place in history would be accorded to the leaders who turn the corner out of the arms race into a peacefully ordered world. But neither good intentions, yearning, nor ambition has drawn any of these leaders— except, at certain times possibly, the Soviet rulers (as the footnote 8 in this chapter indicates)—away from a deadly persistence in policies and modes of thinking which preclude that turn.

The greatest difficulty is not wickedness of national leaders but their drivenness. When I see the film *Hearts and Minds* with its panoramic survey of the roots of United States' warmaking in Indochina, what comes to me most is a sense of the drivenness, the impotence, of those wielders of titanic power. Under them were great numbers of marionettes; but they themselves were marionettes, pulled and jerked by dark forces. One cannot become the master of marionettes without ending up as a marionette oneself. In the nuclear arms competition this is even more fatefully the case. As Fred J. Cook stated almost two decades ago, "Weapons have come to dominate the Military as the Military dominates the State."[11] Former Secretary of Defense Robert McNamara noted "a kind of mad momentum intrinsic to the development of all new nuclear weaponry."[12] As Martin Buber expressed it in an appeal to world leaders: "Now the game plays with you."[13] Only the One who took to himself no marionettes, no absolute power, was able to live in the spirit of the Father's leading and not at all in that drivenness.[14]

Death came as the most obvious negation of ancient rulers' claim to divinity. ("Wilt thou yet say before him that slayeth thee, I am God? but thou shalt be a man, and no God, in the hand of him that slayeth thee"—Ezek. 28:9 AV). So it is with more veiled contemporary claims. A wielder of power over millions of bodies finds himself powerless before some tiny malfunction in his own flesh. The seat of his power is his own slight body, but how easily he can be unseated. The leader is the focus and, also in his vulnerability and death, images the collectivity. He is a sort of negative first fruit: His undoing presages the same for the collectivity. Death is the prime lese-majesty, most radical offense against the dignity of the focal person and of all that finds its focus in him. The funeral must then, by massive solemnities, obscure the offense.

John F. Kennedy was in one moment the most powerful head of state on the face of the earth. In the next he was powerless to raise his head half an inch from the lap of his wife. He who had been Commander-in-chief over the firing of billions of practice projectiles found the chain of command no longer intact. He had saved and doomed others but had not the power to save himself.

Few there were who noticed the dark irony in the funeral. In the ceremonials for this victim of a horrible act of violence marched phalanx upon phalanx of the practitioners of violence—"a military parade the likes of which this city has never seen," as one radio announcer described it. Assassins originally were members of a Moslem order which practiced secret murder, committed under the influence of hashish. But the "Christian" funeral for that assassinated leader was filled with glorified reliance on military strength. As such it represented the full Islamization of an allegedly Christian society. Nationalism is better than hashish for inducing a readiness to kill.

Who could expect Americans to imagine a world without the United States of America, without the national context of their existence? But in an instant this focus, this dynamic image of what America is, went down. We wept not only for Kennedy but for ourselves and for our children. In his death we each, and by intimation the whole populace, were shown to be vulnerable and mortal. We dimly felt the prospect of a coming day when all of us might fall victim to a mad deed.

The most plebeian enemy archer could upon occasion emerge triumphant over a mighty soldier king. The assassins or assassin in Dallas came through as more powerful than Kennedy. The head of a superpower can, at any time, be turned into a wisp of matter in an inferno. The prospective soldier assassin presides over billions of times more explosive energy than strictly needed to dismember the one focal body. An imperiled leader can dissuade by threat of death. But all his power would amount to nothing when pitted against nuclear weapons fired at him.

The President and the national security managers might of course be in the massive underground shelters of the Federal Relocation Arc at the outbreak of a nuclear war—most certainly so in the event of an authorized United States' first strike. But the key priority would be the maintenance of a cohesion of military command and power, and for this there would not need to be any high priority on the survival of civilian leaders. As German theologian Helmut Gollwitzer has pointed out:

> In future the purpose of defense will not be to protect the population; the armed forces will form the core of the state and will fight for the survival of the state. The notion of defending one's country is out of date; anyone who quotes it must be either blind or a hypocrite.[15]

What Gollwitzer describes is already upon us. In terms of the imminence of nuclear war the military is the central substance of the state; the nonmilitary population is subsidiary, and even the President governs as quite dispensable head.

We can each accept marginality to the God and Father of Jesus Christ, or we are caught in marginality to the dynamisms of evil.

Chapter 18

FORFEITED DOMINION

From His patient body pierced
Blood and water streaming fall:
Earth and sea and stars and mankind
By that stream are cleansed all. [1]
Sixth-century Celtic missionary

God formed matter into the splendor of stars, galaxies, sun, and planets. At His command matter formed into a glorious multiplicity of plants and animals. He took dust from the ground, shaped a human being, and breathed life into him. A still greater ennoblement of matter followed. When the Son took as his own the human form, he took matter as part of his being. The One through whom matter was created distinct from its Creator gave to matter the supreme dignity of constituting his earthly body. That body, as part of his psychosomatic unity, opened out toward all the matter of the universe. Atoms and molecules were being continually taken in and thrown off. Specific atoms which were transient components of his body are spread around the surface of the earth—an aftermath in matter of the Incarnation—and certain of them at any given time are within the physical being of each of us.

Jesus was raised from the tomb with a changed body; his crucified body and the matter in it were recreated, transformed. He could be touched; he could eat ordinary food. But his was a corporeality and materiality beyond what the senses ordinarily experience. The hidden glory which rests over our living has its source in the Incarnation and Rising of Jesus; he took our nature, our life, our death as his own in condescension and ascension. All matter—the very soil, rocks, water, air around us—shares mutely in that glory. Transmuted matter is a component of who the Risen Son is for us and all creation.

A pumpkin, a mouse, a child by their very existence show forth the glory of matter. But when any living thing rots away, the debasement of what was is also a debasement of matter itself. Matter shares in this utter indignity which in the Bible is referred to as corruption.

The explosion of a nuclear warhead can be seen as a parody of Jesus'

121

Rising—and even of his Appearing (his Second Coming). Uranium and missiles are raised out of the depths of earth and sea. The inert bursts upward in resplendent, irresistible power. Mushroom clouds of awesome beauty are there for all (not already dead) to see: "and all tribes of the earth will wail..." (Rev. 1:7). Matter is transmuted not into a celestial body (1 Cor. 15:40) but into an immensity of death which instantaneously draws nearby ennobled matter into itself and then spreads to envelop and lay low all within its reach. Matter, rather than being allowed to continue in its dumb readiness to be appropriated for life is impelled into a sort of permanent identity with death. This is sin against matter itself.

Our Lord in his Rising reaches out to draw all creatures, all creation, up into his Life. In a nuclear explosion matter moves up, out, and down as infernal countermovement to that rising.

Physically every human being on earth is already victim of the Bomb in an incipient way. Lodged in the body of each one of us is an infinitesimal amount of plutonium, along with other manmade radioactive substances like strontium 90 and cesium 137. Each such particle, during every breath we take, maintains its microcosmic deadly presence; and because of this hidden radioactivity an unknown number of human beings die each year. The Spirit of the Risen Lord has been given into those who are his, as a first installment, *arrabon,* confirming the promise of more to come (2 Cor. 1:22, 5:5). In a dark parody those bits of radioactive matter within each of our bodies are also a first installment: Far more is to come unless the fatal contract is broken.

As answer to the puzzle of why living cells age and deteriorate toward death, there is the convincing hypothesis, widely accepted among scientists, that cells age mainly from a slow bombardment by natural radiation in the environment (to which in recent decades manmade radiation has been added). If this explanation is correct, it is by radiation that death rules; radiation is death in its most pervasive physical coming. This would mean that nuclear scientists have done more than construct new weapons which kill far greater numbers of people and leave behind deadly aftereffects, some of which persist for hundreds of thousands of years. They have penetrated, taken for themselves, and are about to magnify greatly death's secret permeating presence in nature.

Physical illness generally results from a malfunction of some part of the body or from something like an alien attack by germs, viruses, harmful substances. But cancer is remarkable as an uprising from within the body against the coherence of the whole. A cell begins its wild multiplication, and that initial and most intimate dominion a person has in his own body is slowly lost. The pollution of the environment stemming from the human quest for power brings to more and more persons the excruciating loss of that most basic and precious dominion. Man's rebellion recoils in blighted matter to become cancer's insurgency. A nuclear war would climax the rebellion and enormously increase that insurgency.

God's initial command to the first human couple, "Be fruitful and multiply" (Gen. 1:28), was stated as prerequisite for the complementary command to exercise dominion. The genetic damage caused by manmade radioactivity and other pollutants is a diminishing of the human form which God created for dominion. It images in the body the inner deformity that came with the Fall. World War III would brand tens of millions of survivors with disfiguring scars, and huge numbers of those born later would bear the genetic stigmata resulting from the radioactive piercing of human flesh.

It is often thought that, while the bad consequences of earlier wars could be gradually overcome, the worst consequences of a nuclear world war would persist indefinitely.

This most significant difference can be rightly pointed to with regard to the natural and material environment, but there is the difference only in that dimension. The aftereffects of earlier wars have persisted within the dynamisms shaping the mental and social environment. Indeed, it seems that all those consequences currently merge into the global rush toward annihilation. After World War III the ghastly dominion of radioactivity would give outer imaging to what had been till then chiefly the nonmaterial dominance of the consequences of wars.

A few days after the thermonuclear volleys of a Third World War many areas farther downwind would look nearly as they had before. The visual glory and welcome familiarity would continue, but all would be changed. Without bodily equipment for detecting radiation, residents there might find that change hard to believe: How could homes and the sustaining environment look quite the same and yet be so terribly different?

A nuclear war would bring the destruction or irradiation of a great portion of the artistic creations (fragile dominion over form and color) that have been a nurturing glory in Western civilization—paintings, sculpture, cathedrals, and so much else. Most of the heritage of music and literature might survive in parts of the Southern Hemisphere. But many of the other great works of art are concentrated in those areas most exposed to nuclear obliteration.

God entrusted to man an earth with the calmed atoms of air, soil, water, not the raging atoms of sun and star. In earth's atoms, though, lurked the cosmic raging, which man has now unleashed. The initial temperature in the explosion of a twenty-megaton nuclear bomb is 150 million degrees Fahrenheit—more than four times the temperature at the center of the sun. With what might be regarded as man's climactic subjection of matter to his own will comes a decisive release of matter from "under his feet."

* * *

The titillating exposure of human, mostly female, bodies is a commonplace in contemporary civilization. Lust is the impulse to take what is not given, or cannot be rightly given, in the sexual dimension of our lives or in other dimensions. In any lust we grab at what God or neighbor does not give, or we seize gift divorced from giver—thus not really gift (as in sexual promiscuity). Nakedness before the Fall was part of the full spontaneous mutuality of giving and receiving. Nakedness in marriage can be somewhat of a continuation of that. Adam, fallen, in his nakedness was afraid before God and uneasy with Eve. He was exposed and vulnerable in his pathetic, newly achieved autonomy and nervously uncertain because of that lurking impulse to take or lay burdens. There is in us the desire to take in the nakedness of others and to take others in by means of our bodily exposure. Western societies are vibrant with nudity as power.

A very different nakedness is often mentioned in the accounts by survivors of the atomic blasts that destroyed Hiroshima and Nagasaki. In the immediate aftermath a great many dazed people were going around naked or nearly so, chiefly because their clothing had been burned off them. In the outbreak of World War III there could be hundreds of millions who would be similarly naked—not the nakedness of play with power, but of impotence. This would be the nakedness the prophets warned about: the utter destitution of those who have been brought by a ravaging enemy even to the loss of their clothing. Mesopotamian conquerors relished the nakedness of the vanquished as demonstration of their total victory.

> Pass on your way,
> inhabitants of Shaphir,
> in nakedness and shame.
>
> (Mic. 1:11)

Exposure of the body played a big part in the ancient Near Eastern idolatries, even within Israel. It does the same within contemporary idolatries. The prophets saw the unrecognized shame of this nakedness about to be changed into the undeniable shame of a far different nakedness. If people insisted on being naked, God would let them be naked: "those whom you hate...shall deal with you in hatred, and take away all the fruit of your labor, and leave you naked and bare, and the nakedness of your harlotry shall be uncovered" (Ezek. 23:28–29). The diminution of persons involved with manipulative nakedness ends in the pathos of this extreme diminution.

But we can, with Mary and John, stand near the naked Messiah on the cross. God provided clothes to cover Adam and Eve, but let soldiers strip the garments from the Second Adam. Jesus took as his own the convergence of all our wrong nakedness—the shame, the destitution. Through his nakedness he won the wherewithal to cover ours. We cannot eliminate the possibility of our being stripped naked by adversaries. After the outbreak of nuclear war there would be a sort of nakedness before the spreading radioactivity, clothes being no longer a very protective covering. But we could enter into that in such a way as to share in Jesus' nakedness. Even the post-holocaust actuality of total exposure could be lived out in remembrance of his.

* * *

Paul wrote that "the whole creation was groaning in travail together until now" (Rom. 8:22). Part of this surely is the cry of other living things, especially higher animals, in the travail that is theirs. So much of their woe is needlessly inflicted by man. Human beings were originally given dominion to mediate the rule of a Lord whose tender care embraces all His creatures. Human dominion over the earth derived from man's having received God's likeness.

That dominion receives marginal explication in one of Jesus' parables of stewardship. In Matthew 24:45–51 Jesus' illustration of the two behaviors possible for a steward brings out the antithesis between "absolute power" and Christlike servanthood: The steward can give his fellow servants their food at the proper time, or he can beat them and eat and drink with the drunken. In global perspective the pouring of enormous resources into the military leaves great numbers of fellow servants without the necessities of life and constitutes, alongside a careless affluence, an actual or arranged-for "beating" of countless modern-day servants.

In the proper care of a garden or of animals the master is also servant to plants and beasts. But rule as servant-masters who are accountable to the one Master has so often given way to lording it over lesser creatures. Through the millennia much of the destructive callousness that goes with overindulgence has taken God's nonhuman creatures as its victims. This is even more the case now with environmental pollution, developments like the "death" of Lake Erie, agribusiness, the near extinction of many species, the bleak urbanization of land, recombinant DNA research, the proliferation of nuclear power plants. There has been no satisfactory solution to the problem of the permanent storage of radioactive waste, and there is no prospect of one. Yet in an incredibly reckless jeopardizing of the biosphere, American society is rushing ahead in the production of the one billion cubic feet of nuclear waste which the United States government estimates will be in this country alone by the end of the century. That would be enough to pave a four-lane highway coast to coast one foot deep.

The human anguish experienced during the Indochina War is beyond our comprehension, but the extent of the war's desolation was far wider. The forests were defoliated; the land, poisoned and pocked with craters; bombs, napalm, anti-personnel weapons rained down upon vast numbers of plants and animals given to the care of the human race.

A warning came to Babylonian invaders:

> For the violence done to Lebanon is going to overwhelm you,
> so will the slaughter of terrified beasts,
> for you have shed men's blood and ravished the country,
> the city and all who live in it.
>
> (Hab. 2:17 JB)

Judgment (recoil) falls, not only for the violence done to human beings, but for violence in all its ranges.

God says to Jonah at the very end of the story, "You pity the plant.... And should not I pity Nineveh, that great city, in which there are more than a hundred and twenty thousand persons who do not know their right hand from their left, and also much cattle?" (Jon. 4:10–11). Not one sparrow can fall to the ground without the Father's knowing and caring (Mt. 10:29). This God holds back nuclear catastrophe in a compassion that reaches wider than the human multitudes who do not know what they are doing and embraces all the "cattle" of our planetary Nineveh.

There are many aspects to the current dismal perversion of the

Genesis 1 dominion to which human beings are called. But worst of all is the power and the readiness to turn much or all of God's earth into a waste uninhabitable not only for humankind but for the higher species generally. The tilling of the garden, the naming of the animals has been largely displaced by this preparedness to destroy the creation. In terms of reaping the results of what has been chosen, there would be a certain appropriateness if nuclear devastation sweeps over human beings, but not so for animals and plants. They have done nothing to bring such destruction upon themselves; they are without sin.

Animals and plants were left much more exposed to nuclear tests,. particularly those of the United States in the Pacific, than were human beings. Countless numbers of creatures perished in those infernos. Slow-working genetic damage, sickness, and death because of radiation enter all forms of life, not just the human race. If we take the call to dominion and Jesus' word about the sparrow's fall seriously, a considerable part of the unspeakable pathos of nuclear war lies in what it would be for nonhuman creatures. Vast numbers of animals would succumb to radiation sickness without understanding why. For many species, perhaps for most higher species, that long and marvelous call to be fruitful and multiply would be cut off. *Their* environment would be irreversibly ravaged. More than human blood cries out to God.

It may be that, with the elimination of most or all birds, insects, notably roaches because of their high resistance to radioactivity, will inherit the earth as an unintended bequest from human beings. The biblical motif that the mighty are cast down and the lowly exalted will then have come to fulfilment among the species.

> *I looked on the earth, and lo, it was waste and void;*
> *and to the heavens, and they had no light.*
> *I looked on the mountains, and lo, they were quaking,*
> *and all the hills moved to and fro.*
> *I looked, and lo, there was no man,*
> *and all the birds of the air had fled.*
> *I looked, and lo, the fruitful land was a desert,*
> *and all its cities were laid in ruins.*
>
> (Jer. 4:23–26)

* * *

The prevailing assumption is that what man has devised he can certainly control. This has been the fateful perspective behind the construction of nuclear power plants—in spite of the frightful dangers and the lack even of a reasonable prospect that the problem of radioactive wastes can be solved. Leaders and man-machine control systems have been entrusted with the power to incinerate hundreds of millions of people, power even to end human history. And there is, through it all, the confidence that these creations of human ingenuity with the many custodial safeguards can be trusted too.

We do well, though, in this connection to consider the "elusiveness of soap, the knottiness of strings, the transitory nature of buttons, the inclination of suspenders to twist"—what has been summed up half playfully as "the total depravity of inanimate things."[2] By resisting God, man has drawn the context of his living into patterns of resistance. We set our wills against God, and we find in turn that children and animals set their wills against us. There is also a seeming willfulness in things. The resistance can be very strong in the things human beings fabricate. The obstinacy of clothes hangers, thread at needle's eye, ketchup in the bottleneck, zippers, mimeograph machines, cars in zero weather can confront us with comic imitation of our own stubbornness before God. Dominion has not been taken from us, but running through everything is a refractoriness mirroring our own.

Nuclear weapons systems with their many millions of component parts are the most complex things ever devised by man. Though they constitute his most ambitious attempt at dominion, they have the same refractoriness found in clothes hangers, flashlights, multi-state power circuits. Indeed, the more complicated a machine, the greater the possibility it will malfunction.

There has been a progressive relinquishment of human control over the weapons systems. As the superpowers have worked frantically to retain a second-strike capability, it has been deemed necessary to rely more and more on computerized systems that would proceed to function automatically, even in the absence of human decision-making. There is thus the inevitable, even if supposedly marginal, risk that these systems themselves, through some malfunction, will proceed to blow up much of the world. Such an accident apart from any initiating human action could bring on the end of human history. During and after World War III, it might be impossible to determine how the war started. In that situation people could better recognize that the terrible blame for what happened lay, not with one person, group, or nation, but with the readiness of human beings to construct countervailing nuclear weapons systems.

The danger of malfunction is of course very much recognized, and great technological expertise has been marshalled to forestall or delimit it. Man bolsters his presumption as he strives to be master of the danger. Yet human beings become increasingly the mere attendants of nearly autonomous weapons systems. Austrian philosopher Günther Anders has explained: "Every machine is expansionistic (if we avoid saying 'imperialistic') and creates for itself its own subservient colonial domain, consisting of suppliers, teams of attendants, consumers, etc."[3] A nuclear weapons "defense" system can be seen as one incredibly complex, farflung machine with an expansionism that draws an entire society into subservience.

In the Three Mile Island power plant disaster, what came into view was an infernal creature seizing mastery. The large numbers of real and potential victims had become almost incidental to the dominating centrality of the reactor. That marginality of human beings, other than those involved in trying to reestablish their control, would be dreadfully magnified in a nuclear war.

Man seems to have a fuller dominion over machines than over the other created species which he came to regard as a much too limited realm. Machines, unlike plants and animals which are God's creatures, are entirely man's own "creatures." But the grant of dominion in Genesis 1 does not, even by implication, include machines. When in accord with that primeval command, man's servanthood toward animals and plants remains limited. And seldom does anyone become subservient to a tool like a hoe, hammer, or needle. But machines are substitutes for animals and slaves and have lifelike dynamisms. They need tending, care, service. In God's arrangement, caring servanthood (even if just in granting to other species space for their living) is a decisive part in the form of Godlike dominion. In man's arrangement the expansionism of machines turns a presumed dominion into servitude.

Gambling is one opposite to dominion, man's or God's. Gamblers give allegiance to the lordship of chance. There has been a vast proliferation of gambling as chance dispenses blessing or woe. Subservient impotence is obscured by the relish of standing before those opposites and trying to coax, woo, cajole that lord. Chance's awesome lordship is greatest when the gambler plays with life and death, as in Russian roulette. Much of the appeal of battle and war is the life-and-death stakes being played for.

The nuclear arms race needs to be understood at least partially in this light. Beyond the presumed range of human control and technological reliability is the range of danger, risk, luck, accident, blunder, madness. The survival of mankind is at stake in this roulette. But the stimulation of the gambling stance is a key factor—as can be seen, for instance, in the way the Kennedy Administration handled the Cuban Missile Crisis. Danger in terms of imponderables and chance possibilities, rather than inhibiting, whets the appetite of the gambler. Submission to the lordship of chance has reached the point that World War III and even the end of history may quite possibly result, not from immediate human decisions, but from some chance occurrence. Yet the gamblers stay at the nuclear tables.

Chapter 19

INVALIDATED MODELS

> The point I am making is that, because the advantage of the first strike is so great, the policy of deterrence through superior power is essentially self-defeating. The policy works to prevent war only when both sides are convinced that the other will never strike first. They cannot acquire that confidence; on the contrary, as the race to outbid each other in deterrent power goes on, and as tension builds up, the temptation to try to avoid doom by striking the opponent first with a knockout blow becomes more and more compelling. In other words, the deterrence "race" pushes both the United States and the U.S.S.R. closer and closer to the verge of contemplating a first strike.[1]
>
> *Ralph E. Lapp*

The most common question in discussions about war and pacifism is very probably, "What would you do if someone breaks into your home and attacks your wife and children? Wouldn't you do anything possible to prevent the criminal from killing your loved ones?" In the countries of the West this question is presented as an analogy to the political question: "But what about the Russians? We can't just let them come in and take over."

These basic models of attack and defense play an indispensable part in the undergirding psychology of cold and hot wars. But in the context of the nuclear arms buildup, these models have become quite invalid, if indeed they were ever valid before. This invalidity needs to be shown, even if such analysis does little to diminish their emotionally pervasive power.

First, we need to see that, though the model of the family under attack is taken as a basis for military preparedness and going to war, criminal attacks on specific families add up to only a small counterpart of what sweeps over families in war. If World War III does break out, precisely the reliance on nuclear weapons with their justification in these attack and defense models will bring across whole continents that very destruction of homes and loved ones which was to have been prevented.

But already now our homes have been broken into and our families endangered by low level radiation resulting from trust in nuclear "defense." Already the way in which the drive for national "security" radiates societal violence and draws resources and energies away from dealing with urgent domestic problems is the prime factor behind the rising incidence of violent attacks within American society. The more national "security," the less local and family security.

With regard to the cherished models, however, the American experience of war has been exceptional: The wars that are more within memory have been fought out where the enemy is, to put the "attackers" on the defensive and keep them from reaching and devastating the American homeland. People of the Confederacy experienced the Civil War as defense that did not succeed, as desolation of their country. But since then American wars—those against the Indians too—have been fought off somewhere else, and the American homeland has not been ravaged. The tens of millions of homes attacked or destroyed in these more recent wars have not (with marginal exceptions) been American homes. Most Americans see nuclear weapons as a continuation of that success pattern: The two atomic bombs that were dropped on human populations brought the surrender of an aggressor nation; Kennedy's readiness to go to the brink of nuclear war forced the Soviets to withdraw their missiles from Cuba; U.S. nuclear warheads have held off the communists. The models seem confirmed; the nuclear gun in hand appears to have preserved home, family, country. But set against that confirmation is the imminence of reciprocal attacks that would prove the illogic of the models when it would be too late.

Second: In the scenarios of threat and defense one does not (primarily) kill to defend oneself. That would be too egotistic. One kills to defend others. *But behind the avowed altruism in the models is a familial or collective egotism.* The "others" are those of one's own group, small or large, in conflict with some adversary. What is decisive is not an altruistic caring about others but the delimited solidarity of a *we*.

Third: The model of a family under attack as the analogy for the situation between the United States and the Soviet Union does not correspond to the complexities of the world nuclear situation.

If a family model for that situation is desired, here is a rough one. You and your family are at one end of a long large room. An opponent and his family are at the other end. Earlier you each had a gun leveled at the other and the other's family. But then you both realized that your opponent might be able to shoot fast enough to prevent return fire. You each, with help from the family, frantically proceeded to set up across each end of the room an ever-increasing array of shotguns, rifles, and machineguns, all interconnected, primed for firing also at the pull of triggering wires (which would be tripped even by riddled bodies toppling over) and aimed partly at the weaponry, partly at the people in the other end of the room.

As you each work away at the ingenious buildup of firearms, you shout warnings toward the other end of the room. There are times of heightened tension when each thinks that the other may be at the point of firing first in the hope of coming through at least somewhat better that way than if he were fired upon first. There is the constant danger that some gun may go off by accident, that a triggering wire may be pulled unintentionally, or even that an intruder may burst in. The two of you have shouted to each other across the length of the room about the possibility of a partial or total dismantling of the two countering weaponry setups; but neither of you sees any feasible way this could be done. So each of you keeps adding the leveled guns and the triggering wires across his end of the room because the other must be prevented from concluding that he might be able to fire first and get away with it.

From the American side the objection may come that the United States has resorted to its nuclear arms buildup because this was the only way to keep the communists from attacking. But chronologically it was the United States that first "broke in" with atomic weapons aimed and ready to fire; the Soviet Union was only later able to reciprocate. And the U.S. has led in every new development in the nuclear arms race. In the popular models the S.U. is the criminal nation, whereas in the actual world there is so much good and so much evil in each country.

Fourth: In the two-part model it is assumed that the power resorted to will be sufficient for avoiding impotence. Psychiatrist Sanford Gifford holds that fear of being helpless, impotent, at the mercy of others is stronger than the fear of death itself and plays a crucial part in the psychology of the Cold War.[2] This fear of being impotent infuses the attack-defense models, and so it is that power to avoid that impotence must be asserted.

The decisive and astonishing assumption in the model, whether familial or national, is that resort to violence is the sure way through. But this assumption is highly questionable even in terms of an attack on a family. The attacker already has his weapon aimed; for this is what constitutes the attack. Unless the defender carries a gun all the time, he would have the problem of getting his hands on one. If he does succeed in grabbing a gun, he would need to be the equal of a Wild West hero to outshoot the attacker who has his gun already aimed. Or is the father defender, as in a television drama, to come with gun blazing through the doorway of the adjoining room? In real life situations there is occasionally that sort of possibility. But far more often there is no weapon at hand or, if there is, a person would be most foolhardy to use one; a nonviolent response is the only sensible option. In some situations resort to shooting brings on a murder of loved ones which otherwise would not have come.

From a biblical perspective the type of thinking implicit in these models that shape public attitudes and policies constitutes an Adamic grabbing at omniscience and omnipotence: The threatened know the one and only sure way to defend, and will (at least quite probably) bring it off. But how can one be certain about just what the attacker does have in mind? How can one be sure that he is determined to kill? How can anyone know in advance that striking at the life of an attacker is the only way to stop him, that it will indeed stop him, that there would be no other way to get through to him, that killing him is better than failure otherwise to prevent him from murdering others? Similar questions could be asked for the antagonists in any war or cold war. Christians should be able to see that such presumption amounts to rebellion against the plain command of God.

But the irony that fully dashes the power motif in the models lies in the fact that fear of being impotent in the hands of others has, through the nuclear arms buildup, led into unprecedented and unfathomable impotence in relation to what those others can now do. As John H. Herz has summarized the world nuclear situation: "Utter permeability now negates the traditional territoriality of units, and it is exactly the most powerful nuclear powers which as targets of other nuclear powers become the most vulnerable. Utmost power coincides with utmost impotence.[3] Thus, New Zealand has more "national security" than does the United States; Costa Rica, much more than the Soviet Union; Togo, far more than France or Great Britain. The impotence of an individual citizen of a superpower can be contemplated in relation to the explosion of a thermonuclear bomb or an advancing front of radioactive fallout. To defend is to imperil. The ultimate model of threat and sure power to defend is illusion, and with it the lesser models.

War has been the chief way for measuring the relative power of collectivities and has served therefore as the most highly regarded indicator of the superior power collectively sought. Commitment to and fascination with that indicator drive nation-states ever onward toward a final measurement which will make irresistibly clear what is already the case: that supreme lethal power over others coincides with total impotence before the equivalent power wielded by those others.

Fifth: Though most people see the nation as their preserver, sustaining context, and source of security, precisely the opposite is becoming more and more the case: The nation is the prime jeopardizer, the main threat, the chief source of peril.

Each human being desperately needs a niche, a place, a sustaining context. Home and family in the first attack-defense model represent that niche. But that in its turn needs a wider sustaining context— which for most people is the nation. The feared collapse of the nation is seen as almost certainly bringing with it the loss of one's personal niche. What then could be more important than the preservation of this wider context?

I can express, for myself, the understanding that one's own nation-state is the primary jeopardizer rather than chief Preserver. I care very much about my wife and children and about the concentric circles of those I love, know, know of. I, too, nestle in the niche that is mine and fear losing it. But nuclear catastrophe is the supreme earthly danger hanging over all I care about. The continuing Cold War pursuits of the United States (plus those of the Soviet Union and other nations, although I look first toward the nation-state within which I live) will probably at some point bring death to me and my family and an end to much that I care about. The military defense imposed on me is for me no defense; I wish passionately that I could be without it, for I am convinced that these military policies, if continued, will take us into a nuclear holocaust. The United States is, in certain ways, a determining wider context for me, but this is a somber fact, full of forboding for me. If I think of the various dangers that threaten the life and security of my family, I don't think first of a berserk murderer or of communist divisions. I think rather of the United States military overlords, the American initiation of and continued leadership in the nuclear arms race, the Cuban missile crisis, an accelerating arms buildup oriented toward readiness for a first strike.

The scenario outlined before, of proliferating gun arrangements at the opposite ends of a long room could be modified somewhat. Instead of two father defenders would be two competing gangs; instead of the families, those who find security in their gang and throw themselves into the effort to defend it. And some of us would be like bystanders trapped at one end of the closed room, dismayed by such "defense," yet not able to escape it.

Sixth: From whatever lips the old questions about defending family and country come, God's absence and the implicit atheism sound through. The models—and through the years I've heard them thousands of times—are set on a terrain without God. Man is there, competent to make out on his own, or at least needing to make out on his own. If God's presence in the midst of that terrain is recognized, the stock answers supporting resort to violence can no longer be given.

For any dire crisis that may come, disciples can take the promise given by Jesus in Scripture and repeated to Pascal: "I shall act in thee if it occur."[4]

As it is, the terrible laughter of God inundates the models and the model builders, in merciful warning before ghastly inundation.

Chapter 20

LATTER-DAY JERUSALEM

What is transpiring is that the nation—Rome or Nazi Germany or America—lusts to be the holy nation, the Church. And, thus, the Church living in her Jerusalem vocation is an alien in a hostile land.

The American vanity as a nation has, since the origins of America, been Babylonian—boasting, through Presidents, often through pharisees within the churches, through folk religion, and in other ways, that America is Jerusalem. This is neither an innocuous nor benign claim; it is the essence of the doctrine of the Antichrist.[1]

William Stringfellow

The claim that America is the new chosen people, the righteous and uniquely ordained nation, the modern Jerusalem, has shaped the history of this country and the outlook of most Americans. The churches have widely supported that claim. I believe we should accept the Jerusalem claim (as biblically explicated) and view the United States as being, more than any other country, the current, latter-day Jerusalem.

Throughout much of the Old Testament a cry rang out against the wickedness in Israel, Judah, and most of all Jerusalem. It was a unique wickedness because this people alone among the nations had been shown so much of God's intent, yet by and large disregarded it. God's gracious call was seized and distorted into collective presumption. God had ventured into the condescension of attaching His name, His identity, to this people, and what came of it was mostly a profanation of that name. "The name of God is blasphemed among the Gentiles because of you" (Rom. 2:24). There was through the generations a faithful remant. There were occasions of mass repentance and renewal. But most Hebrew and Jewish history can be seen as successive veerings into apostasy and disaster. The culmination of the darker side of Israel's nationhood came when the Jerusalem oligarchy, supported by the populace, brought about Jesus' crucifixion. "His own people [and all God's covenanting intent underlies those words] received him not" (Jn. 1:11).

Church history since the earthly ministry of Jesus can be seen as a rough recapitulation of the biblical sequence. The church of the first centuries had some correspondence to the patriarchs, Moses, Samuel, and the early David. But in the Constantinian arrangement collective ethnic presumption grasped God's call to the church as its own. In contrast to peoples unaware of God's central saving acts in history, the Constantinian and post-Constantinian collectivities, past and present, have proliferated the originally unique and terrible sinfulness of Israel. Biblically, deafness and blindness toward God is at its worst in the context of an abounding outward familiarity with God. Christendom provided a continuation of that context. God ventured to risk His name and that of His Son, and the profanation of His name by vain collective taking of it has filled the christendom/post-christendom centuries.

This is not to say that christendom/post-christendom has been all bad, anymore than one would say this about Israel/Judah in the biblical period. There have been many life-serving societal dimensions in education, health care, human rights, help for the neediest; in art, architecture, music, literature. A remnant church has witnessed, served, and given warning. The mostly hidden reality of God's Rule taking form in human life has always been present in the midst of christendom. But as Jewish history, centered in Jerusalem, converged into the execution of Jesus, war with Rome, and the destruction of the city and country, so christendom/post-christendom history has converged into two world wars, the nuclear arms competition, and the imminent annihilation of much or all of the human race.

In the Constantinian assimilation, the churches became "themselves parts of the sundered cultures, their spokesmen, justifiers and prisoners."[2] The wedding of church and lethal violence received its frankest representation when Germanic chieftains at mass baptisms of their troops had the men hold their sword arm up out of the transforming water. Persecution of non-christians and of any regarded as heretics, crusades, warrior bishops, glorification of martial violence, the doctrine of the just war—all this has decisively shaped the planetary situation in which we so precariously live. The just war position has been accepted by nearly all churches, with the remarkable record through more than sixteen centuries that no subscribing church has ever clearly and cohesively resisted as unjust a war being fought by *its* side. For five hundred years Western "Christian" countries—and by heritage, even the Soviet Union as a heretical deviant can be counted among these—have been the chief makers of world history. There has been colonial expansion, the nation-state, the industrial revolution, modern technology, the initiation of two wars that engulfed most of the planet, multinational corporations, client allies around the world. The profanation of Christ's name has been many-faceted.

Jewish political power was centered in Jerusalem. Western political and economic power centers in the United States. As Jerusalem had its outlying towns, so the United States has its allies and satellites. Jewish religion had its focus in Jerusalem. In terms of material means, activity, social and economic leverage, it is the United States that has the prime contemporary concentration of people, groups, and institutions that bear the name of Christ. In this, too, the United States is Number One. (And it is widely supposed that a country so blessed with this numerically unprecedented concentration can't be anything except basically good.)

With only marginal exceptions the churches and church people in the United States have meshed supportively or acquiescently into American participation in two World Wars and into the awesome march of United States nuclear efforts. The sanctification of the country and the American way has been easily stretched to include the thermonuclear arsenal. With regard to nuclear weapons there have been a number of official denominational statements that pointed in the right direction. But these statements did not have the support of a committed cohesive body of believers. And no denomination within the just war tradition has tried to live out an obvious conclusion from even that doctrine: that its members as followers of Christ dare not be part of the United States armed forces, which are based on weapons of mass annihilation.

In mass media preaching and in the dominant theologies there has not been for Christian discipleship a clarity out of which could have resounded a decisive No to nuclear (and other) arms. As Herbert Butterfield has written, with reference to the Old Testament prophets,

> It is not difficult to see the parallels, furthermore, when the ancient writers cried out against the blind leaders of public opinion in their day—the false prophets who told the people that all was well and that they would have peace, who called evil good and good evil, and who flourished by giving men the comfortable doctrines they like to hear. If judgment comes on twentieth-century democracy, that will be partly because it encouraged—and in fact erected into a system—that whole policy of flattering human nature.[3]

Most of populist religion and preaching in the United States can be seen as a living out of that policy.

A majority of American national security managers have seen themselves as Christians. More than sixty million Americans consider themselves born-again Christians, and additional tens of millions claim to be Christians without the "born-again" designation. The great majority in this large segment of the population have given a vigorous or a reluctant Yes to the Bomb. If World War III comes, it is highly probable that American leaders who see themselves as upright Christians and who may very well have been in a church service the previous Sunday will give the firing orders (quite possibly for a first strike). The United States would be the Jerusalem for this global crucifixion.

I believe that if the American religious sanctification of the country and the military is scrutinized in the light of God's Coming in Jesus Christ, less severe conclusions can hardly be reached. It is, however, important to make clear that none of us and no Christian group have an unjeopardized vantage point. We are all heirs of damning collective legacies. We each have a personal history of power strategies, self-flattery, presumption, and complicities in such things as the neo-colonial exploitation of the world's poor. If we offer prophetic resistance to the rush toward annihilation, we do this not as the few who are righteous but as persons whom God is extricating from those legacies and entrapments.

In Japan, there is a noteworthy designation for weapons that destroyed Hiroshima and Nagasaki: the Christian bomb. Paul pointed to the unthinkable grotesqueness of acts in which bodies that are part of Christ's body unite with the bodies of prostitutes (1 Cor. 6:15). Is it not even more grotesque when bodies and minds, members of the very body of the Risen Jesus, are merged with weapons, when they are merged now in systemic fusion with weapons of mass annihilation? Jesus Christ is drawn into union with those infernal bombs and delivery vehicles. I am reckoning with the possibility that some at least of those in these man-weapon fusions are really of Christ's body.

Jesus, speaking of his own followers in the Endtime, said: "And then many will fall away, and betray one another, and hate one another. And many false prophets will arise and lead many astray. And because wickedness is multiplied, most men's love will grow cold" (Mt. 24:10–12). Each phrase has a Western (and an Eastern) fulfilment in the East-West struggle. As Judas betrayed Jesus by handing him over for execution, American and other Western church people have handed

over to their Sanhedrin and Caesar tens of millions of Christians in
the Soviet Union and Eastern Europe for nuclear arrest and possible
execution. How could this have been possible except by a precipitous
diminution of faith and love in a new context where previous bounds
to human wickedness have been removed by technology. If praise of
God dies out in the Soviet Union, this will be the result, not of
communist persecution, but of a strike with thousands of the nuclear
bombs generally accepted by church-going people in the West.

The Bomb is "Christian" no less than the Crucifixion was "Jewish."
"By undertaking the execution of the Messiah in defense of the
majesty of Caesar the mystery of iniquity is consummated, and the
blasphemy of the Jews is complete."[4] For "the Messiah" one could put
"much of the human race," and for "the Jews," "the churches." The
mystery of iniquity as the preparation for the slaughter of hundreds of
millions infuses the time and space within which we live. To look on
Soviet cities with a lustful readiness to annihilate them (and there
cannot be the readiness without some lusting) is to have annihilated
them already in one's heart. To fight a nuclear war would not greatly
increase nuclear sinning beyond what it is now; it would simply expose
the sin that is already there. Some imaginative recognition of the
horrors of a nuclear war can help us to a sense of how colossal the
sinfulness is which shapes the pre-war present.

Our Lord's confrontation with his Jewish contemporaries remark-
ably prefigured his current encounter with humankind in the nuclear
arms buildup. Or, expressed differently, the present encounter was
subsumed in and elaborates the earlier confrontation.

As the hosannahs of the triumphal entry were dying away, Jesus
gazed on the teeming city before him and wept over it, saying, "Would
that even today you knew the things that make for peace! But now
they are hid from your eyes. For the days shall come upon you, when
your enemies will cast up a bank about you and surround you, and
hem you in on every side, and dash you to the ground, you and your
children within you, and they will not leave one stone upon another in
you; because you did not know the time of your visitation" (Lk. 19:42–
44). Jesus could feel ahead into the nearing cataclysm; he could see the
Roman siegeworks looming up, the later slaughter of countless
persons there under his gaze, the razed, rubble-strewn heights of
what had been the beloved city. He knew what was in these people; he
saw a stiff, self-righteous ethnic group veering further into a
nationalistic violence that would bring on complete destruction. With
all the intensity of his being, Jesus had been trying to call them into a

different way. He would be their weaponless, donkey-riding king, their mother-hen leader. The people would be transformed into the equivalent of a brood of chicks under his "wings" (Lk. 13:34). His venturing again into the city at extreme risk to his life was a renewal of that impassioned call to his way of peace: "Would that even today you knew...." He threw himself against their catastrophic course. They destroyed him—and themselves.

Jesus took proleptically upon himself the political doom that was hanging over and soon to descend upon his fellow Jews. He was condemned as an insurgent against God and handed over to Pilate as an upstart insurgent against Roman rule. These he was not, but he accepted the penalty of *their* insurgency. Part of his passion on the way to the cross was the awareness that his execution was sealing their collective doom: "Daughters of Jerusalem, do not weep for me, but weep for yourselves and for your children.... For if they do this when the wood is green [if the Romans do this to me who am not an incendiary], what will happen when it is dry?" (Lk. 23:28,31). And he by whose execution Jerusalem fell was crucified again when Roman troops rampaged through the flaming city.

Now too there is the triumphal entry: the easy shouts of acclamation; thick carpets rolled along sanctuary aisles; forests of young evergreens felled in salutation of his coming; multitudes carried along in positive but shallow response.

In faith we can know that Jesus gazes upon our world and weeps. The siegeworks and catapults for overwhelming a thousand cities are already in place. He sees the multitudes about to be slaughtered and the skylines about to be obliterated. His compassionate call keeps ringing out to turn from the mad nationalisms and all that goes with them and come instead to his way—"the things that make for peace." The new direction away from catastrophe could be taken "even today," at least by those who claim to be God's people. But Satan-Peters protest against submission to suffering at the hands of others (Mt. 16:22–23). Shouts of "Crucify!" reverberate into the temple. Not knowing the day of visitation nor the things that make for peace, the manipulated throngs confirm the politicians' strategy, which amounts to the cry, "Their blood, if it comes to that, be upon us and upon our children"—vaporized, radioactive blood descending in fall-out. It seems Jesus says again to agents of governmental violence, "This is your hour, and the power of darkness" (Lk. 22:53). The crosses of cloud are about to tower up.

The decision of the Jerusalem populace became final when they cried for the release of Barabbas and the crucifixion of Jesus. Luke stressed the fateful irony: Pilate "released the man who had been thrown into prison for insurrection and murder, whom they asked for; but Jesus he delivered up to their will" (Lk. 23:25); "you...asked for a murderer to be granted to you, and killed the Author of life" (Acts 3:14,15). Barabbas, that other "son of the father" (which is the meaning of the name), represented ardent nationalism in its recourse to lethal violence. The decision for Barabbas confirmed the national course toward that crescendo of insurrection and violence which ended in the destruction of the city.

Though seldom recognized, the choice between Jesus and Barabbas has continued through the centuries and now takes on a fatefulness for all people comparable to the fatefulness which that choice there in Jerusalem had for the Palestinian Jews. The Jerusalem multitude did not realize that they were rejecting God's Messiah, rejecting His salvation, and were choosing their own doom. Those in the West and in its Jerusalem center who claim to be the chosen people and proceed within the outer motions of the New Covenant do not realize that their Yes to NATO arms, Pentagon budgets, "defense" by weapons of mass annihilation is a resounding cry for Barabbas and a fateful No to God's Way in Jesus, the only path out of death into life. That clamor for Barabbas amounts to the cry, "Crucify Jesus!," for he is—and will be—Victim in the midst of all victims of governmental violence.

* * *

If the United States is to be seen as a latter-day Jerusalem ready to bring on a worldwide crucifixion, what is to be said about the Soviet Union and secondarily about the East European socialist countries and China?

At times I think there could be nothing more overweening and colossal than American collective self-righteousness. But when, by travel or otherwise, I survey East European news media and official attitudes, I become uncertain. The accusing outcries there are still more strident, and the affirmation of collective righteousness even more blatant. That style is used because many people still need to be persuaded. The Western media are far more subtle. People by and large are already persuaded and stand in solidarity with the prevailing system; they need only to be manipulated.

Byzantium tried to be the successor of Rome as the world's political center and of Jerusalem as the world's holy religious center. Moscow, many centuries ago, appropriated for itself this Byzantine merger. Russian communists proceed unwittingly within that tradition, though their religion is one without God. Much of the world is polarized around two Rome-Jerusalems; and these two poles are united as the surfacings of a single axis, that is, as the two chief expressions of what the world turns on politically. (If we see the United States as a successor to Rome, it is significant that what fell at the beginning of the Dark Ages was not Rome, the persecutor of Christians, but Rome the seducer of the church.)

In the East there is the programmatic effort from the top down to integrate all into a socialist whole. The possibilities for legal dissent or standing apart from that integration are very limited. (In communist countries churches are usually the only organizations that are autonomously separate from the government.) In Western countries a coalition of power structures and interest groups works so effectively at national integration that opportunities for dissent can be offered— and kept marginal. Our thankfulness to God for that range of opportunity (not to be confused with the freedom given us in Jesus Christ) will hardly be greater than our use of it.

To the constant accusations from either side about the inhumanities of the other, it can be said: "The supreme inhumanity the other side is capable of, you are (or are striving to be) even more capable of. Readiness to perpetrate the ultimate inhumanity gives a false ring to any cry against lesser inhumanities."

The shared political ethic of East and West was vividly summed up by Nikita Khrushchev when he quoted a Russian proverb: "When you live among wolves, you need to act like a wolf." The snarling back and forth has continued so long now that it is difficult to ascertain whether any are only acting the part. Even most of those who were expressly sent out to live as sheep in the midst of wolves adopt, for international affairs, that proverb.

The communist take-over of the United States has already occurred. The worst in communism—the readiness to resort to any means and to sacrifice any number of people in what is proclaimed as the public interest has come to dominate the national posture of the United States. And communist countries have fallen to the forces of reaction, for they are shaped primarily not by their own best ideals but by reaction to Western military pressures. In the spiraling nuclear arms competition each side erodes and undermines the remaining good sense, high hopes, and humaneness of the other. The vitriol that envelops both East and West etches on each side the mirror image of that which is feared and deplored in the other.

Chapter 21

DEATH'S MASQUERADE

> Suicide is the ultimate and extreme self-justification of man as man, and it is therefore, from the purely human standpoint, in a certain sense even the self-accomplished expiation for a life that has failed. This deed will usually take place in a state of despair, yet it is not the despair itself that is the actual originator of suicide, but rather a man's freedom to perform his supreme act of self-justification even in the midst of this despair.[1]
>
> *Dietrich Bonhoeffer*

As psychiatrists, philosophers, and theologians have sought to understand the current world situation and the prospect of nuclear catastrophe, much attention has been given to the lure of death and the impulsions to mass suicide. What is usually missing in such analyses is anything akin to a recognition of the central irony within the biblical understanding of man. This irony is most vividly expressed by Jesus: "For whoever would save his life will lose it; and whoever loses his life for my sake and the gospel's will save it. For what does it profit a man, to gain the whole world and forfeit his life?" (Mk. 8:35–36 and parallels).

If a friend intervenes and saves my life from death by fire or drowning, the person saves *me,* the totality of who at that time I am as an individual. The dissolution of this specific entity in all its contours and substance is postponed. *Psyche,* the Greek word translated "life" or "soul" in the passage (and behind it the Hebrew *nephesh*), does not refer to something that animates a body but to the coherence of the entire entity.

Jesus' words of warning express what was depicted in the story of the Fall. God was the source of Adam's moment-by-moment living. The garden was filled with the fruits and life given by God. But Adam (and surely Eve as well) chose to venture out on his own, to secure by *his* initiative a life fuller than the one of which he had been simply the recipient. Because Adam in the venture found himself largely cut off from the embracing whole he had been a part of, he sought to make his

145

own pathetic littleness into the dominating center of all things. Jesus' phrase, "gain the whole world," far from being an oriental hyperbole, graphically characterizes Adam's attempt and the hidden longing, subdued but persistent in each of us.[2] In imperial nation-states this pursuit comes most clearly into view. Individuals, blocked from gaining the whole world, proceed, in collective alignment, with the attempt.

If covetousness is seen in its depth as "the desire to possess life without receiving it from God,"[3] the last of the Ten Commandments, "You shall not covet" (Ex. 20:17), is in a sense the summary of the preceding negative commandments.

Jesus' words about trying to save one's life point toward the extreme situation of persecution and danger in which a person, to save his own skin, acts in such a way that his relationship to God as source of his life is broken off. But that type of decision is an occasional and more dramatic form of the choice that pervades and distorts so much of human existence: the preoccupation with possessing life without receiving it from God. Jesus' words about saving and losing one's life also apply to that choice in its more general and elusive forms.

Adam's intent was to lay hold of life; in fact it was death that he took into himself, death disguised as life. There can hardly be for the present human situation a more revealing negative image than this. Overconsumption, ease, control, entertainment, titillation, spectacle, drugs are pursued as *life*. Advertising comes as reiteration of the serpent's primeval prompting to reach out and possess. Most writers and artists seize something to put before the public rather than welcome a gift meant for sharing with others. Religion becomes *gnosis*, know-how, for taking on and taking over life. The nation-state with its military might is looked to as context and bulwark of this "life." The machinery of death is amassed and justified as regrettably indispensable for "life."

The forbidden fruit with all that is enclosed in it is alluring, delicious, pleasurable—and fatal. Because it is unitary, the manifold modes of reaching to grasp it mesh together and interlock, in the individual and in the nation-state. This overwhelmingly powerful merger of personal, social, economic, and military dynamisms parading as attainment of life bears us toward a vastly magnified fulfilment of God's original warning about the fruit. On the day of that climactic clutching at "life," death would come to hundreds of millions, and survivors would look back to their pre-war surroundings as a relative paradise.

Any partial rending of death's disguise, any emerging awareness as to what has actually been chosen, is typically countered by an intensified pursuit of "life," most of all in the activity where that rending has come: alcohol and other drugs, random sex, power over others, etc. The intensification impels toward a final unmasking. Two-digit inflation is exposure of Mammon's lie: What is so greatly valued continues to decrease in value; the more it is sought, the less it can buy. Death's masquerade reaches its most preposterous extreme in "security" through nuclear arms. Of the multiplicity of masks this one is thinnest, and that is probably the chief reason why collective energies and resources are directed most of all toward keeping it intact.

A most significant strategy in death's masquerade has been the great effort, throughout the Constantinian centuries, to see the death of soldiers as at least somewhat parallel to the death of Jesus: "As he died to make men holy, let us die to make men free!"; or, on innumerable plaques listing war dead some such verse as "Greater love has no man than this, that a man lay down his life for his friends" (Jn. 15:13). "Let us kill to make men free!" doesn't sing very reassuringly. But there is a deeper inappropriateness to that parallel. In any hot or cold war the governmental and military command is prepared to sacrifice the lives of soldiers, and soldiers proceed in a voluntary or imposed readiness to lay down their lives. This laying down of life has in it much that deserves our empathy and respect. However, the preparation or attempt to kill adversaries in war necessarily involves a readiness to risk being killed. This stance in soldiers and in others *for* soldiers does not correspond to that of Jesus as he went to the cross but rather, in considerable measure, to that of a person who threatens suicide in order to impose his will on another. In war and in combat the overridingly important relationship, individually and collectively, is with the enemy, not with those who are being defended. The goal is to impose death and devastation to entail defeat of the other side. One's own death in combat or the death of soldiers under one's command is not chosen as such. But the desired power over the enemy cannot be achieved without the readiness to risk and suffer death.

The fact that Jesus was not trying to kill others as he went to his death was the result of his having chosen not to seize or grasp for power over others. His willingness to die, unlike that of soldiers, was not oriented toward such power. The life he had received from the Father he laid down for others that they might be drawn into that very receiving. Life received in Christ as gift will not be used as power threat or medium for inflicting death. Adam reached out to possess, even before he violated love for another. The wrong in individual or collective killing which is prior even to the negation of love is this Adamic attempt to *have* life. Fighting in war is contrary to the love of Christ. But what is still more decisive, it is utterly contrary to the way Jesus lived his life as gift to be received from the Father. In the confrontation with his Jerusalem adversaries, he did not grasp the gift but looked to One Who would give back more than what could be taken from him.

The Jews were hoping for a messiah who would venture out to gain the whole world for them. Jesus could not be drawn into such Adamic grasping. The key to Jesus' life, as Hans Urs von Balthasar has so well expressed, was this:

> The Son's form of existence, which makes him the Son from all eternity ([John] xvii 5), is the uninterrupted reception of everything that he is, of his very self, from the Father. It is indeed this receiving of himself which gives him his "I," his own inner dimension, his spontaneity, that sonship with which he can answer the Father in a reciprocal giving.[4]

"Jesus said to them, 'Truly, truly, I say to you, the Son can do nothing of his own accord, but only what he sees the Father doing; for whatever he does, that the Son does likewise'" (Jn. 5:19).

This One has come into the midst of the human scramble after life to live out that receptivity. Jesus Christ is God's central Gift. To receive him is to be drawn away from the seizure of "life" into that very receptivity which is salvation. His incarnation, ministry, death, and resurrection are the foundational clarification of what he meant by the words, "whoever loses his life ... will save it." Jesus was willing to lose his life in the expectancy that his Father would give it again. God set that solitary willingness of his against the fatal momentum of the universal human attempt to *have* life.

Paul could write,

> For his sake I have suffered the loss of all things, and count them as refuse, in order that I may gain Christ and be found in him, not having a righteousness of my own, based on law, but that which is through faith in Christ, the righteousness from God that depends on faith; that I may know him and the power of his resurrection, and may *share his sufferings,* becoming like him in his death, that if possible I may attain the resurrection from the dead. (Phil. 3:8–11)

This passage brings out what the whole tenor of the New Testament indicates. *Lose/save* as salvation by God's grace (not by one's own achievements) and *lose/save* as the willingness to go with Jesus into loss of everything at the hands of enemies (not relying on carnal defenses) are most intimately related aspects of faith's wholeness. Self-justification before God and security through weapons over against enemies are the inner and outer culminations of our human attempt to save ourselves. For Jesus, confrontation with adversaries ready to kill him brought him the supreme test of his receptive readiness to follow the Father's lead. There is for the followers of Jesus in this latter part of the twentieth century a comparable test.

* * *

Individual suicide is not so much a choosing of death as it is the climactic confirmation that what had long been chosen was death.

Suicide generally is to be seen as culminating prosecution, directed as a rule not so much against other persons as against "life" (death's masquerade). A person tries to prove his case by taking his own life. Extreme depression, self-condemnation, self-punishment, fascination with dying and with the power to put an end to all one's capabilities may enter into the act. But the most widespread and characteristic dynamism is this prosecution. One's self-inflicted death is meant as a supremely cogent accusation against "life." When a suicide is directed against another person, for example a lover who has turned away, there is so plainly the prosecution of the person. But broader and deeper than that is the prosecution of what was grasped at and yet could not be possessed—life. As in all prosecution there is the attempt to counter condemnation by others and by oneself. By this prosecution of "life" and possibly of others, the suicide would seize, not life any longer, but an ultimate self-justification. The person in all his seeking after life reaches this end to his losing of life; and the word for the deed becomes the final characterization of the person.

The flicker of fascination with the power to kill another or oneself— the person near me with knife or hammer in my hand, the momentary swerve into head-on collision, the jump from a high place or from the night deck of a ship (how easily done the incomprehensible deed!)— that fascination is the primeval lure to savor without limit. The threshold into boundless power ("the knowledge of good and evil") seems to lie at the easily-crossed margin of a human life, someone else's or one's own. There is a range of power that can be experienced only through the act of taking a life. That lure alone seldom impels into the deed. But conjoined with the more powerful dynamisms we are considering, it can become even the precipitating factor in a suicide, a murder—or in the start of a nuclear war.

The type of suicide most relevant to the East-West struggle is that of the person who tells someone else, "If you do that (or don't do that), I will commit suicide." The power of the threat depends mainly on whether the individual is perceived as "crazy" enough, heedless enough of his or her life, to carry out the threat. When a suicide comes as the fulfilment of such a threat, it is meant as prosecution of the one who has not complied. West and East have been saying to each other, "If you overstep too far, we will choose for vast populations in both power blocks mutual suicide." Though this threat in its political abstractness and technological hiddenness dominates the world, the one time when it was dramatically and intensely experienced by hundreds of millions of people was during the days of the Cuban Missile Crisis in 1962. The prevailing attitude in the American populace as shaped by the government and the media was: "We've set our course. We are right. We're going ahead, no matter what." And there was within this, though hardly articulated, a general collective readiness to go down in mutual suicide if it would come to that.

The stunned, compulsive interest around the world in the mass suicide-murder in Jonestown, Guyana, may derive in considerable measure from the mostly unrecognized fact that the nation-states of West and East have nuclear arrangements and even drills for comparable suicide decisions by their leaders. It is not without significance that leaders and led in the Jonestown portent were Americans. Indeed, it is probable that after a Third World War poison depots would be set up wherever there was still the possibility for doing that, to facilitate suicide by survivors who would be impelled to that step.

Underlying both individual and collective threats of suicide is a low valuation of life. If one's own life and the daily living of it is received as gift from God, one can choose, as Jesus did, to lay down that life, precious as it is, for others. But the individual or collective attempt by threat of suicide to command others can only arise out of a depreciation of life. In the context of that depreciation one is ready, in the attempt to impose one's will, to risk forfeiting one's life. If the attempt does not succeed, the impulsion toward carrying out the threat derives not only from the commitment to do so but also from this latest failure to seize what was willed. There can be a determined collective forfeiture of life as a final accusation against "life" that has slipped out of the common grasp. All human effort to *have* life veers sooner or later toward the conclusion that life isn't all that great anyway. This repressed but pervasive conclusion in the American and the Soviet public outlook underlies the nuclear threats and the readiness to carry them out. Violence and war are often chosen as a way out of boredom.

An American nuclear first strike as an attempt to *win* by knocking out virtually all the retaliatory capacity of the adversary could be carried out only with great risk to the American population and would thus still come within the range of this analysis. (Indeed, the insanity of a first-strike capability is revealed by the prospect that, even if such a strike were "successful," the fallout from it, carried by the prevailing westerly winds, would probably render the United States unfit for human habitation.) If a nuclear war breaks out because of some technological accident apart from precipitating governmental maneuvers, it will be preceded by the readiness to set up those vast systems. If a nuclear war is initiated, without authorization, by one or more nuclear functionaries, that person or persons would be taking just one further step in the progression of many steps already collectively taken.

In Mark 10:29–30 and parallels, Jesus gives examples of losing and saving: "Truly, I say to you, there is no one who has left house or brothers or sisters or mother or father or children or lands, for my sake and for the gospel, who will not receive a hundredfold now in this time, houses and brothers and sisters and mothers and children and lands, with persecutions, and in the age to come eternal life."

Disciples give up much, but they receive a hundredfold more already in this life. In persecutions they may need to give up their lives, but following that too, they are to receive life in far greater measure.

It is important for fuller understanding of Jesus' warning about saving and losing one's life to know that behind the Greek verb translated "lose" is a Hebrew verb meaning "bring oneself to destruction."[5] The losing of one's life is not just something that happens to a person as a result of the attempt to save it. The person, though intending otherwise, is actively engaged in bringing himself to total ruin. What Adam was told before the Fall echoes within each of us, though we may largely drown it out. Any of us can resolutely persist in swallowing the lie and grabbing to ourselves death's "life" disguise. The momentum of that persistence carries a person toward the brink at which the unconfessed self-destroying becomes terminated destruction. For the neck of each human being there are, in the imagery of

Jesus, two contrary possibilities: the welcoming embrace of the Father (Lk. 15:20 AV) or the strangling pull of the millstone into the depths (Lk. 17:2).

A suicide is so awesome because here more plainly than anywhere else the earthly endpoint of the losing of life, the bringing of oneself to dissolution, comes into view. What looms up is not any cogency of intended prosecution or self-justification but the dark pathos of this conclusive refusal to receive life as gift. A comparable awesomeness would enshroud the planet after World War III.

Chapter 22

AS IN THE DAYS OF NOAH

As the enemy drew nearer to Moscow the attitude taken by its inhabitants in regard to their position did not become more serious, but, on the contrary, more frivolous, as is always the case with people who see a great danger approaching. At the approach of danger there are always two voices that speak with equal force in the heart of man: one very reasonably tells the man to consider the nature of the danger and the means of avoiding it; the other even more reasonably says that it is too painful and harassing to think of the danger, since it is not in a man's power to provide for everything and escape from the general march of events; and that it is therefore better to turn aside from the painful subject till it has come, and to think of what is pleasant. In solitude a man generally yields to the first voice; in society to the second. So it was now with the inhabitants of Moscow. It was long since there had been so much gaiety in Moscow as that year.[1]

Leo Tolstoy

And he said to the disciples, "The days are coming when you will desire to see one of the days of the Son of man, and you will not see it. And they will say to you, 'Lo, there!' or 'Lo, here!' Do not go, do not follow them. For as the lightning flashes and lights up the sky from one side to the other, so will the Son of man be in his day. But first he must suffer many things and be rejected by this generation. As it was in the days of Noah, so will it be in the days of the Son of man. They ate, they drank, they married, they were given in marriage, until the day when Noah entered the ark, and the flood came and destroyed them all. Likewise as it was in the days of Lot— they ate, they drank, they bought, they sold, they planted, they built, but on the day when Lot went out from Sodom fire and brimstone rained from heaven and destroyed them all—so will it be on the day when the Son of man is revealed.

Luke 17:22–30

In his summary of the stories of Noah and Lot, Jesus draws a dramatic contrast between "days" and "the day." The former was a long period when human affairs seemed to be proceeding in customary

153

fashion; the latter was the cataclysmic destruction from God for those who had been complacently absorbed in their own pursuits. And yet this day of destruction was also one of rescue by God for those who heeded His warning about what was coming and acted accordingly. Jesus does not point to the violence which filled the earth in Noah's time (Gen. 6:11, 13) nor to the infamous sins of Sodom. Though the wickedness of such a period is what stands out for God (as in the Genesis stories), the prevailing experience of the doomed generation is that of immersion in the daily round of ordinary human pursuits. Eating, drinking, marrying, buying and selling, planting and building are not forbidden activities. But the error even more decisive than participation in the gross wickedness which calls down the catastrophe is the thoughtless, self-satisfied absorption in these busy routines at a time when overwhelming disaster is about to strike.

As God called Noah and Lot out of those routines, Jesus, speaking to his disciples, does the same; for the time before the glorious Appearing of the Son of Man will be filled with heedless absorption in commonplace activities. This is the picture given by Jesus in the Luke 17 passage and in the parables of the unexpected thief, returning master, and the arriving bridegroom (Mt. 24:42–25:13). In 1 Thessalonians 5:2–3, Paul so vividly expressed the same view: "For you yourselves know well that the day of the Lord will come like a thief in the night. When people say, 'There is peace and security,' then sudden destruction will come upon them as travail comes upon a woman with child, and there will be no escape."

In contrast, the book of Revelation and certain passages in the synoptic gospels seem to indicate that the period just prior to Christ's Appearing is to be one of great upheaval and tribulation. If we see this contrary picture as pointing to developments that stand out only for those who with eyes of faith discern what is happening and as pointing in part to aspects of the Endpoint cataclysm itself, we are left with the basic image for the Endtime of deceptive quiet and business as usual. John's visions unveiled the dark dynamisms within the Roman Empire and later mutations; but most of his contemporaries in the Empire were blind to all that he saw and remained complacently absorbed in what might best fill the emptiness of day after day.

The pre-nuclear-war present is astonishingly like "the days of Noah" and "the days of Lot." The wickedness and the forces that impel the world toward doom are mostly out of sight or not recognized for what they are. Few see even partially with God in His seeing (as the Hebrew prophets did). Most human beings live out day after day absorbed in consumption, production, commerce, self-gratification. And each such day moves inevitably on—unless there is a human turning around—toward that day which will be overwhelmingly unlike all the ordinary days preceding it, that day of sudden inundating cataclysm, that day of fire and worse than brimstone raining across continents.

Throughout the Bible there is a vivid sense of the suddenness with which total destruction can come. Again and again the prophets cried out to the people around them, nearly all of whom were lulled by the seeming calm and caught up in their own affairs.

> *Therefore this iniquity shall be to you*
> *like a break in a high wall, bulging out, and*
> *about to collapse,*
> *whose crash comes suddenly, in an instant.*
>
> (Is. 30:13)

> *And ruin shall come on you suddenly,*
> *of which you know nothing.*
>
> (Is. 47:11)

> *Make mourning as for an only son,*
> *most bitter lamentation;*
> *for suddenly the destroyer*
> *will come upon us.*
>
> (Jer. 6:26)

> *Suddenly Babylon has fallen and been broken.*
>
> (Jer. 51:8)

Ancient Near Eastern political and military actualities were such that premonitions like these received fulfilment. In the siege of an ancient city the terrible change from security to destruction would come in a single hour. On the day the central city of a small invaded country fell, all fell. And the typically brutal thoroughness of the victorious army was pictured by Jesus: they "will dash you to the ground, you and your children within you, and they will not leave one stone upon another in you" (Lk. 19:44). In modern wars defeat has been more drawn out—at the very least (as with Poland in 1939) a matter of a few days. But in a nuclear war destruction would come with the suddenness of old. The demolition of the social fabric and basic structure of even the largest collectivities can come in part of a single day.

If the "days" and "the day" of Noah and Lot are prototypes for the nuclear present and its imminent end, then what is happening now and what is ahead can be added to those biblical stories as prototype for the "days" and "the Day" of the Son of Man. It is not given us to know the relation between the day of the Bomb and the Day of the Son of Man. His Day could precede and prevent the day of the Bomb, though biblical apocalyptic would seem to point away from that possibility. But if we discern what the days of the Bomb are like, we can understand the days of the Son of Man. As such it is filled with frantic consumption and with immersion in the commonplace and in diversions from the commonplace. The undercurrents of anxiety around the world drive people, not to turn-around, but to an intensified seizing of day after day.

There is the possibility that prior to a Third World War there will be one or more relatively localized nuclear disasters through accident or very limited use of nuclear weapons, perhaps by nonaligned countries. Accidental nuclear explosions have almost occurred a number of times, as in 1961 when a B-52 bomber with two 24-megaton bombs crashed near Goldsboro, North Carolina, and five of the six interlocking safety devices in the one bomb were triggered. The hope has been sometimes expressed that such a disaster, by confronting the peoples of the world with the actual ghastliness of the destruction, suffering, and death hanging over us all, might bring on the change of heart and mind needed for the worldwide halt and turning back. Such a result is possible. It may be that under God even this climactic warning and opportunity will come.

There would be vast news coverage of such a disaster, horror and fascination in every country, an upsurge of good intentions and high-sounding appeals. But after the assassinations of John Kennedy, Martin Luther King, Jr., and Robert Kennedy it still was not possible within the United States to enact desperately needed gun control legislation. The decisive start toward general disarmament, even after a relatively limited nuclear disaster, would be a move fraught with far greater attitudinal, technological, and counter-lobbying difficulties. A turn back from the development of nuclear power plants might come following the shock of a great power plant disaster, for national and personal "security" as threatened by enemy groups would not be directly at stake. But the immense momentum of nuclear weaponry would very likely override whatever increased resistance might result from a limited nuclear disaster. Except for the immediate victims there would be a general and gradual return to living out the contemporary counterpart of the "days" of Noah and Lot.

For Noah's contemporaries and the people of Sodom there were no experiential or commonsense grounds for supposing that a flood or fire was about to sweep them away. There was only the warning. We have no commonsense grounds for expecting the Day of the Son of Man. We have only his word. The days of the Bomb are in this regard different. Common sense, reason, political analysis, if directed toward the current world situation, show that, in the long run, continuation of the nuclear arms race and its vertical and horizontal proliferations will almost certainly bring catastrophe on much or all of the human race. But day-by-day immersion in consumption, getting ahead, and building (weapons most of all) holds both general populations and political leaders back from taking a long-range view.

The image of travail is frequently used by the prophets for the sudden agony of a day of destruction. The preceding "days" and the people who teem within them are a womb widening with the dire pregnancy which convulses into travail and birth on the concluding day. It is in this fashion that the day of the Bomb and the doom of the last Day are hidden within these ever so ordinary days. People who say, "There is peace and security," are trying to put to rest their anxieties.

> The word of Yahweh was addressed to me as follows, "Son of man, what do you mean by this proverb common throughout the land of Israel: Days go by and visions fade?
>
> "Very well, tell them, 'The Lord Yahweh says this: I will put an end to this proverb; it shall never be heard in Israel again.' Instead, tell them:
>
> 'The day is coming when every vision will come true.'" (Ezek. 12:21–24 JB)

In any succession of "days" there is for each day, in the balancing of general human experience, a chronological sameness. They are experienced as "duration leading nowhere."[2] But that bland sameness is illusion. For each day feeds into the next in an unrecognized progression toward the *day*. Each deposits into a mounting cumulative weight like layer upon layer of further snow on a steeply sloping mass. Each increases the tautness which draws the trap (as the biblical image has it) to its springing point. We experience these days of the Bomb as commonplace succession, one after another. But closer analysis, quite apart from Christian faith, shows them to be progression—toward the unknown day. With the daily passage of time the momentum increases, bearing humanity onward in the nuclear arms buildup, relations between the countries of the world become more destabilized, and the obstacles to disarmament become still more formidable. The turn toward disarmament could have been made so much more easily in the fifties than later. Wiser political leadership in the United States (which might have resulted from other election returns) could have actualized what was quite feasible. Dissipation of days and years has brought a constant narrowing of what seems feasible politically. As even more sophisticated weapons systems (most notably the cruise missile) are developed one after another, the prospects for fully reliable inspection and thus for any reasonable assurance about national security in a disarmament process grow ever dimmer.

The determinative content of "days" is the uneasy optimism that things will continue as they are. Yet current preliminary refutation of this is to be found in the fact that on the underside of these "days" enormous changes, from 1950 to 1960 to 1970 to 1980, have been taking place. There has been almost the worst imaginable technological progression humanly achievable, apart from wholesale firing of the weapons. And as Ralph E. Lapp pointed out, the real test of deterrence is not whether it has worked till now but "the shape of the world it has created—and the outlook ahead."[3]

Warning of that Day which is to come like a thief, Jesus urged, "And what I say to you I say to all: Watch" (Mk. 13:37)—be alert as a sentinel, expectantly reckon with a Return at any time, discern the inbreaking nearness of wrath and rescue. The lulling succession of ordinary days makes that very difficult. But if in these days we recognize the imminence of the holocaust, discernment of this sequel to the "days of Noah" can stimulate us to heed that command, "Watch!" The nearness of that technologically arranged-for day intimates the same for the Day beyond all human arrangement or postponing. And if we are drawn out of the somnolence of days into watching for that Day, our reckoning with nuclear holocaust should become a secondary aspect of that vigilance.

But consider a strange puzzle: Could there be, after a Third World War, the commonplace "days" of the Son of Man and circumstances that people would describe by saying, "There is peace and security"?

For any human being there is the shorter or longer succession of days and then the day of death. When people have the outlook, "Let us eat and drink, for tomorrow we die" (Is. 22:13; 1 Cor. 15:32), awareness of a day for dying impels them to seize the fleeting days.

Biblically, generation follows generation. Some generations never experience a focal collective day of judgment. A generation passes because through the years death takes persons away, one by one. But then there comes the generation of Noah, of Lot, of Jeremiah, of Jesus, and a day of destruction overwhelms it. Out of the sowing of the wind through unsmitten generations comes the whirlwind which strikes down that generation. God's encounter with the generation brings to a new culmination the dynamic legacies of rebellion and guilt, a climactic calling down of the day. "Therefore also the Wisdom of God said, 'I will send them prophets and apostles, some of whom they will kill and persecute,' that the blood of all the prophets, shed from the foundation of the world, may be required of this generation, from the blood of Abel to the blood of Zechariah, who perished between the altar and the sanctuary. Yes, I tell you, it shall be required of this generation" (Lk. 11:49–51). To the persisting stain of all that past blood they added for themselves the blood of Jesus and of his followers. On them the day of Jerusalem's doom came. How somber to be in a generation (and all too much a part of it) which is actualizing on planetary scale a repeat fulfilment of those words.

Sodom's destruction intimated the last Day. But for the people of Sodom who perished on that day there is still the more awesome and determinative Day: "I tell you that it shall be more tolerable on the day of judgment for the land of Sodom than for you" (Mt. 11:24). For each of us, beyond whatever nuclear fire may sweep over us, there looms a far more intensely trying fire: "Each man's work will become manifest; for the Day will disclose it, because it will be revealed with fire, and the fire will test what sort of work each one has done" (1 Cor. 3:13). We will each be refined by that fire of love—or will be shown to be, to the innermost of who we are, dross.

Prelude to that Day is *today*, as opposite of "days." "Behold, now is the day of salvation" (2 Cor. 6:2). "Exhort one another every day, as long as it is called 'today,' that none of you may be hardened by the deceitfulness of sin" (Heb. 3:13).

Chapter 23

WHY THE POSSIBILITY FOR THE BOMB?

He is the great stone flung out of Heaven that smites the image of human empire so that the iron and brass, the silver and gold, are broken in pieces and become like summer chaff. The supreme act of judgment in the Cross remains as the abiding force to determine all history, and every crisis in human affairs falls under its action and reflects its meaning. Let us make no mistake about it. The Cross of Jesus Christ is still in the field. Jesus Christ still holds the sovereign initiative in history. No doubt the fire rages in the world, but in the heart of the fire there is one like unto the Son of God, and out of the heart of it there comes the shout of a King: Be of good cheer, I have overcome the world."[1]

Thomas F. Torrance

Why evil? To that most difficult of questions Christians answer that inherent in the freedom God has given man is the possibility of evil. God allows this. Such evil acts are often preceded by what the Bible refers to as the devising of evil, the remarkable ingenuity (for personal and collective aggrandizement) in discovering ways to blight and crush human life. Within what God permits, that ingenuity has now produced devices far beyond anything achieved earlier. These overshadow the many scientific discoveries that generally enhance human life.

But the development of nuclear weapons raises for biblical people a question of a different order from those having to do with God's permitting the worst that has been devised and perpetrated from the dim past till now. For God certainly could have created the universe and the earth without uranium and thus without the possibility of these technological breakthroughs that have given human beings the capability of turning the planet into an uninhabitable waste. We need to ponder this. Within "the depth of the riches and wisdom and knowledge of God" (Rom. 11:33), He created the uranium isotopes as the natural culmination of the elements. God set us in the midst of a creation which contained that very hidden and most terrible possibility. Why?—when He could so easily have withheld it from us.

The answer comes partly by considering why among the abundant variety of trees in the garden He made to grow that one additional tree. Man was to cleave to his Creator and live life out of what He gave. Man was to obey. The splitting of the atom is like a postponed swallowing of the tough core of that original fruit. We wanted to grasp, to have, to act, without limit. God's No to the boundlessness of our craving has been given in the biblical revelation but not in matter itself. Uranium mediates God's interim "So be it" to the limitlessness of our rebellion.

It is assumed in the teaching of Jesus and throughout the New Testament that there will always be those who turn and become his disciples and those who do not. He extends his call into discipleship to all people. Faithful discipleship is expected of those who heed the call and turn.

Liberal pacifism, based in the Anglo-American churches and cresting during the nineteen-thirties, was largely shaped by the hope that the nations would come around to living by the nonviolence of the Sermon on the Mount. That optimism was generally shattered by the Second World War and by the theological critique of Reinhold Niebuhr. As Niebuhr pointed out, there had been too little awareness of the dynamism of sin in social structures. There was also in those peace movements not very much of the New Testament understanding that the way of Jesus can really be lived out only by those who in faith receive power for that. The church of the first centuries expected its members to live by the Sermon on the Mount; it did not expect nor urge the Roman imperial apparatus to do so. This church/world differentiation was revived and continued by the Anabaptists who judged nominally Christian governments "by their fruits" to be obviously unchristian. For them faithful discipleship was to be expected in the New Community, not in structures that were manifestly unredeemed.

From a biblical perspective a most remarkable and ironic dimension has emerged in the past decades. There is no way to avoid global catastrophe except through some degree of public readiness in certain countries to face enemies without violence as Jesus did, and thus risk the worst that they might do (the cross). This development negates the mainline christendom/post-christendom perspective of excusing rulers from Christ's way of love, but it also impels us beyond the Anabaptist view. Some limited general readiness for the way of the cross, which was scandal and folly even to Jesus' closest friends at first and persistently so for those outside the Christian community (1 Cor. 1:23), is the only alternative to nuclear doom. This is expressed in Martin Luther King's words: "Today the choice is no longer between violence and nonviolence. It is either nonviolence or nonexistence.[2]

The nuclear arms race will continue to its unimaginable conclusion, or there will be a halt and the determined movement back to general disarmament. Arms control is a mix of hoax and illusion.[3] But disarmament or more advanced steps toward it cannot come without some willingness to enter into unaccustomed risks of vulnerability and possible impotence in relation to an adversary. Inspection arrangements, no matter how ingenious and comprehensive, cannot fully eliminate the possibility that the other side might cheat, strike with remaining weapons, and invade the country. A technology that produced such immense arsenals of destruction cannot, for any dismantling of them, eliminate the risk of a cross. There are brilliantly conceived plans for the disarmament process whereby the risks could be very much reduced.[4] But the great problem is not such risks in themselves (which inspection could very possibly reduce to a quite acceptable marginality). It is rather the fact that the big majority in each of the major powers are so deeply convinced that the adversary cannot be trusted and that entering into the risks of a disarmament process would be complete folly.

A surgeon can tell a patient that he runs probably a 20% risk of dying in the needed open heart surgery but that he has the virtual 100% certainty of dying quite soon if he does not undergo the operation. Nations could make a commonsense decision comparable to that of the patient and take the lesser risk. The worst that might come in a disarmament process would not be nearly so bad as what will almost certainly come through continuation of the nuclear arms buildup. There could be disarmament by unilateral steps, planned to elicit reciprocal action by adversaries. There could be massive preparations for nonviolent defense against invasion, preparations that could make the prospect of invasion or successful occupation rather unlikely. Such pragmatism could turn the human race back from nuclear death.

The new outlook which is so urgently needed would not need to be a worldwide recapitulation of Jesus' trust in the Father as he faced adversaries who were determined to do away with him. He moved not into a risk but toward a virtual certainty. For a disarmament process there would be risk, but possibly quite limited risk. Apart from trust in

God, assurance could be grounded in transnational inspection arrangements, nonviolent defense strategies, and the progressively recognized humanity of the other side.

Yet it is hard to see how such a commonsense choice of the far lesser risk could win an effective majority of the American people. The lure of military preparations lies in their being experienced as the crucial effort at saving, securing, guaranteeing the national "life." Disarmament proposals can be ever so reasonable and demonstrably less risky than continuation of the nuclear arms buildup. But to most people they seem like a crazy step into vulnerability and impotence. The possible dangers in a disarmament process loom up to cut off a vision of what disarmament could bring with it for the human family. In the military stance the far greater dangers are obscured because attention is focused on the efforts to counter them.

Jesus confronted his fellow Jews with the alternatives of a general turning to him or catastrophe at the hands of the Romans. His cry, "Repent!," was to the Jewish people as a whole, and not just to individuals.[5] We can hardly envision what that turning would have looked like, had it come, or what would have developed beyond that for an ethnic entity ruled by Jesus of Nazareth. But as Jesus saw it, his rejection by the Jews would lead to a fatal collision with Roman military might. Apart from a turn to Jesus as the Messiah, Palestinian Jews after 30 A.D. could have followed a moderate commonsense political course, which would have avoided that collision. But the dominant public attitudes which led to the rejection of Jesus led also to the rejection of that moderate course and thus to the destruction of the country. Is not the present world situation comparable?

Jesus said, "All authority [*exousia*] in heaven and on earth has been given to me" (Mt. 28:18). The hollowness and impending collapse of every contrary *exousia* can be discerned in the world around us. Now, even pragmatically, it is only within his authority that rescue for the race can be found.

* * *

The nuclear arms buildup has been compared to alcoholism. This is a most revealing analogy, if pursued further than is typically done. All that is wrong with the person converges into the alcoholism, which becomes the central dynamic pulling the person down into ruin. All that was collectively and individually wrong in Germany in the 1920's and 1930's fed and converged into the dark side of Nazism, which in turn was the embracing dynamism that took the German people to catastrophe. All that has been wrong in the superpowers and the middle-range powers—grasping in all its individual, economic, and social dimensions, with the resultant hardening of attitudes—finds unifying convergence in military "defense" and the nuclear arms buildup. For an analogy to the East-West struggle one could think of a husband and wife who in a collapsing marriage turn to alcohol, which compounds their problems and comes to loom as the most pressing problem.

The good work of the Alcoholics Anonymous movement is based on the insight that before a liberation can be brought about, a chronic alcoholic has to recognize: I am an alcoholic; I need help; that help needs to be from a Power greater than I am. An alcoholic cannot (usually at least) accomplish his own liberation, because his alcoholism is the impelling center of all that is wrong in him.

If contemporary militarism and the compulsive acquisition of arms is a societal equivalent to alcoholism, then for any conversion out of that a society must, it seems, come to a prevailing outlook something like, our alcohol is weapons; we desperately need help—from a Power greater, overwhelmingly greater, than we are. Throughout the Bible it was this type of outlook (not of course necessarily with primary reference to weapons) which provided the indispensable prelude to God's rescuing those who together turned in suppliant longing to Him.

When I try to discern biblically what the immensity of the nuclear arms race is, not only in itself, but as the convergence of all other *save/lose* dynamisms, I can see hardly any prospect for breaking out of its ensnarement unless there is a general turn to God comparable to what is recorded in a number of Old Testament stories. Many leading thinkers have warned that there will have to be a revolutionary change in the worldwide human outlook if doom is to be avoided. Christians at least should know that such *metanoia* comes only as persons and groups turn to God so that He can turn them around.

I am most ready to admit that it is hard for me even to imagine the political emergence and ascendancy of such an outlook in the United States or in any other country. All the more so because that *metanoia* in its societal application is quite marginal within the churches. What is difficult to believe in the story of Jonah is not the role of the big fish but the mass repentance of the Ninevites. That story, however, profoundly points to the alternatives set by God before any Nineveh and the turn by a whole society through which alone the impending destruction can be averted. It is important to keep in mind that this turn did not of itself achieve the rescue. It was God who could and did, when they turned. The Ninevites did not view their repentance as something that put God under obligation to save them: "Who knows if God will not change his mind and relent, if he will not renounce his burning wrath, so that we do not perish?" (Jon. 3:9 JB).

But the churches generally, rather than heading with Jonah for Tarshish or even belatedly for Nineveh, have been flourishing as esteemed priesthood within the great city. If a wide segment of the churches in the United States would really take up the Jonah task, who knows what might happen? If this turning would come in the United States, who knows what that might mean for the world?

Though God could have created the earth without the chemical possibility of alcoholism, His special mercy to the alcoholic finds focus in that progressive and nearly undeniable disclosure that he is losing out and is in extreme need of help. In nuclear armaments and also in overconsumption and the effects of that on the environment and on the poor of the earth there is a comparable disclosure: The major powers and indeed all of humanity are losing out and desperately need help to turn around. Only in a blindness equivalent to that of the advanced but unconfessed alcoholic can there be denial of this. Even if such blindness prevails, the disclosure proceeds as intimation of God's merciful plea. In the gospel narratives the persons who gravitated to Jesus were most notably those that could hardly deny they were in great need. "Those who are well have no need of a physician, but those who are sick" (Mt. 9:12).

An alcoholic has many good intentions, high resolves, commonsense insights. But the momentum of the alcoholism as convergence of all that is wrong in the person overpowers these. To suppose that there can be a wide enough mustering of pragmatic good sense to achieve a reversal of the nuclear arms race implies inadequate recognition of the momentum of the military convergence and the immensity of the societal wrongs that feed into it. One problem is of course that the mass media are to a great extent controlled by the vested interests that pursue current policies and that they would largely remain so until such a political breakthrough. There is too the dark prospect that, if a disarmament candidate would, say, be able to win the Presidency of the United States, an unconvinced military elite would resort to a coup, as in *Seven Days in May*. If the relatively limited threat posed by the candidacy of George McGovern in 1972 had not been dependably blocked by manipulation of the public, there might have been resort to assassination.

* * *

The immensity of the approaching nuclear cataclysm makes biblical sense only if it is seen as the consequence of a comparable immensity of sinning around the world. Rachel H. King pointed to a similar correlation in the recent past:

> If the world is thought of as under the power of God so that nothing happens in it without his permission, and if the war is thought to be permitted by God as the result of and judgment for the sins of men and nations, consideration of the magnitude of the misery caused by World War II creates a dilemma. We are faced with the alternative either of believing God to be cruelly capricious, a deity who judges sin with a retribution far greater than the sin itself; or we must concede the sin, of which the war was the judgment, to have been of enormous proportions.[6]

We turn away from considering the wrath of God just as we turn away from the prospect of nuclear catastrophe. This prospect encroaches upon us little though we may consciously realize it, and, in doing so, intimates God's wrath—the awesome extremity to which His No to sin will reach. In Jeremiah 4 we can read the prophet's vision of a totally desolated earth and sense it as a possibility all too near us. But when he writes,

> *I looked, and lo, the fruitful land was a desert,*
> *and all its cities were laid in ruins*
> *before the Lord, before his fierce anger,*

(Jer. 4:26)

we draw back uneasily, not wanting God to be that directly and decisively related to such desolation.

This problem of "before his fierce anger" meets us again and again in the Old Testament and also, though less obviously, in the New Testament. And yet, with our thinking shaped by the prophets and by Jesus, we need to see that the desolation of a nuclear war would come upon us "before the Lord, before his fierce anger." If, as we should gratefully recognize, nuclear war has been held back till now, not basically by human rationality and cleverness, but by God's merciful hand, it would be by "His formidable non-intervention" (His wrath)[7] that the day of the Bomb would at last come. Indeed, nothing else is at all so formidable as God's nonintervention. There cannot be that sovereign mercy apart from the prospect that God will at some point decide to let the worst come. "Therefore—Yahweh says this: You have disobeyed me, by not each granting freedom to his brother and his neighbor. Very well, I in my turn—it is Yahweh who speaks—leave sword, famine and plague free to deal with you" (Jer. 34:17 JB). Pointing to God's wrath, Paul in triple reiteration wrote, "God gave them up" to what they were so intent on (Rom. 1:24,26,28). As psychiatrist Fredric Wertham has pointed out, "Nothing in history has ever been prepared more thoroughly, both materially and psychologically, than the next world war."[8] How long for such a world as ours will God stay His wrath?

God's mercy in holding back engulfing perdition so as to give the opportunity for repentance creates a time lag that can easily be misinterpreted as a confirmation of the primeval lie, "You will not die" (Gen. 3:4). But as disaster upon disaster throughout the biblical period shows, God does not allow that illusion to hold sway for very long. He is the source of all life, and no individual or group can withdraw from Him without eventually collapsing.

Paul said to the Athenian crowd, "The times of [idolatrous] ignorance God overlooked, but now he commands all men everywhere to repent, because he has fixed a day on which he will judge the world in righteousness by a man whom he has appointed, and of this he has given assurance to all men by raising him from the dead" (Acts 17:30–31). In the nuclear era we have come into an added fulfilment of that "now he commands." Through thousands of years God in His patience allowed to the nations a certain latitude for their violent pursuits. But that time is at an end. There is no way ahead unless the peoples of the world turn from those pursuits to the One He has appointed.

The opposite of the sin of which nuclear war would be the consequence is trust in God, the cleaving to Him and to His Son. A simple inference then is that only if that immensity of sin is, to a wide extent, replaced by its opposite can the consequence be avoided.

Popular evangelical preaching and writing in this country does give some attention to the possibility of a nuclear war as punishment and to the imperative need for a repentance that would embrace multitudes. But that preaching and writing with reference to these issues is generally unbiblical and unprophetic. Imminent disaster is seen as punishment chiefly for individual sins in aggregate. There is little discernment of the convergence of these into the sins committed collectively. Most church people are aligned with the political, economic, and military status quo. Nuclear disaster is seen as hanging over us because of such things as sexual promiscuity, drug abuse, dabbling in the occult, street crime (the sins of *others*) and because of

the political, economic, and military perverseness of the other side—
but not because of a corresponding perverseness in the West. One
could just as well hold that the destruction of Jerusalem in 70 A.D.
came only because of the private sins of the people and the
ruthlessness of the Romans but not because of the militant Jewish
nationalism.

There could be a mass American turning away from all those private
sins and even a general public turn to God in such fashion as is
typically called for, and the country would proceed in political,
economic, and military matters very much as it does now. The
Pentagon is honeycombed with prayer cells. The entire country could
be one ardent honeycomb of comparable prayer cells and move even
faster to the day of God's fierce anger.

On that day of wrath something more substantially biblical than
popular evangelicalism would be needed for Christians to make any
sense of what had happened. Collective self-righteousness more than
anything else impels toward nuclear disaster and would tend, more
than anything else, to keep survivors from making any sense of that
chaos. Yet dozens of times in Ezekiel as imminent horrors are pictured,
there comes the strange and somber refrain, "*Then* you will know that
I am the Lord."

But if already in this pre-war period we see the impending nuclear
desolation as the starkest indicator of the immensity of our collective
sinning, this can point us more to God's love than to wrath. He loves
us each and all, yearns over us, lays down the life of the Son for us.
Apart, though, from discernment of the wrath we remain largely
blinded to the marvel of His mercy.

We sense the threat of nuclear annihilation. But there is a mightier,
more determinative threat, the one felt by the Dark Powers: the
onrush of their annihilation as God makes His final move against
them. As we view the human situation, the threat we should be most
keenly aware of and celebrate is the one those Powers tremble at. We
too can learn something from the shrieking demons in the gospel
exorcisms. Theirs was a panicky, convulsive resistance as Jesus moved
to cast them out. We are confronted now with something comparable
on a world scale.

"But woe to you, earth and sea, for the Devil has come down to you
in great fury, knowing that his time is short!" (Rev. 12:12 NEB). We
may feel that time is running out. But really it is only for the devil, for
those aligned with him, and for those who might yet turn from him
that time is running out. The convulsions of this century have their

deepest source in that infernal fury of the one and the many whose time is at an end. We cannot know beforehand (and possibly wouldn't as survivors) the time relationship between a nuclear paroxysm and the final day for the powers of evil, but we can know that this paroxysm, this derivative intercontinental crucifixion, would— contrary to all appearances—be an event precipitating that end.

Why, under God's sovereignty, the Bomb? Because God chose to let our rebellion be limitless; because He has chosen to give this culminating disclosure that apart from Him we are doomed; because He is, in this dread time, calling all peoples to recognize that "there is salvation in no one else, for there is no other name under heaven given among men by which we must be saved." (Acts 4:12).

PART IV

THE KINGDOM AS PEACE MOVEMENT

Chapter 24

ONE'S NICHE

Ordinary men are only a puff of wind,
important men delusion;
put both in the scales and up they go,
lighter than a puff of wind.

Psalm 62:9 (JB)

Lighter, less substantial than a puff of wind: this I may resist admitting with all my might. But how infinitesimal my might. I may strive to become an important man—no longer an ordinary one. Even if I succeed, I have not escaped the irony of my insignificance.

I want my life to have weight and that weight to be felt. I want whatever scales there are to register *my* being on them. But I cannot fully exclude an awareness that possibly they do not register this at all: in the astronomical reaches of space and time; or even on this speck of a planet, in the sweep of history, or within a huge national population. "Lighter than a puff of wind," a psalmist sighed; and now scientists can calculate that in the earth's atmosphere there are more than one million tons of air for each human being alive.

I am dogged by an awareness that my life has virtually no weight. From my shoes and through my eyes I seem to be center of the universe. But I can't find a single other person to confirm that view. Persons around me have almost no weight either; but I am outweighed easily by any of them banded together against me.

How many times will you come rushing at a man,
all of you, to bring him down
like a wall already leaning over,
like a rampart undermined?

(Ps. 62:3 JB)

The dynamism of even one person moving against me causes me to reel. I secretly extrapolate from the one to the ominous many; and behind even one lurk the many.

Each of us tries to find and maintain a niche: family, friends, house or lodging, work, income and what it can buy—the more immediate physical and human context of one's living. (Much of the beauty of childhood has to do with the fact that the small child is largely spared this niche-making effort.) We direct our energies toward having a spot. Yet there are so many dangers that could bring partial or full collapse of whatever place we have made for ourselves: loss of job, financial reverses, fire, natural catastrophe, sickness, accident, divorce, disintegration of other key relationships, economic and social upheaval, war. Whatever else may not come, death comes in the end to take from us each our place.

I can seek to let my imperiled near-nothingness merge into the substance of a nation-state so that I may be part of something that has undeniable weight. But according to the prophetic word, the nations too "are accounted as the dust on the scales" (Is. 40:15). And even apart from any biblical warning, we can hardly escape the unsettling premonition that the nation-state within which we would find asylum from our weightlessness is hardly more than a mirage projection of our individual weightlessness.

A Christian reply to the standard questions about attack and defense must go deeper than pointing to the possibility of meeting the killer or the collective adversary with love, deeper even than pointing to the command and example of our Lord. It must speak to the immeasurably compelling human need to have and to preserve for oneself a place.

> Do not be afraid of those who kill the body but cannot kill the soul; fear him rather who can destroy both body and soul in hell. Can you not buy two sparrows for a penny? And yet not one falls to the ground without your Father knowing. Why, every hair on your head has been counted. So there is no need to be afraid; you are worth more than hundreds of sparrows.
>
> So if anyone declares himself for me in the presence of men, I will declare myself for him in the presence of my Father in heaven. But the one who disowns me in the presence of men, I will disown in the presence of my Father in heaven. (Mt. 10:28–33 JB)

These words of Jesus speak more decisively to the attack-defense questions than probably anything else in his teachings—including the command to love enemies. This counsel comes near the close of the instructions to the Twelve as Jesus sends them out to be heralds and agents of the Kingdom. Jesus warns of the rejections, betrayals, persecutions, interrogations they will encounter. To go forth without material resources into *that* is, humanly considered, the complete opposite of maintaining one's niche. What does Jesus set over against the loss of all achieved security and the fear of adversaries who may, with lethal might, take from disciples the last earthly thing they have? Sparrows—and God's care for them. Even the sparrows have their place before God. How much more do disciples of Jesus!

It is no surprise to be told that we are of more worth than hundreds of sparrows. We naturally assume that importance for ourselves. If, though, sparrows have virtually no worth, as we are inclined to suppose, the starting point for the comparison gives no basis for reassurance. We need to unlearn that assumption and take in what Jesus affirms. Each sparrow is dear to God—and each of His human children far more. His love and caring surround a sparrow in its dying—and us ever so much more. If we trust this Father, we can, with courage, face the threat of death at the hands of adversaries. Ultimately there is no solid basis for the worth of human beings other than the Father's care for them. This worth is not achieved or maintained; it is simply recognized and cherished.

In Matthew 10 Jesus was giving his disciples a task, a work to do in his movement. Their role and place before other human beings was that of manifesting the in-breaking reality of God's Rule. In that frontier position they would often be right next to the closed-minded, to fanatic persecutors and skeptical rulers. On that exposed, perilous frontier they would have nothing that from a merely human viewpoint could be considered a niche. But before God they had a place—in His caring for them and in His work for them.

For myself I would put it like this. The Father knows me and cares for me; this means that I have a place before him. To the extent that I am a disciple of Jesus, God's Kingdom is the only large-scale context that really counts for me. His encompassing Rule becomes the determining context of my life. That Rule is on the move—in, among, toward persons. In that movement I have been given a place. Insofar as this place is forward, exposed, imperiled, I can fill it only as I discern God's encircling love making of it a bulwark.

The Old Testament motif which corresponds to this teaching comes out so vividly and frequently in the Psalms: God is looked to as rock, refuge, fortress, stronghold. The only secure niche is the place He gives us within His caring, not any territory we stake out for ourselves. And He is the defender of that place. The eschatological fulfilment of this motif is pictured in Micah 4:4:

But they shall sit every man under
his vine and under his fig tree,
and none shall make them afraid;
for the mouth of the Lord of hosts has spoken.

From this perspective the standard attack-defense models look quite different. The preservation of the United States isn't for me a compelling concern, because I don't see this country as the sustaining large-scale context. If I did, it could make sense to resort to any means in trying to preserve it. I am not clinging to something that may collapse, but to God's Kingdom.

Similarly for my personal small-scale context. I may indeed lose my job, possessions, home, status. I may lose members of my family and my own life through illness, accident, murder. But all that I might lose does not constitute my place. These are God-given components of that place. But His gift of place is prior to and not dependent on those components. So it is that nothing whatever that comes against those components can separate us from the love of God in Christ Jesus our Lord or destroy the place given us in that love.

It becomes a question of which pillar of cloud and fire we look to. The pillar of cloud by day and of fire by night led the Israelites out of Egypt and stood between them and the pursuing army. The Lord, manifested in the pillar, rescued His people from their enemies and brought them to their allotted place. Those without eyes of faith to see that guarding pillar and its fulfilment in a column of wood and impaled flesh, look for protection to the thermonuclear pillar of fire and cloud in its proliferating multiplicity.

There is for us a far worse possibility than death at the hands of persecutors or other enemies; there is an ultimate peril, stated grimly by Jesus as God's destroying both soul and body in hell—the complete loss of one's place before the Father, the fall away into no place. This worst is said to result from disowning the Father's Son in the presence of men. Jesus had been warning about conflict with enemies of the Kingdom. It is most of all on the frontier of facing enemies and the suffering or death which they may inflict that the ultimate peril lies: that of disowning the Son, in thinking, word, deed. The Son is most clearly disowned when hard-pressed believers publicly renounce their faith in him; Jesus' words about disowning refer most of all to that. But Peter broke with his Lord by violent deed before he did so in words. If, when confronted by personal or transoceanic enemies, I go against all that the One I call Master has showed me about meeting enemies, I disown that Master "in the presence of men." In encounter with enemies I must remember that the extreme danger lies not in what they can do to me but in what I might do—disown the Lord.

I can, however, in the way I face enemies, declare myself for the Son and point others to him. As for the berserk attacker, communist army, or postholocaust scavenging band breaking into my niche, I have the hope that I would sense the loving rule of God in the situation, that I would be open to His freeing me from terror into faith and love, and that I would be given the grace to show something of Christ's love to whoever is moving against me. This is my hope for my family and for the New Community.

The objection may come that this passage is concerned with facing persecutors, not the enemy in the form of a rival country. To this the following can be said. If a church, in the Constantinian pattern, aligns itself with the governing elite, then it almost certainly removes itself from the danger of domestic persecution (as long, at least, as that elite remains in power). Jesus' words about facing enemies who persecute cannot be relevant since there are none. The only notable enemies are those beyond the frontiers who are designated as such by the governing elite. Church people in their fear of those enemies may view them as potential invaders who will become their persecutors. But here too Jesus' words are not seen as relevant, because the church meshes into the front of social-military solidarity over against those enemies, with preservation of religious freedom as the lofty rationale justifying this. Participation in that solidarity is the clearest evidence of the alignment through which domestic persecution is avoided. This alignment insures against persecution and moves the church away from any circumstances in which Jesus' teaching about facing perse- cutors and other enemy groups would be seen as relevant. The decisive frontier has come to be that of the nation-state, not the open frontier of the New Community turned outward in love and service to those beyond it. If an enemy country successfully invades (or a revolutionary movement takes over), what may follow is not, by and large, persecution of Christ's church but repression of this part of the defeated front.

The teaching about a pre-tribulation rapture of the church, which first appeared only in the nineteenth century, is for many people a means by which success in avoiding persecution and cross-bearing is projected into an apocalyptic future. It has considerable political significance. This presumed prospect is a sort of ultimate air raid shelter for many conservative church people aligned with the political, economic, and military status quo: before something as terrible as a nuclear war takes place, true believers will surely be caught up to be with the Lord. The history of Israel, Jesus' teaching that his disciples need to reckon with bearing a cross, and a closer examination of the relevant texts point away from such an easy exit.

Where Christians are forthrightly unaligned with the ruling elite, Jesus' words about facing persecutors are usually very relevant. Nonaligned Christians refuse to be part of a national front pitted against the designated enemy. Or, to put it positively, they are willing to meet possible invaders with nonviolent suffering love. Such Christians, especially if they are very numerous, will be seen as a grave internal threat. Faced with the danger posed by a rival country, people feel that there must be the strength of national unity. Any group that stands apart seems to be undermining the united front so vital for resisting the enemy. A church with a nationist, military stance avoids persecution. A church with an actively non-nationist, nonviolent stance usually encounters persecution. We accept a place, assailed by human beings but given and secured by God; or we join in laying hold of a place given and secured by a great mass of human beings but assailed by God.

Chapter 25

THE SCANDAL OF DEFENSELESSNESS

Jesus said to them, "Tonight every one of you will lose his faith *because of me.*"

Matthew 26:31 (Phillips)

Our minds are unable to comprehend the pathos of those words. The Son of Man had come to save the lost, to lift the fallen. But here others, far from being lifted up, fall away *because of him.* "Anyone who is an obstacle [stumbling-block] to bring down one of these little ones who have faith, would be better thrown into the sea with a great millstone around his neck" (Mk. 9:42 JB). But here Jesus himself causes others to fall from faith. He is the stone of stumbling *(skandalon),* and he feels the weight of the ponderous millstone.

Dostoevsky's Grand Inquisitor said to Jesus, "Thou art proud of Thine elect, but Thou hast only the elect, while we give rest to all."[1] Jesus had rejected a political strategy for mobilizing and lifting up the many. With gaze still upon the many, he had turned to the few. But now he has no longer even the few. The few, on whom the future of his mission depends, are about to fall away—*because of him.* Peter does not fall away because of the number of swords over against his. He and the others collapse into grave sin because of Jesus himself, Jesus in his defenselessness. Peter is ready to go down fighting. But he is utterly unready to go down not fighting. What breaks Peter and the others is not the overpowering concentration of armed might sent against them in the garden, and not the danger of death. Rather, it is the way Jesus meets that armed mob, reprimands Peter for the attempted defense, and goes as a lamb to the slaughter. The disciples fall away precisely because of who they perceive Jesus to be at the time of his arrest.

The Son obeys the Father, but because of his obedience his disciples most terribly disobey. He sees that in going to the cross he exposes his followers to grave physical danger and the most extreme moral peril. They will either go into the jaws of death with him or desert him. He knows they will desert him. The prospect of himself being a *skandalon* is for him a *skandalon*.

Jesus knew what was in man (Jn. 2:25), but he moved into the turbulent center of the human situation, he put himself in human hands, he gave himself over into the power of his enemies. His coming was God's ultimate exposure, defenselessness, vulnerability. Reconciliation between God and His adversaries could come, not through His annihilating them, not by His overpowering and coercing them, not by His keeping them at a safe distance or His maintaining a shield to hold off their mad attacks. Reconciliation could be brought about only if He drew near to the enemy, met them, spoke with them, showed Himself to them. It could come only through defenselessness, vulnerability, the cross. God did not defend Himself. The Father did not defend the Son. Jesus drew near his enemies; he met them. He was wounded, smitten, pierced, done away with by human beings. When we had done our worst, God came back with His best.

But death on the cross was not the end of the wounding. The Resurrection did not terminate the vulnerability of Jesus. The Risen One had still visible wounds. He put the question, "Saul, Saul, why do you persecute me?" (Acts 9:4). Paul later saw the sufferings of Christians as extension of the sufferings of Christ (1 Th. 2:14–15; 2 Cor. 1:5–7; 4:7–12; Col. 1:24; 1 Tim. 1:13; 2 Tim. 2:3,10–12). In the Old Testament, God was drawn into the sufferings of His people. In the New Testament, Christ's people are drawn into his sufferings. The vulnerability of Jesus Christ does not stop just with him. The healing, deliverance, and power of his triumph go out into others, as do his weakness, his defenselessness, and his suffering. "While we live we are always being given up to death for Jesus' sake, so that the life of Jesus may be manifested in our mortal flesh" (2 Cor. 4:11).

Jesus was *skandalon* not only to his disciples during those several days; he has remained a *skandalon* for the many in each generation. "Christ crucified" was "a stumbling-block to Jews and folly to Gentiles" (1 Cor. 1:23). The Jesus of Gethsemane and Golgotha is the stone of stumbling (Rom. 9:33; 1 Pet. 2:8; Gal. 5:11). Jesus must also have discerned the long-term scandalousness of his going to the cross and been torn by it.

From this perspective, Jesus as the *skandalon*, we can now deal further with that most difficult question of attack and defense. Neo-Cain says, "I am my brother's keeper and therefore must kill." When thus laid bare, the attitude of military custodianship isn't very attractive. But what is the alternative? Are we to leave others undefended? Can God expect of us an obedience which would leave others exposed to whatever evils our adversaries might choose to inflict? We know (perhaps) that we ourselves should be ready to suffer; but are we to keep our hands clean even if this means the suffering and the ruin of others?

What we usually forget is that Jesus in the desert and in the garden faced these very questions. Their persuasiveness was pressed upon him by Satan himself. Direct from the Evil One he learned the subtleties of the lesser-of-two-evils argument: You have to resort to some regrettable actions to prevent what would be far worse; don't fall into the pride of an obedience which brings the ruin of others. Jesus in Gethsemane met the marshaled pathos and power of all these considerations. The Son obeyed the Father. In weakness he faced the might of the enemy and went down. He became the *skandalon*. That child was "set for the fall and rising of many" (Lk. 2:34). The Son scandalously obeyed the Father, and through his rising many rose.

To refuse certain modes of defending loved ones, thus leaving them seemingly more open to attack by adversaries, is a scandalous stance. So is the rejection of lethal modes of combatting a perverted and perverting system like Nazism, whose wider victory might bring spiritual ruin to additional tens of millions. But the great difficulty and scandalousness of the Christian pacifist position is closely derivative from the scandal of God's weakness in Jesus Christ, the weakness needed for God's "reconciling the world to himself" (2 Cor. 5:19). The dark *skandalon* of Jesus on the cross was soon illuminated—for those with eyes to see—by the light of the Father's raising up the obedient Son. This same light illuminates the scandalous defenselessness accepted by the community of disciples when they understand that they are to meet enemies as God in Christ has met them.

Jesus did not resort to violence, but he did, in other than the usual sense, defend those who were his. In the last hours Jesus defended those dearest to him by praying for them. "Simon, Simon, behold, Satan hath desired to have you [plural], that he may sift you as wheat: But I have prayed for thee, that thy faith fail not" (Lk. 22:31–32 AV). That prayer was not a feeble second-best, marginal to the central need in the situation. Jesus' prayers for Peter and the others, and not twelve legions of angels to hurl back the enemy mob, were what the disciples most of all needed. Jesus' praying followed those who deserted him.

Jesus defended those he loved by cleaving to the Father rather than resorting to a wrong line of action which could have kept him and them from the cross. His obedience was the *skandalon* pressing his dear ones toward ruin. But his disobedience would have opened the abyss of ultimate ruin for all. Discernment of this can help free us from supposing that through readiness to kill we can neatly hold back ruin from loved ones. In the attack situation the turn from Jesus Christ to kill the attacker with one's private pistol or through the national army can be more deeply damaging to the ones defended than the harm the attacker might otherwise have inflicted. We can surmise that the alignment of churches with lethal defense through the centuries has issued in more spiritual ruin for those being defended than would have been inflicted by invaders, had there not been that alignment.

Jesus acted decisively to defend any under attack, but not by crushing the attackers. There is in the gospels an incident somewhat comparable to the situation asked about in the ever repeated question, "What would you do if somebody attacked your wife, mother, sister . . . ?" Jesus was on the scene when the life of a defenseless woman was about to be taken (Jn. 8:2–11). Stones were in those tensed hands ready for hurling at the terrified adulteress. Jesus did not stand by and do nothing. But neither did he call down fire from heaven or rally his disciples to grab up whatever defensive stones they could find lying around. He halted their drive to crush the life out of her. He met their lethal force with a far different kind of power. There was no crushing of the attackers. True, his was a limited triumph that day. His initiative did not draw those men into fellowship, but it did hold them back from total negation of fellowship. Jesus stood between the woman and the attackers. In effect he took the brunt of their attack upon himself. The bitter madness which extinguished his life was in part the very madness which he had held back from that woman.

Similarly, Jesus in Gethsemane defended the disciples by drawing the attack to himself: "If you seek me, let these men go" (Jn. 18:8). He defended them by absorbing the evil that was pressing toward them all.

When defense is needed, Christians should look to Jesus as the model. In Jesus we are shown what it is to be the kind of person God wants. "He who says he abides in him ought to walk in the same way in which he walked" (1 Jn. 2:6). Would God ever expect from us a mode of defense which we do not at all see in Jesus?

The questions with regard to a hypothetical attack often focus on the prospect of the rape of a man's wife, mother, sister. But there could have come a rape attempt on the mother or a sister of Jesus with him nearby. Jesus would have met that enemy in love, *or* by his own standards he would have sinned. The intent of the hypothetical questions is to show that there are situations in which it is necessary to resort to a lesser evil inflicted on the attacker. But if this is indeed the case, Jesus was without sin only because of his good fortune in not having had to face that type of situation; and he was therefore not tempted in every respect as we are (cf. Heb. 4:15).

The *skandalon* for the church through most of its history has not been the defenselessness of Jesus (which has been regarded as necessary for the salvation drama) but rather the corollary that his people should be defenseless in the same way. The prevailing protests within the church against acceptance of that defenselessness have come as a modified echo of Peter's outburst: "God forbid, Lord! This mustn't happen to *us*." Peter with his plea was for Jesus a *skandalon* (Mt. 16:23), a lure tempting him to turn from God. In wrongheadedness too he was a representative first start for the church; and for followers of Jesus that modification of Peter's plea against suffering at the hands of adversaries has continued to be the primary lure away from God.

If we try to defend others with violence, we replay Peter's reliance on the sword, which was really the turning-point in his abandonment of Jesus. If Peter had stayed with the threatened One without resort to violence, his action could have been a model for how Christians are to stand with any who are threatened. Christ stands weaponless with them. His disciples are to do the same.

Jesus Christ is Head of the community, and Christians are bound together in a corporate vulnerability derivative from his. Only when this is discerned, can there be right thinking about defense of those attacked. Others may join together in military "defense," but Christians must stand together in shared vulnerability. In that common stand there are elements of defense. But in Gethsemane the disciples pulled out of this corporate vulnerability; they broke with the body rather than be broken themselves. And that has been the continuous pattern of christendom/post-christendom history down to the present.

For the Eleven, Jesus was temporary *skandalon*. For Judas he was *skandalon* into eternal ruin. There is for Christians the awesome possibility that their very obedience may enter crucially into the terrible drama of the final ruin of other persons. Jesus gives sternest warning against sin that undermines the faith of another. Christian obedience, though, like that of Jesus, will not cause the collapse of another person's faith. It can only be a blow to inadequate faith or, as with Judas and the Pharisees, bring to the surface the dominant underlying rejection of the Son. Yet the uncertainty as to what might result partly from our faithfulness, specifically in not using lethal violence to fend off evil, should impel us to pray for those most affected.

In the imagery of Ephesians 6, attack by invisible powers, not by flesh-and-blood adversaries, constitutes the central danger for us and those around us. The same understanding was expressed in Jesus' words to Simon Peter, "Satan hath desired to have you." Resort to the "lesser evil" of violent resistance cannot really counter *that* danger, but rather augments it. There is in all of us an inclination to see the use of tangible weapons to fend off physical attack as more real, substantial, and practical than the spiritual warfare described in Ephesians 6. But the most decisive battle in history was the one between Jesus and the Powers of Darkness; his was the supreme defense of us all. If in biblical perspective we truly see that and the relative indecisiveness of all military battles, we have a basis for discerning what for us and those dearest to us is the critically needed defense: "They have triumphed over him [Satan] by the blood of the Lamb and by the witness of their martyrdom, because even in the face of death they would not cling to life" (Rev. 12:11 JB). When Christians confirm that triumphal defense by Jesus, even to the point of letting their life blood be added to his, the main imperiling attack is countered and overcome.

Chapter 26

DESERTION AND REGATHERING

Jesus answered them: "So you believe at this moment? See! the
hour is coming—it has come—when each of you will be scattered to
your own homes, and you will leave me alone. And yet I am not
alone, because the Father is with me. I have spoken these things to
you that you might have peace in me. In the world you will have
tribulation. But courage! I have conquered the world."[1]

John 16:31-33 (William Barclay)

These words are given in the Gospel of John as the last recorded
teaching of Jesus before his arrest, trial, and execution. As such they
deserve far more attention than they usually receive.

The disciples had just stated their faith in him. Jesus does not reject
that affirmation, but he discerns how unsteady their faith is and puts a
question to them prompted by his knowledge of what is about to
happen. Here they *are,* with him, bound to him and to one another by
their common faith in him. But within several hours that unity is to be
undone. Each disciple is about to flee into his own private realm. One
disciple had already deserted, and collapse into desertion has already
begun in the others. They are now to be scattered, each into an
isolation, which will be the opposite of their present gathered oneness
around Jesus.

The main factor that swept those first disciples into desertion was
fear, fear that came when encounter with adversaries and collapse of
faith coincided. Desertion from Christ has taken many forms. But for
those who have seen themselves as disciples of Jesus, the most
powerful factor again and again has been that same fear.

The disciples in their desertion, their flight, their scattering, represent all humankind from Adam and Eve hiding in the garden to the
vast lonely crowds in our contemporary world. That desertion is part
of the truth about each of us and about any segment of the Christian
church. Two diagrams can help bring out the universal drama pointed
to in Jesus' words.

184

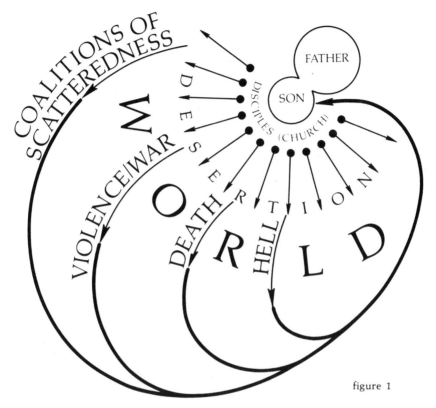

figure 1

In figure 1 all God's human creatures, disciples included, desert from the Center into scattered isolation. The world, mentioned twice by Jesus in this passage, can be seen as the context of dynamisms that impel human beings away from the Center into desertion and scatteredness, but also draw them into pseudo-unities.[2] Violence and war, death, and hell are the farther reaches of the flight from him who is Center. Violence and war are the collision of different courses of flight. Death is the climactic isolation, the dissolution of all that has been brought together in a human being, the visible endpoint of man's running from the Center. Hell is the ultimate scattering, isolation, and dissolution. All these forces merge and veer around for the supreme assault on Jesus, assault that in the desert and in Gethsemane aimed at drawing him too into desertion from the Father and that on Golgotha sought to annihilate him as incarnate extension of the Center.

"You will leave me alone." Jesus is to be isolated and to face by himself the might of those Infernal Powers.

"And yet I am not alone, because the Father is with me." The Father is with Jesus, and Jesus with the Father. Everything, very literally and universally everything, depends on this unbroken bond between them. All else has collapsed into desertion and scatteredness. Only because the Son does not desert and is not deserted by the Father can there come the reversal.

"I have conquered the world." This claim by a hunted man hours before his execution was the most unlikely statement ever made by Jesus or anyone else. *Ego nenikeka ton kosmon.* The Greek perfect tense indicates action already accomplished with the result continuing in the present. His Death and Resurrection are so near that they can be viewed as accomplished. But more than that, Jesus' faith-obedience to the Father is the victory already achieved over the infernal dynamisms of the world. In that emphatic, audacious *ego* of one who is selflessly obedient to the Father, even unto death on a cross, there is no egotism. Jesus' conquest of the world is God's counterstroke to the Adamic drive to gain the whole world.

"I have spoken these things to you that you might have peace in me." The opposite of this peace is scatteredness and chaos. Jesus speaks of the scattering, then of the bond with the Father, then of peace. Peace is what will overcome their desertion, what will bring them together again. Peace is their being back together in wholeness of relationship to him and to one another. His teaching points them to a peace grounded in his victory, a peace the essence of which is the corporate union with him. And to be in union with the Victor is to live out that victory.

In figure 2 we see that peace is the frontal momentum of Christ's victory bringing human beings and all creation together again out of scatteredness. Peace is his triumphal might overwhelming the forces of desertion. In this peace movement comes the fulfilment of all the connotations of that most extraordinary Hebrew word *shalom*—the wholeness, unity, harmony, abundance of life, fearlessness, salvation, that God brings about.

We each choose between two supremely contrary Emmaus events. There Judas Maccabeus won his decisive first victory over an army of Antiochus IV (1 Maccabees 4:1–25). There Jesus appeared in his triumph to regather two of his scattered band (Lk. 24:13–35).

"In the world you will have tribulation. But courage!" Jesus speaks of peace, of tribulation, then of courage because of his victory. As the disciples are drawn together again beyond their brief desertion, there is the prospect that adversaries will give them a hard time. In union with

figure 2

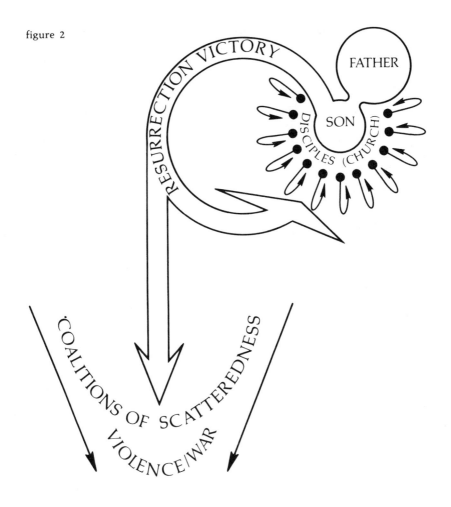

DEATH

HELL

Jesus the disciples will accept the suffering they flee from now. They will be able to face it with the strength and courage that come from his victory.

Probably the most difficult element in the passage for us to incorporate into our understanding and lives is that about peace: peace not as the absence of war or conflict, not as the desired result of negotiations, not as inner tranquillity; but peace as the opposite of scatteredness, peace as union with and unity in Christ, peace as the continuing forward momentum of Christ's victory, present in those who have been already regathered and moving toward all who are yet to be regathered. Unbiblical conceptions of peace, like the ones just mentioned, dominant as they are in churches generally and also in many Christian pacifist circles, impede God's will for peace. There may be no more important passage than John 16:31–35 to set against such misconceptions. Only as Christ draws groups of us together in nearness to him can we be part of his peace movement. Only when we keep in mind that we are repeatedly regathered deserters, can we have the humility appropriate to that highest of callings.

A nuclear war would bring unprecedented scattering and isolation of survivors. Those tides of chaos would swirl over surviving disciples too. We should be praying already that, even under the onrush of those tides, we would hear Jesus' ringing cry. "Courage! I have conquered the world." We need now to give ourselves into the fusion which is Christ's body on earth if we are to stand against the imminence or actuality of nuclear holocaust.

Chapter 27

STANDING WITH THE CENTRAL VICTIM

[The prophet experienced] the overwhelming impact of the divine pathos upon his mind and heart, completely involving and gripping his personality in its depths, and the unrelieved distress which sprang from his intimate involvement. The task of the prophet is to convey the word of God. Yet the word is aglow with the pathos. One cannot understand the word without sensing the pathos....

An analysis of prophetic utterances shows that the fundamental experience of the prophet is a fellowship with the feelings of God, a *sympathy with the divine pathos,* a communion with the divine consciousness which comes about through the prophet's reflection of, or participation jn, the divine pathos.

Abraham J. Heschel

Israel was shown God in His vulnerability, God living a turbulent history with His people, deeply involved with them, acutely touched by their follies and sufferings, God in anguish. On earth there is no love without vulnerability; and this is supremely so for God. Compassion is not painless, least of all for Him. The Lord God walks near in the blighted evening garden. He goes into a strange land with Abram and with Joseph. From the transfigured bush on Horeb He says to Moses: "I have seen the affliction of my people who are in Egypt, and have heard their cry because of their taskmasters; I *know* their sufferings, and I have come down to deliver them out of the hand of the Egyptians" (Ex. 3:7–8). God is moved by the pleas of Hannah, David, Elijah, Habakkuk. He who is far more pleading than pled with, cries through the lacerated Hosea (11:8 JB):

> *Ephraim, how could I part with you?*
> *Israel, how could I give you up?*
> *How could I treat you like Admah,*
> *or deal with you like Zeboiim?*2
> *My heart recoils from it,*
> *my whole being trembles at the thought.*

God trembles not for Israel alone. He who chose a Moabitess to pour her blood into the veins of David and the Son of David could say also of perishing Moab:

> *Therefore I wail for Moab;*
> *I cry out for all Moab;*
> *for the men of Kirheres I mourn.*
> *More than for Jazer I weep for you,*
> *O vine of Sibmah!*
> *Your branches passed over the sea,*
> *reached as far as Jazer;*
> *upon your summer fruits and your vintage*
> *the destroyer has fallen.*
>
> (Jer. 48:31–32)

Wrestling with Israel in the long Peniel of Old Testament history, God is worsted again and again, but out of that worsting issues the blessing which turns back disaster.

All those Old Testament images that point to God's intense compassion for his people climax in him who is God's Image. The Incarnation is ultimate empathy: "he has borne our griefs/and carried our sorrows" (Is. 53:4); "we have . . . one who in every respect has been tempted as we are, yet without sinning" (Heb. 4:15); "by God's grace he had to experience death for all mankind" (Heb. 2:9 JB). He went down in the doom we are too frail and constricted to experience. He has plumbed the depths of an anguish which the rebels hanging next to him (and all of us to some degree) only began to feel. All that human sin calls down enveloped him.

Jesus in his earthly life lived out a vulnerability limited by his humanity. The Resurrection did not bring transcendence over that vulnerability. The Risen Lord could be present everywhere and to all, and one aspect of this has been a compassion, a vulnerability, an anguish as wide as that presence. The insight given Pascal, "Jesus will be in agony even to the end of the world,"[3] is implicit in the words of the resplendent Son of Man (Mt. 25:31–46) to the innumerable hosts of those being judged. "As you did it (or did not do it) to one of the least of these my brethren, you did it (or did not do it) to me."

Jesus stands in close, caring identity with the outcast, the hungry, the sick, the imprisoned, the destitute. In this somber century the Victor-Victim has stood with uncountable victims, with all who do not count. These have been most of all victims in war and cold war. More people have been killed in wars since 1945 than the estimated fifty-two million who died in World War II. The suffering poor of the world remain that way mainly because of the compulsive militarism and callous nationalism that divert resources from them. The rich nations spend more each year on military "defense" than the total income of the poor countries. But the suffering of all victims becomes the suffering of God's Son.

A mother, watching by the bed of a dying child, strains with the tormented, tossing body. Each groan of the child is a groan within her. The child has the disease, but the mother bears it too. In her love she may experience the awfulness of the disease even more fully than the child. What that mother is, our Lord is far more.

To flee from God is to vanish into the void. The prospect of nuclear holocaust as fire and lifeless waste gives intimation of that void. On the cross Jesus, who never for a moment stopped cleaving to God, vanished into the void—ours—but then returned with his loving arms stretched wider than our lostness to stop our fleeing further. This Jesus stands across the path of our individual and collective flight into the void, and thus across that part of the path which leads into the nuclear void. But when there is no halt to the fleeing, he himself is pressed back toward the abyss.

The horrors of nuclear war seem to have little effect in causing people to turn back, or in bringing about active resistance to the insanity of the nuclear arms race. Only by strenuous mental attention can we imagine those horrors even a little. But for Christians there is something nearer and far more accessible that can draw us into prophetic action: Jesus Christ interposes himself between all victims (including us) and that annihilation and holds back doom. He moves in the midst of the urban throngs of unknowing, unknown prospective victims in Moscow, Berlin, Glasgow, Washington, Peking, and a thousand other cities. He takes in the imminent horror they cannot. As God's love drawing close, he sees and yearns over each one, partly in terms of what can so soon envelop that person. His caring embraces children and others less guilty, but also those more guilty: "Father, have mercy—they don't know what they're doing."

If as disciples we are drawn close to this Lord, we will be drawn into his anguished compassion for those moving into catastrophe. God was able to involve lone prophets in His agonized cry. The Son draws those who are his. Full knowledge of the doom so near ahead shapes the ways his love comes. Our Lord does not ask that we stare heroically into the nuclear abyss; he asks that we look toward him and let our sight become aligned with his.

If we have really heard the Old Testament prophets, we can know, by inference, that God's love for this teeming human world must now be heavily occupied with the imminence of nuclear war. Stronger yet and deeper than that inference is the command of the risen victim and his call, as in Gethsemane: "Watch with me." The mob with weapons readied for a worldwide crucifixion, is nearing the darkened garden. Our Lord is in anguish now because of what is coming on others; yet already, in that anguish, it comes upon him. "Jesus will be in agony even to the end of the world. We must not sleep during that time." We dare not sleep, if, as with the first disciples, Easter and Pentecost have banished drowsiness.

What was coming upon the Eleven was too much for them to enter into beforehand with imagination or understanding. Jesus did not expect it of them. He simply asked that they be watchful and pray near him as the armed throng came through the night. He does not ask less of us. Psychologists can analyze the processes that turn us away from facing what a nuclear war would be. Our Lord calls us to turn to him, who is beyond those processes, that we may discern with his discerning and care with his caring.

We are to love as he has loved us. It is most of all from his earthly life and death that we learn how he loved. But beyond that we can consider how he loves all of us in the human family *now*. Surely a central part of Christ's love now is his standing with all who are about to be the victims of nuclear war. Will we love near and far neighbors as he now loves us? Will we see any who come within our vision, partly as overshadowed by nuclear guilt and the approach of nuclear war? Will we put our lives on the line, his line, against the onrush of chaos?

Chapter 28

DEFENDING THE COUNTRY

The word of the Lord came to me: "Son of man, speak to your people and say to them, If I bring the sword upon a land, and the people of the land take a man from among them, and make him their watchman; and if he sees the sword coming upon the land and blows the trumpet and warns the people; then if any one who hears the sound of the trumpet does not take warning, and the sword comes and takes him away, his blood shall be upon his own head. He heard the sound of the trumpet, and did not take warning; his blood shall be upon himself. But if he had taken warning, he would have saved his life. But if the watchman sees the sword coming and does not blow the trumpet, so that the people are not warned, and the sword comes, and takes any one of them; that man is taken away in his iniquity, but his blood I will require at the watchman's hand.

"So you, son of man, I have made a watchman for the house of Israel; whenever you hear a word from my mouth, you shall give them warning from me. If I say to the wicked, O wicked man, you shall surely die, and you do not speak to warn the wicked to turn from his way, that wicked man shall die in his iniquity, but his blood I will require at your hand. But if you warn the wicked to turn from his way, and he does not turn from his way; he shall die in his iniquity, but you will have saved your life."

Ezekiel 33:1-9

"I have been looking for someone among them to build a wall and man the breach in front of me, to defend the country and prevent me from destroying it; but I have not found anyone."

Ezekiel 22:30 (JB)

In the common view the great necessity is to defend the country. Those who refuse to align themselves with that military defense, are seen as shirkers, traitors, or possibly as marginal idealists to be magnanimously tolerated. Many who refuse, while grateful for the toleration extended to them, would like very much to escape a "defense" which they see as a steady movement toward catastrophe. But escape, except perhaps through emigration to some remote place in a southern latitude, is hardly possible.

A country is most of all the conglomeration of human beings who live in it at any particular time. Pacifist disciples, though not willing to participate in military "defense," do care about the country as composed of persons loved by God. That caring does not stop at national boundaries; it reaches out toward all the human family. However, because we cannot be omnipresent, our participation in God's caring, will, as a rule, more readily reach and take in those he has put us closer to geographically. Within this perspective disciples can rightly have special concern for the national population they live in the midst of.

The great difference in outlook has to do, not with the country's need to be defended, but with what defense the country really needs and how this can be carried out. The two passages in Ezekiel bring into view the biblical understanding of prophetic defense of a country.

In Ezekiel 33 the image is that of a fortified town with peasants working in the fields round about. The watchman in a high tower can see beyond what those workers see. If he spots a raiding party, he is to blow the trumpet so that the workers can rush back into the protection of the town walls. In the actual situation a watchman who gave no warning would have been held responsible for the deaths of persons killed outside the safety of those walls.

Throughout the history of warfare watchmen, sentries, scouts have had a key role; it was imperative to be informed about the moves of an adversary so as to be able to make appropriate countermoves. Reconnaissance flights, satellite surveillance, early warning radar systems, spy networks have taken over the watchman's role. But in Ezekiel 33 the watchman's warning about a raid or an invasion is not at all directed toward calling forth necessary military measures. No military defense is alluded to, and no attention is given to whether the symbolic town withstands an attack. (Jerusalem was, right at that time, under siege and about to fall to the Babylonians.) In the imagery of the passage, the place of security is that of trust in Yahweh and obedience to Him. When a person hears the prophet's warning, he can turn back from the exposed, imperiled position where his sin has taken him. The great danger is not the approaching "sword" in itself, but rather the prospect that any person should die "in his iniquity." The turn to God leads a person back out of that. The image focuses on each erring person and the need for the return to Yahweh. But the interpretation widens toward all Israel as a collection of such persons: "turn back, turn back from your evil ways; for why will you die, O house of Israel?" (Ezek. 33:11).

In the impassioned words of Abraham J. Heschel: "It is generally

assumed that politics, warfare, and economic activities are the substance and the subject matter of history. To the prophets, God's
judgment of man's conduct is the main issue; all else is marginal."₁ The
warning call within the institutional churches and beyond should be
within the perspective of Ezekiel 33 as restated by Jesus in Luke 13:5:
"unless you repent you will all likewise perish." The greatest danger is
not the continuing approach of the nuclear sword, but rather the
prospect that many hundreds of millions will die in the iniquity which
is bringing on that sword. This is a far different outlook from that of
an evangelism which rejoices that Johnny got saved before he went to
Vietnam to fight and be killed. We must reject an evangelism which is
concerned with souls but hardly with the nuclear peril, an evangelism
that would leave untouched and unresisted the involvements in the
dynamisms which are bringing nuclear doom closer. We must stand
against the "evangelism" of the Far Right that feeds directly into those
dynamisms.

"Why will you die, O house of Israel?" Individuals make up the
collectivity. In both there can be the obstinate sinning which brings on
destruction, or there can be the turn back which makes possible God's
rescue. Prophetic warning now must point to the supreme danger, to
the urgency of a break with the iniquities that are leading toward
nuclear war, and to the security that God offers. "The life of someone
who pays attention to the warning will be secure" (Ezek. 33:5 JB)—
within God's eternal care. Throughout the prophetic writings, the
well-being and survival of God's people were seen as dependent on
repentance and obedience, not on military strength. A prophet calling
his people to repentance was therefore the key defender of the
country. National disaster could be avoided only by heeding his
message. In the nuclear era, reliance on nationalist military defense is
doom, and a country's true defenders, its only sure early warning
system, are those who cry out to the nation to turn back.

The watchman, along with God, sees what is coming. The dark
pattern of sowing the wind and reaping the whirlwind he knows, not
as historical rule, but as the nearing roar of the tornado behind the
whistlings of current breezes. Judgment is for the watchman a massive
momentum hurtling nearer, like the enlarging front of an immense
locomotive. He cannot assess the remaining distance but simply
apprehends how the ominous oncoming shape spreads larger still. He
discerns behind that frontal shape the infinite weight of God's
movement against sin. In what fills his vision there is stark intimation
of the End. Yet he cannot tell whether what sweeps nearer is the End

or a lesser end leading toward the final one. Because the last trump ceaselessly sounds in his ears, he too must blow to strike awe and courage into the hearts of all who will listen.

Every Christian is meant to be part watchman. Followers of Jesus bear witness as successors to the Hebrew prophets ("so men persecuted the prophets who *were before you*"—Mt. 5:12). If we fail to warn as the prophets and Jesus warned, the ominous prospect is that we may be struck down in this sin of omission. In Ezekiel 33 this sin is viewed as so grave that by itself it brings ruin to any who are guilty of it. Especially those who have taken up the task of Christian preaching, teaching, writing should, by all means, consider whether they are or are not transmitting the warning God has for people of this nuclear age.

In Ezekiel 22 God lists the vile sins of the inhabitants of Jerusalem, sins that are described as collectively committed. Most notable is the killing, the oppression, the confiscation of property carried out by the governing elite. Then come the penultimate words, "I have been looking for someone among them to build a wall and man the breach in front of me, to defend the country and prevent me from destroying it; but I have not found anyone." Then Yahweh utters words of judgment that are the only fitting conclusion to what has just been surveyed: "Hence I have discharged my anger on them; I have destroyed them in the fire of my fury. I have made their conduct recoil on their own heads—it is the Lord Yahweh who speaks."

In ancient warfare the worst thing that could happen to defenders was a breaching of the walls of the city. A besieging army had the goal of breaking through the walled defense at one point. Through that breach their troops could pour in and overwhelm the city. The contemporary extension of those possibilities takes the form of "missile gaps," anxiety as to whether NATO forces could repel an attack by Warsaw Pact divisions, the lure or specter of a technological breakthrough in weaponry that would make feasible an incapacitating first strike.

But in Ezekiel 22:30 the awesome breach is not a literal one made by a ravaging adversary. Rather, the intended wholeness and cohesion of God's people has been torn apart by crimes that dominate the city. Jerusalem's safety depends on the intangible walls of God's protecting presence. But massive, shameless sin has breached those walls. What is about to sweep in through that breach is the recoil of their sins. Yet Yahweh it is who seeks someone to stand in the breach and hold back this onrush of His wrath. Events have evidently gone so far that not even Ezekiel or Jeremiah can fill the breach.

What is so desperately needed is not defense against an earthly adversary, but defense against God's anger. Yet He is the One who moves to set up that defense. We are not likely to feel comfortable with this imagery; and it is hardly intended for our comfort. With it, however, we come again to what we have encountered several times before. The greatest danger is not nuclear holocaust but God's impending judgment. The fateful breach caused by sin's rending things apart widens.

Abraham interceded for Sodom (Gen. 18:22–33). Led by God, he gained from God the promise that He would spare the city if even ten righteous persons could be found in it. Abraham strove to defend Sodom. Even ten righteous persons in the midst of it would have rounded out the defense. But these weren't there.

After the Israelites had committed the abomination of worshiping the golden calf, Moses

> *stood in the breach before him,*
> *to turn away his wrath from destroying them.*
>
> (Ps. 106:23)

He pleaded with God and most of the people were spared.

Ultimately only one person was found who could stand in the gaping breach. In Jesus, God did what no one else could do. But the walls of protection Christ raised over the breach circle the New Community— not old Jerusalem or those who refuse to turn and come within the walls.

Defend the country? We do—or we can, by pleading with God and with people around us: with God that He not yet make "their conduct recoil on their own heads"; with those around us that they flee the city of breached walls and enter another.

From the story of Abraham's intercession for Sodom we can infer that the most important defense for any country against nuclear desolation may be that provided by a remnant of people within it whom God sees as righteous. This is the defense Christians are called to take part in.

Chapter 29

"SHALOM!"

On the evening of that day, the first day of the week, the doors
being shut where the disciples were, for fear of the Jews, Jesus came
and stood among them and said to them, "Peace be with you." When
he had said this, he showed them his hands and his side. Then the
disciples were glad when they saw the Lord. Jesus said to them
again, "Peace be with you. As the Father has sent me, even so I send
you." And when he had said this, he breathed on them, and said to
them, "Receive the Holy Spirit."

John 20:19-22

In a hospital waiting room members of a family sit in suspense,
praying for the loved one who is being operated on. At last the
surgeon comes in, smiles, and says, "All's well."

Or after the removal of a tumor from a young mother, there is the
test for malignancy. What will the test show? Life—or death? The
report is given: Not malignant. And to relatives and friends, who have
been waiting apprehensively, the great news is spread: "Everything's
all right!"

In the Hebrew or Aramaic of biblical times, one word could have
expressed in either of these situations all that needed to be said:
"Shalom!" As the word for peace, it had as one of its meanings, "All's
well. Everything is all right!"

When Absalom revolted, his father, David, and those loyal to him
fled from Jerusalem. Later, after the decisive battle, David sat at the
gates of Mahanaim in an agony of waiting for news of what had
happened. When the runner Ahimaaz drew near, he cried out to the
king (2 Sam. 18:28), "All is well," as translations have it, but in Hebrew
simply, *"Shalom!"* (a strange and indeed highly inaccurate summary of
the result of a battle).

Similarly, "Peace to you," could encourage and reassure a person
filled with fear: "There is nothing to fear; you are safe, all's well for
you." The Lord said to Gideon, "Peace be to you; do not fear, you shall
not die" (Jg. 6:23). A heavenly being said to Daniel, "O man greatly
beloved, fear not, peace be with you; be strong and of good courage"

(Dan. 10:19). And Joseph needed to say to his fearful, guilt-ridden brothers, "Peace be to you, fear not" (Gen. 43:23 AV).

The central fulfilment of this biblical motif is recorded in John 20:19–23. On the evening of the first Easter Sunday the disciples were together back in the upper room. They were still crushed by the execution of Jesus and terribly afraid that they also would be arrested and executed by the Jewish authorities. The doors were locked for what little protection that could give. Suddenly the air around them became vibrant with an overwhelming presence; and Jesus, in the midst of their pathetic, fearful huddle, said, "Peace be with you!" or, as the disciples would have understood it in the Aramaic, "There's nothing to fear; you're safe; all's well for you." *Shalom!* All's well. Don't be afraid. Ahead of you, coming upon you, is not death but life. The battle has been won; the infernal enemies vanquished. I'm here—with you and for you. Courage; be strong.

Twice Jesus said to them, "Peace be with you," the first time more to calm their fear, the second more to describe what he was infusing into their lives. And he expressed the same thing in a different way when he breathed on them and said, "Receive the Holy Spirit."

After the initial greeting, "Shalom to you," Jesus "showed them his hands and his side." *There* were the wounds from the nails and from the Roman spear. The disciples could know for sure that this being in their midst was the one who had hung on the cross. Jesus, after having been condemned, tortured, executed, was back with them! And they were filled with joy.

This encounter and this greeting, "Peace to you," with all that went into it, were the most decisive beginning point for the church of Jesus Christ. Pentecost came soon after as an expansion of this. Too little attention has been given to what is clear in John's account: Our Lord's very first resurrection word to the disciples as a gathered group was "Shalom!" With that word he constituted the New Community. "Shalom!" was the way he called them out of their fear of enemies and death; it was his cry of reassurance because of triumph achieved, his embracing invitation into a new corporateness filled with that Life of his, now lifted out of the grave. He was giving them his peace to reshape them and make of them the manifest frontier in the actualizing of what God wills to establish on the earth.

The terrible unfaithfulness so dominant in the later church can be seen as derivative from deafness to that constitutive "Shalom!" Thus there could be all that drivenness by fear of enemies and what they might do, all the attempted personal and ecclesiastical triumphalism within human perspectives cut off from his triumph, all the rampant collectivism and individualism in the church as fill-in for the harmony, wholeness, unity Christ draws disciples into.

Those with ears to hear that word, have eyes to see the wounds he holds into view. Part of the significance of those abiding wounds is this: He who is Lord of the universe died defenseless at the hands of his enemies, but precisely because he stood obediently defenseless against the chaos, madness, and doom of rebelling human beings and institutions, God raised him as victor over that darkness. In showing his wounds, the Lord calls disciples to confront that darkness just as he did, but he also gives the decisive assurance that ultimately all is well, for his light has overpowered the darkness and continues in the faithfulness of his people to overpower it.

Christians in any particular historical period are confronted by a prime negation of the Gospel. Those who live and spread the Good News of Jesus Christ must be emphatic in their No to the prime negation within their particular period and setting. This is precisely what Paul did in writing to the Galatians. Judaizing legalism had come in as denial of the essence of the Good News. Everything was at stake: the cohesion of the Christian fellowship, the validity of the Christian mission in that area, the eternal destiny of the Galatian believers. Paul presented the Good News as counter to that perverting bad news.

Several passages in 1 John were written to counter a different prime negation of the Gospel that had been finding its way into some other Christian groups. In later periods assimilation of idolatrous practices, church-sponsored persecution, slavery and Nazi ideology, to name just a few, have been the prime negation penetrating into the church. I have sought to show that for most Christians in the most powerful nations the prime negation currently is that of reliance on violence, war, nuclear weapons, because of an absolutizing of the nation-state. Just as Paul or John showed God's No to the primary negation infiltrating some Christian churches then, so must we, with regard to nationalist military "defense" and the dimensions of unfaithfulness that converge into it. Now, too, everything is at stake.

What we are pointing to here is quite different from the pragmatic conclusion that nuclear war is the supreme threat to the human race and the attempt, therefore, to draw churches and Christians into a movement working against that threat. The chief negation of the Gospel in our time and thus the central provocation of God's judgment lies in the attitudes which impel the nations toward nuclear war. It is crucial, therefore, that the Gospel be presented in a way that will counter that negation and liberate us from it.

The terrible difficulty (prefigured by the typical periods of Hebrew and Jewish unfaithfulness in the Old Testament) is that, by and large, the churches are ensnared in that primary negation. Nearly all denominations are partly caught; so are the overwhelming majority of congregations. As I see it, what needs to happen and what is happening more and more is the emergence of a Confessing Church similar to that in Nazi Germany. Configurations of Christians are being drawn together into faithfulness over against the regnant lie. These are often groupings distinct from the ensnared traditional structures, yet in constant witness to them.

Each Old Testament prophet stood in communion with God, but alone, or nearly so, among an unfaithful people and thus prefigured the One who was to go to the cross alone. But Jesus died "to gather into one the children of God who are scattered abroad" (Jn. 11:52). His body and fellowships within it are to be characterized by "being of the same mind, having the same love, being in full accord and of one mind" (Phil. 2:2). It is doubtful whether God calls any Christian to be a lone prophet. His intent is that faithful, cohesive shalom communities echo His call, resist the nationalist-military negation in all its breadth, and live as beachheads of His shalom in the midst of encircling chaos.

If average congregations are of "one mind" about military defense, nuclear weapons, wealth and poverty, this is very likely a oneness conformed to majority opinion in the country—over against the mind of Jesus Christ. If disciples who do see and heed the implications of the Gospel for these matters are part of a congregational mix with "defense" industry workers, veterans still proud of having fought for their country, and zealous anti-communists, there can hardly be more than the witness of individuals from within that confusion. In the New Testament, Christian witness, evangelism, outreach are mainly corporate endeavors of the fellowship of disciples. The pointer toward Jesus as Lord is most of all what outsiders can see in a united, loving fellowship.

The crucial matter is not a certain form of Christian "community" or community of goods. It is rather that disciples, in spite of failures and groping, are being drawn into a common mind which images that of Jesus, for nurture and witness: "Have this mind among yourselves, which you have in Christ Jesus" (Phil. 2:5). What we are up against in the forces of prosecution, violence, and acquisitiveness, is dreadfully powerful. It is as collective magnitudes that they impinge upon us. We can hardly, even for ourselves, resist their domination unless we are part of a corporate group united in Christ over against them. A fellowship even of two or three, if it is the primary one for those in it, can provide the sustaining context for being "strong in the Lord and in the strength of his might" (Eph. 6:10). Disciples who are not part of such a group should ask God to guide them into an existing shalom community or to draw together a new one. God is calling the vast human multitudes to repent, turn from the march into doom, and yield to Jesus as Lord. That call can be resoundingly echoed only from within fellowships that strive for a coherent living of that *metanoia*.

Chapter 30

SHALOM COMMUNITIES

> Jesus did not bring to faithful Israel any corrected ritual or any new theories about the being of God. He brought them a new peoplehood and a new way of living together. The very existence of such a group is itself a deep social change. Its very presence was such a threat that He had to be crucified. But such a group is not only by its existence a novelty on the social scene; if it lives faithfully, it is also the most powerful tool of social change.[1]
>
> *John H. Yoder*

We can venture to sketch what a shalom community looks like as it lives out God's Yes to His human children and His No to the forces of death.

The community worships not an American or West European success-giving god, but God who became the victim of the Rebel Powers and emerged Victor over them. Worship is the vital center of the life together. The Lord who is praised opens the eyes of believers to discern the spreading darkness. That discernment can be borne only because, through worship, His light shines all the brighter over against that darkness. Awareness of God's wrath imminent in the awesome perils threatening humanity opens the way for a sense of wonder at the earlier and present coming of Jesus. To *hope* for a person, a group, a world, is to see God in His seeking to be related to them. But there isn't the cheap optimism of supposing that God will not allow a nuclear war to break out. There is praise of Him who till now has held back cataclysmic wrath to give time for the turning-back which could dispel the imminence of that wrath.

For the community there is clarity that discipleship to Jesus Christ makes unthinkable any alignment with the military or with other forms of violence; clarity that there can hardly be a significant nonalignment except in the form of determined resistance to the dynamisms of violence within and without; clarity that the fleshing out of God's Yes in self-sacrificial identification with the least of Christ's brethren is the other side of that No to death. There is recognition that in individuals, groups, and nations any turn from trust in violence to reliance on nonviolence has to have correlated with it a transformation of outlook and practice in economic matters. The community in its own economic life seeks to point toward the radical redistribution of available resources with the goal of worldwide "equality. As it is written, 'He who gathered much had nothing over, and he who gathered little had no lack'" (2 Cor. 8:14–15).

This clarity with regard to violence so pervades the life of the fellowship that it would make no sense for persons who reject this clarity to become members or to remain in membership. Any within the fellowship who persist in rejection of this clarity are to be dealt with in the steps of loving discipline outlined by Jesus in Matthew 18:15–20. Go alone to talk with the person; take one or two others with you in a further effort to reach the person; bring the matter to the gathered fellowship. Any step that brings a breakthrough to the other person does away with the need to proceed further in the sequence. But if the person rejects all these initiatives, he is to be seen as an outsider who needs to be won to the faith again. There can, of course, be dimensions of unfaithfulness other than those we have been considering which trap Christians and bring on the urgent need for the initiatives Jesus outlined. But if the primary negation of the Gospel at present has been rightly identified, there clearly should be central attention to it as a lure away from discipleship.

Like the Ephesians 6:18 call to "pray at all times in the Spirit, with all prayer and supplication," the prayers of a shalom fellowship are in the context of combat with the Rebel Powers. Resistance to those Powers as concretized in political, social, economic, and military structures has its center and source in prayer. Out of the prayer-combat comes understanding as to what further modes of resistance need to be taken up. Alert confession of individual and group collaboration with those Powers opens the way for disengagement from them.

Intercession reaches out to victims of overt and systemic violence around the world: victims of repression and torture by ruthless governments; exploited victims of multinational companies; victims, scarred survivors of earlier or current wars; dying victims of human recklessness with nuclear testing, nuclear power, nuclear weapons; destitute victims of surfeited military establishments. Intercession moves out to embrace the prospective victims of a Third World War in their hundreds of millions. Depth of intercession comes as we find ourselves drawn into the yearning of God and His Son that surrounds all in this world.

Intercession for *"all* who are in high positions" (1 Tim. 2:2)—also those on "the other side,"—will be more than the easy request that God bless them. It will proceed in the recognition of their general subservience to the Dark Powers and will seek full or at least partial emancipation of rulers—for the sake of the multitudes imperiled by their power and for their own sake. Disciples will sense the extreme spiritual jeopardy of those in high positions, especially those who profess to be Christians. The media bring them close before our eyes. Prayer resistance to the eternal ruin pressing upon them should be an inner part of outward political resistance to the ruin they are bringing on others.

Humanly considered, there seems so little prospect of stopping the rush toward nuclear annihilation. But communities of disciples will not, because of this, be immobilized or impelled into frantic activism. World War III is not inevitable. The God of Scripture continues to make His offer of rescue in utter seriousness and His is a sovereignity of surprises. A group of disciples, listening together in prayer, will be able to discern forms and acts of witness God wants of them.

In New Testament perspective, the word of warning is given first within the church, and especially within a confused, disobedient church. Disciples need to be alert for God's leading. They can converse with those who have not caught on and give them things to read. They can invite groups of unconvinced persons into their homes. They can do draft counseling and lead out in preaching, teaching, meetings, retreats, discussion with local pastors and congregations.

A possible approach within a congregation is that members be asked to commit a period of time to study the issues of nuclear arms in the light of Christian faith. Excellent study materials are available.[2] If such a period is entered into, the possibility that God is calling all the congregation to a forthright common stand (full trust in Him, but none at all in weapons) should be struggled with. Such a time, though intended for corporate discernment, could prove to be divisive. But that risk is dwarfed by greater ones. There is the deep resistance to reconsidering attitudes which are central to a person's view of what constitutes security. Yet it does occasionally develop that a congregation which is quite divided about the content of discipleship in our time is renewed and drawn together under Christ's Lordship.

For disciples who seek to warn others, the threat of impending spiritual ruin stands out even more than that of nuclear conflagrations. God's constraining love lays siege within the churches to the citadels of blind rejection of Christ's way. "For though we live in the world we are not carrying on a worldly war, for the weapons of our warfare are not worldly but have divine power to destroy strongholds. We destroy arguments and every proud obstacle to the knowledge of God, and take every thought captive to obey Christ" (2 Cor. 10:3–5). Only those wielding the weapons of the Spirit can overwhelm such strongholds as we have been surveying. The Pentagon as a building is the central concretized stronghold into which a vast array of immaterial citadels have converged.

Out of worship and prayer must come the rekindling of evangelistic passion. We get our eyes opened to see with Jesus the crowds (within the churches too) so wretchedly lost without the true Shepherd and being misled straight into nuclear doom. Our unclogged ears can hear the call, "Go, make disciples, baptize, teach them all that I have commanded you." Our minds are alerted to sense the slipping away of the days before the day of the Bomb (and the Day of the Son of Man). The nuclear peril cannot properly mobilize disciples. But God uses that peril to amplify what has, though nearly two thousand years, been his imperative. The church and the world around it are together *in extremis*. The unction needed is that of the Spirit of him who gives Life.

The message, "Repent, turn around!," must make clear what is to be turned from—not for most hearers currently the legalisms of Jewish piety or the nothingness of pagan idols, but the enthralling dynamisms for seizing and securing life, most of all with nuclear weapons. For Palestinian Jews in 30 A.D. repentance meant turning to Jesus *from* the attitudes and dynamisms that were leading into cataclysm. It means the same now. The Good News to all is this: Jesus stands as Life against all the might of Death. He calls you to live in that Life—but you must let him free you from every alignment with Death's dominion. God in Jesus Christ loves you, forgives you, is ready to empower you to live with others His Life over against Death. Choose Life in this Lord—or be warned that more than nuclear death is coming upon you.

Though transformation of basic outlook is the key dimension, Christian peacemakers can also point to what choosing life would look like politically. It is imperative that the nuclear arms race be halted. The United States should declare a two- or three-year freeze on all further testing, production, and deployment of nuclear weapons and of those missiles and new aircraft designed primarily to deliver nuclear weapons. The Soviet Union would then be invited to do the same. The United States should end its nuclear testing. It should pledge never to be the first country to use nuclear weapons—a pledge it has so far, in spite of Soviet prodding, refused to give. Although any of these steps could come by bilateral agreement, there is much more prospect of breaking out of the current deadly spiral by taking these steps as unilateral intiatives. These would be peace signals to the Soviet Union and a stimulus to bring reciprocal steps. Negotiations would serve more to confirm the results of such initiatives and responses to them. If there comes the political will for halting of the nuclear arms race, the present escalation could give way to the momentum of reciprocal steps toward a disarmed world.

Hebrew prophets were typically sent to stand right next to the architectural and institutional center of religious practice, there to proclaim God's warning. The contemporary equivalent of that could be witness to churches in the national capital that have concentrations of the governing elite in their memberships; witness at denominational headquarters, mass conferences and rallies; encounter with popular religious leaders.

God is surely calling disciples into far more of the sort of peace witness carried out by persons from the Post-American community (later Sojourners Fellowship) and the Mennonite Central Committee at the huge Explo '72 conference in Dallas, Texas:

> And on the second day some Campus Crusade officials in charge of the exhibits called the messengers of peace in for a meeting, and questioned them concerning the literature they were distributing, saying that some of it was not in harmony with the purpose of Explo. And the officials lifted out samples of objectionable materials, including brochures on Conscientious Objectors and a quote from Menno Simons, "The regenerated do not go to war...."
>
> And the messengers of peace questioned the officials concerning the basis for their judgments, and testified to them of Christ the Prince of Peace, and requested further dialog with officials concerning the attempted censorship. And after further consultation, the officials granted permission to continue the distribution of literature of peace.
>
> And some of the messengers of peace made signs saying "Stop the war in Jesus name" and "The 300 persons killed by American bombs today will not be won in this generation" and "Choose this day— make disciples or make bombs, love your enemies or kill your enemies." And they walked among the people with their signs.
>
> And some people said, "Amen" and others were offended, saying, "Why bring peripheral issues to Explo? We are here to witness to the Lord." And officials of Explo asked the messengers of peace not to carry signs inside the buildings.

One evening the celebration in the Cotton Bowl included a Flag ceremony with "presentation of colors" by military personnel. And while thousands watched the spectacle in awed silence, the messengers of peace unfurled two banners reading "Cross or Flag" and "Christ or Country" and started chanting, "Stop the war! Stop the war! Stop the war!"

And policemen came running, and officials of Campus Crusade came asking, "Who's in charge of this group?" And one of them replied, "The Holy Spirit." And there was vigorous discussion between the Crusade people and the messengers of peace about loyalty to Christ and loyalty to country.[3]

Shalom communities also find ways of breaching the political barricades that demarcate the planet: prayer for, contact and fellowship with, Christians on "the other side" as the living-out of a unity that will not be cut through; gifts of food, medicines, seeds, and implements (even if against the law) to "enemies"; discovery of ways to manifest the humanity of those who live in the target areas of Western bombs.

The message in word and action to the managers of a thermonuclear society is: No! We disengage ourselves from your doomsday machine. None of us will tend or support it. We refuse payment of taxes to finance it. We put our bodies on the line against it.

Jesus was a master of symbolic action. There should be much more corporate waiting for his guidance into symbolic acts that point to the awesomeness of God's No and the wonder of His Yes.

Most of these national security managers in Western countries claim to be Christian. Yet the managers proceed in what amounts to the assumption that Christian faith and ethics have no determinative relevance to the conduct of foreign affairs or other matters of state. This judgment has been tacitly accepted by most Christians and Christian groups that have sought to influence government toward a more humane foreign policy. Their appeals have so often been in terms of the hard-headed pragmatic perspective dominant in the government. Occasionally the basis has been that of generally recognized human values.

There is a place for appeals and arguments calling actions and policies into question on the basis, say, of national interest, or for doing that in terms of the professed ideals of an administration, such as on human rights. But try to imagine the Hebrew prophets speaking simply within the dominant perspective of a disobedient government so as to be more effective. What there is currently rather little of and what I believe there should be much more of, is witness to government leaders that issues directly and clearly out of faith in Jesus Christ as Lord—in face-to-face conversation, in letter-writing, in the giving of testimony, in symbolic action.

What can be expressed is something like: You too claim to follow this Lord. We take that claim seriously. We speak on this matter out of what, as we see it, following this Lord must surely involve—and not involve. We appeal to you under the Lordship of Jesus Christ. What basis do you find as a Christian for support of the manufacture of still more nuclear weapons? What basis at all for nuclear deterrence as a national policy? Can you answer to this Master for your support of this policy, with its increasing risk that this country will kill and desolate hundreds of millions of human beings? Where are you yourself in relation to this Lord? Christ has a better way. You could be one who points to that way.

Making disciples of governmental leaders who profess Christian faith can be truly done only when there is guidance from the Holy Spirit and when there is the gift of a deep caring for them. "What you are to say will be given to you in that hour; for it is not you who speak, but the Spirit of your Father speaking through you" (Mt. 10:19–20).

Chapter 31

WATCHFULNESS
AND THE TAUT TRAP

Watch yourselves, or your hearts will be coarsened with de-
bauchery and drunkenness and the cares of life, and that day will be
sprung on you suddenly, like a trap. For it will come down on every
living man on the face of the earth. Stay awake, praying at all times
for the strength to survive all that is going to happen, and to stand
with confidence before the Son of Man.

Luke 21:34–36 (JB)

If shalom communities repeat for our world situation the warning of
Jesus, "Unless you repent you will all likewise perish" (Lk. 13:3,5),
there goes with this a recognition that repentance may not be
forthcoming and nuclear cataclysm will at some point sweep over
much of the earth. To the extent that we take seriously God's
judgment on human wickedness, we will reckon with this prospect and
brace ourselves spiritually for it.

Psychiatrist Robert Jay Lifton has commented, "Certainly in my
Hiroshima work I was struck by the inability of people to find adequate
transcendent religious explanation—Buddhist, Shinto, or Christian—
for what they and others had experienced."[1] This inability would
surely assume still more overwhelming intensity in a situation where
the wider social coherence of country after country had been largely
shattered and hopefulness about a tolerable human future, nearly lost.
There might be no broader surviving social context to try to get one's
bearings by. There would be terrible pressures to view the nuclear
horrors as evidence against God.

People in the midst of that desolation would be able to make some
biblical sense of it only if they could see it in terms of sowing and
reaping, God's warning rejected, nationalist apostasy in the churches,
wrath as God's decision no longer to intervene against the full recoil of
human sin, and in the midst of all this Jesus Christ as victim, yet still as
Lord. Those who help spread this message now will know it well if the
day of the Bomb comes. Surviving disciples would need, again and

again, to deal from these biblical motifs with the question, Why? Whenever true witness to God's call to turn from doom to His rescue in Christ is given, a basis is being laid for survival in faith or for discovery of faith on that day.

There are within the New Testament varying evangelistic stances. The one that runs through the book of Revelation and could be characterized as corporate faithfulness unto death is probably the stance we need most of all to ponder, as the form of the present world is so near to passing away.

An exercise of Christian piety through many centuries (but rather obscured at present) has been a person's contemplation of the time of his death and prayer for grace and strength to remain in faith, no matter what that time might bring. There was widespread awareness of the infernal power of onslaughts that could come and the physical diminution of a person's resources for meeting those onslaughts. Christians often prayed that they be delivered from sudden (instantaneous) death that would afford no opportunity for crucial dialogue with God just prior to the termination of life.

In New Testament perspective that emphasis comes rightly, but derivatively, within the urgent command to watch and pray, eagerly awaiting the Lord's Appearing. Sudden death is an individualized intimation of the unexpectedness of Jesus' Appearing. The spiritual struggles prior to a person's death are an individual equivalent to the upheaval and distress which will precede that Appearing. A Christian in watchfulness and prayer can look toward both Jesus' Appearing and the time of his own death and seek to be prepared for whichever comes first.

The church teaching that one's eternal destiny is determined by one's spiritual state in the final moments of one's life is not found in the New Testament. What is found there is the call to be alert, watchful, and spiritually prepared for whatever end to one's earthly life may come. In a nuclear war tens or even hundreds of millions of people might be instantaneously vaporized without knowing what hit them. That immense danger should bring us to recognize how imperative it is that we seek to be prepared for sudden death or for the moment of Christ's Appearing.

Also among Christians nuclear war is thought of largely in terms of survival or nonsurvival—personal, national, and human. Biblically the far more crucial question for each person is whether or not one can stand before God in the judgment. But this perspective is not the same as the prevalent zeal for being saved and getting people saved, quite apart from any transformation of outlook with regard to such matters as nuclear weapons and world poverty. If nuclear war ends the earthly existence of vast multitudes or even of all human beings on the planet, survival in the judgment will be very much related to the stance each person had within the dynamisms which brought on the war.

The watchfulness Christ draws us into reckons with the day of the Bomb, with instantaneous, earlier-than-anticipated nuclear death, and with the Day of Judgment beyond that day. This is no resignation to the coming of nuclear war. The watchful throw themselves against the forces that bring it closer and plead with all who might listen to *turn*, not so much because vast annihilation impends, but because God's judgment does. What is so little understood even within the churches is that among all that can be set over against the approach of nuclear catastrophe, nothing has such substance and weight as God's Word of imminent judgment and offer of rescue in Jesus Christ.

As the End draws nearer and nearer, disciples are to pray "for the strength to survive all that is going to happen." (One of the most foreboding sentences from the lips of Jesus is, "Nevertheless, when the Son of man comes, will he find faith on earth?"—Lk..18:8). We can know that any of us surviving the initial nuclear volleys would be in desperate need of strength for spiritual survival and for physical and spiritual ministry to others. The Eleven were too exhausted to watch and pray with Jesus—and they fled. Holding fast in an extreme test of faith ordinarily is the result more of the prayers which precede that test than of prayer in the midst of it. We are to pray now for strength to face even the horrors of the aftermath and for strength to live a love that would still then be chief evidence of Christ's triumph.

The plea in the Lord's Prayer about "temptation," "Put us not to the test, don't give us over to dire testing," was probably intended most of all in reference to eschatological testing and trial at the close of history. Apart from some sense of that meaning—the awesome possibility of coming into extreme spiritual jeopardy, with the Day of Judgment breaking in—we will hardly grasp the crucialness of that plea for our day-to-day living. The nuclear desolation, if not a testing at the End, would be a greater intimation of it than anything previously. We can pray, in the breadth of the Christian *we*,

> Give us not over into that unspeakable testing,
> drive us not into that desert,
> from that apparent planetary triumph of the Evil One deliver us.

Prayer for deliverance weighs against the coming of that day, but would also accompany us into it. In prayer now, there can grow the staying power to pray even then.

There is another dark prospect alongside unexpected instantaneous obliteration or a period of brief or longer survival after the main volleys. There might for large groups of people in some target areas be a forewarning and fleeting minutes before the flash. It is not too early to consider how one might use such minutes. But we have God's forewarning now and the longer, yet dwindling time He gives.

Disciples who understand that Christ, in all situations, calls them away from resorting to violence generally find themselves in a paradoxical position. They cannot avoid standing within a relatively stable "order" structured by violence as they plead for a countering of violence with Christian love. It seems that the main dimensions for trying that are very firmly occupied by political configurations that proceed in contrary fashion. Opportunities for nonviolence seem marginal.

After the outbreak of nuclear world war, surviving disciples would in this regard face a drastically changed situation. The "order" would be largely disintegrated, but concurrent with that would be the grim effort to reestablish "order" by stern military rule, with much display and use of the constraints of lethal violence (conceivably by a foreign occupying power). One model of response within such dissolution of "order" is that of the father with submachinegun guarding the entrance to the family fall-out shelter. For survivors committed to the opposite of that model, there would be a testing of that commitment at every turn. Private firearms, which have been such a hallmark of American civilization, would assume unprecedented dominance—a bleak postholocaust resurgence of the Wild West heritage. Attackers as in the hypothetical defense-of-the-family question would be all around, many in marauding bands trying to get food or shelter. How would disciples respond?

There might be a sort of terrible necessity in the effort to reestablish "order" by strong-handed military rule and presence. That inhuman "order," though perhaps preferable to unchecked social chaos, would be one that disciples might find themselves led to question or resist at many points: and thus again the problem of how to meet an inundating violence.

Shalom communities should reckon with the prospect of these inundations within a thermonuclear deluge and try to do some counting of the possible cost of nonviolence. There can perhaps be little training in nonviolence that enters into projected postholocaust situations. But intensified training now in nonviolent resistance to the momentum of nuclear and other violence would constitute preparation for the time after. In this dimension also, prophetic witness against the coming of the deluge is preparation for faithfulness in the midst of it; and the witness is the opposite of fatalistic resignation.

If human history continues much beyond a Third World War, there will be the question of the shape of the church of Jesus Christ on the earth *then*. If the human race is only partially destroyed, the Christian church will probably have been harder hit than other world faiths— except Judaism. Not only would the total numbers and resources of the churches as official bodies be much reduced; the areas that for many hundreds of years had been the expanding heartland of the church would be largely, if not fully, devastated. Judgment would have begun where there are the largest concentrations of those claiming to be "the household of God" (1 Pet. 4:17). The central nations in the genocidal conflict would be those of christendom/post-christendom. And to the extent that professing Christians and churches have aligned themselves with nuclear weapons, there would be apparent basis for blaming Christianity for what had happened. Relevant here are the Old Testament glimpses of God's hesitation as He contemplates what pagans will conclude from judgment falling upon His people.

The only earlier judgment in church history that can be seen as having had a remotely comparable magnitude was the Moslem conquest of much of the Christian heartland of the early centuries. That development had been preceded and prepared for by the general collapse of faithful discipleship and witness into acculturated establishment religion hallowing the various collectivities. A continuation of that judgment has, humanly seen, been slow in coming. But World Wars I and II brought nearly all of Eastern Europe under communist dominion. Nuclear desolation of the heartland would be recapitulation and terrible expansion of what the destruction of the Temple and the city of Jerusalem was for the Jews.

The fact that disestablished churches under Islam or communism have had such great difficulty in unlearning christendom habits and strategies gives little basis for encouragement about the immense unlearning and return to gospel faithfulness that would be appropriate for surviving churches in a postholocaust world. Yet the emergence of the Confessing Church in Nazi Germany and some believers' church developments in Eastern Europe do intimate the possibility of decisive renewal after the collapse and discrediting of the main seductive illusions of the present. It could be that great numbers of earnest Christians, finally discerning, with regard to violence, God's way and judgment, would break with the nationalism and militarism which had brought on the worst of all wars. The more monstrous a government, the more readily Christians can understand that they must obey God rather than men. This aid to discernment might be more widely and manifestly at hand than ever before.

Disciples would probably find themselves, also spiritually, in a sort of postholocaust catacomb situation. Within the overall dissolution of the old securities (and denominations), small, mostly new configurations of Christians would come together for desperately needed mutual support, witness, service to the suffering. Radioactivity and the cumbersomeness of maintaining church buildings in the midst of general societal collapse would erode the unbiblical identification of church with edifice.

For those who call themselves by Christ's name there would probably come a drastic division, a sifting of wheat from chaff (as in earlier times of persecution), and this most of all in relation to the inundations of violence. Some would be drawn into the grotesque rampaging of violence—in chaotic upheaval or in the ruthlessness of postholocaust "order"—rendering extreme denial, even if still unrecognized, of their Lord. Others would together become, far more than they had ever been before, the Lord's sheep in the midst of ravening wolves, sheep evidencing the reality and nearness of the Shepherd. Immense wrath hangs over us; God's judgment as division presses upon us throughout each today. As we reckon now with that sifting, we prepare to face man's and God's terminal shaking of earth and heaven (Heb. 12:26).

World War III would plunge survivors into a time of shattering negative evidence against hope, against a livable future, against God. In the New Testament the two comparable times for disciples are the period immediately after the crucifixion of Jesus and the chaotic, persecution-filled Endtime pictured in Revelation. In the earlier situation Jesus was manifested in his new Life and sovereignty. The negative evidence was transmuted into positive. Out of the terrible deed perpetrated by human beings God had fashioned His rescue of all who accept it. In Revelation the Appearing of the Son at the End overwhelms the turbulent immensity of what would most naturally be taken as evidence against God. But before that, the faithful remnant, grounded in the initial and continuing evidence of Jesus Risen, are instructed to see the most awful rampages of wickedness and devastation as signs, not of God's defeat, but of the in-breaking completion of His triumph.

The biblical sequence, *rage—wrath—rescue/peace,* receives clearest expression in Psalms 2 and 46. Thus in the middle of the latter (vs. 6–7):

> *The nations rage, the kingdoms totter;*
> *he utters his voice, the earth melts.*
> *The Lord of hosts is with us;*
> *the God of Jacob is our refuge.*

The close of the earthly ministry of Jesus was central fulfilment of that sequence: rage of the nations against him (Acts 4:25–27); wrath—God's "formidable non-intervention," His not holding back the totally undeserved recoil of human wickedness on the Son; rescue/peace—God's triumph, through wrath, over the raging of the nations, and His Lordship as God-with-us reaching out to embrace all into the New Glory. Disciples surviving the initial nuclear conflagration could live in the recognition that the consummately vast rage-wrath actuality which had now come upon the world lies within the all-determining scope of the fulfilment of that sequence in the death and Resurrection of Jesus.

Each day for some, casualness of faith in God is suddenly overshadowed by dire events. Persons are then impelled away from that casualness into still less or no faith; or they are driven back into a deeper grounding for faith. On the day of the Bomb, all survivors who claim Christian faith—and many others too—would be pressed in one of these directions.

The supreme earthly magnitude within range of our present experience is death—unless we come to the one mightier magnitude, the Rising of Jesus Christ. In human history till now there has been the wide possibility for denying or ignoring death's dominion. Nuclear war, because of its terrible intensification of that dominion, would to a large degree (at least in many countries) eliminate any possibility for such denial. And this would constitute the most decisive change in the human situation.

That war would be the climactic coup for him who was "a murderer from the start," but would, precisely in that, largely negate his primeval and all-encompassing deception, "You will not die." That lie is like the benevolent rhetoric of a wicked despot which infuses and mediates the despotism. As the despot comes to rely increasingly on total repression, the rhetoric loses all credibility; people are no longer yielding to the lie really, but to that repression. The rhetoric, the lie, fades out into what it has mediated.

But for any who, in the midst of shattering events or apart from them, see through the lie, there is something that can be set against the dominion which the collapsing lie otherwise confirms: to hear the voice of the sovereign Lord, "Fear not, I am the first and the last, and the living one; I died, and behold I am alive for evermore, and I have the keys of Death and Hades" (Rev. 1:17–18); "Because I live, you will live also" (Jn. 14:19). Not Satan's offer that we can live and not die; but God's, that, even though we die, He gives us life.

The metal keys which command-post functionaries would take hold of, insert, and turn to fire the dread missiles are literal keys of Death and Hades. They can lock the entire planet shut as an enclosure of immediate or slower doom. But there is "the holy one, the true one, who has the key of David, who opens and no one shall shut" (Rev. 3:7).

Robert Jay Lifton in his studies of Hiroshima survivors points again and again to "the immersion in death."[2] Across the intercontinental spread of that immersion after the outbreak of a nuclear war, the age-old consolations with regard to death (like survival in one's descendants, in one's achievements, in the persistence of one's positive contribution to the human story) would go down in the general devastation. The resurrection of Jesus is not consolation really, though it has, in the churches, been very widely made into that. It is *the* Victory which outweighs the immensity of death's winning out at every other point. But, in this, to have been defeated at one point is to have been *defeated.* Jesus Christ lives as the One who is stronger than death. Human life in his resurrection surges into hope, courage, spiritual combat, and joy.

With the culminating manifestation of death's dominion coming ever closer, we should yearn all the more for the counter-unveiling of the still greater power. It is the constant glory of the sky above us that into this Jesus ascended and into this will flash the splendor of his Appearing. In the night sky we see how far the country and vast the domain into which he has gone: and in the blue of day, the far-nearness of his Going and Coming. Every cloud illumined by the sun is lesser comrade to the one that hid him from the disciples' sight and to those that will usher in his Appearing. But down through the glory of this sky, in parody of his Coming, would hurtle the engines of our doom. The monstrous radar eyes peering up are weird mimicry of the watchfulness of Christ's people. Into this overarching intimation of his glory is soon to swell the brilliance of infernal clouds.

The resilient hope we have been pointing to can be very easily cheapened—and often is: If nuclear war comes, I have the assurance anyway of going to heaven; even if nuclear war comes, God can be counted on to clean up the planetary mess. There is this cheapening unless one's life is drawn into His resurrection advance against the defeated but still rampaging last enemy. Only when, in the momentum of that resurrection advance, we face death, press in upon death, and cry out its annihilation, can we, without shallowness, point to life beyond and to a new earth, after whatever human folly may bring upon this one.

The time in my own life when the power and the splendor of Jesus' Rising was most real to me was when my sister Jane died of cancer at fourteen. There pressing upon the ugly, dismal awfulness of death's triumph was something far stronger that brought us who were most bereaved into the glad exhilaration of hope in the Risen One. Christians throughout the centuries have discovered that precisely when death demonstrates its power, they are borne up by the might of One who is concluding his victory over death. Such occasions intimate that same possibility even for the time when disciples would be confronted by an overwhelmingly extensive demonstration of death's power.

In this perspective too, it is clear that any alignment with lethal violence turns a disciple into a defector from that resurrection advance, into one who would promote death's claim and dominion. Throughout this book I have been seeking to set forth a stance of living Christ's resurrection life as combat against death and its sway. This stance is the ground and essence of Christian nonviolence. God in His people will continue to press that combat even if nuclear war ravages the earth.

We are to look to Jesus, who "for the joy that was set before him endured the cross, despising the shame, and is seated at the right hand of the throne of God" (Heb. 12:2). Converging into that cross was God's empathy with all His suffering creatures, Christ's standing as victim through all the years and days with those whose plight he took and still takes as his own; converging into it also would be the nuclear crucifixion of our Lord with the multitudes of the least of the earth. But the destination, the end-fulfilment beyond all that, is the joy, the new glory, the harmony of all within the Father's caring. If the oligarchs and masses of our time bring on that further crucifixion, the Lord moves even through it to that joy. In the day and days of the Bomb, disciples would stand with the One standing as victim in the midst of all. "Let none of you suffer as a murderer, or a thief, or a wrongdoer, or a mischief-maker" (1 Pet. 4:15)—not as an absolutizer of the nation-state, an adherent of weapons systems, or an enemy of the designated adversary. "Yet if one suffers as a Christian, let him not be ashamed, but under that name let him glorify God" (1 Pet. 4:16). Christians can become, with Christ, victims of the madness. Not that disciples are without grave guilt, but they have been summoned by the righteous victim to stand with him.

To endure with him, though, is to have eyes fixed on the coming joy. If all history is to lapse into crucifixion as did that of Israel, there is to be, for human history, resurrection that is completion of Christ's rising. The full joy of the New Age is still "set before him" and thus before us.

We believe that, twisted and erring as we are, the Risen Lord raises us out of that. Ours is the confidence that he will lift us out of death's abyss. Blessed are those who, in the midst of whatever may come, live in yet more ardent faith that the Risen One, at the moment of God's choosing, will lift a resurrected earth, a new humanity, out of the shambles of the old.

> So shall Babylon the great city be thrown down with violence, and shall be found no more.
>
> Hallelujah! For the Lord our God the Almighty reigns.
>
> Behold, he is coming with the clouds, and every eye will see him, every one who pierced him.
>
> Then I saw a new heaven and a new earth; for the first heaven and the first earth had passed away, and the sea was no more.
>
> And I heard a great voice from the throne saying, "Behold, the dwelling of God is with men. He will dwell with them, and they shall be his people, and God himself will be with them; he will wipe away every tear from their eyes, and death shall be no more, neither shall there be mourning nor crying nor pain any more, for the former things have passed away.
>
> He who testifies to these things says, "Surely I am coming soon." Amen. Come, Lord Jesus!
>
> (Rev. 18:21; 19:6; 1:7; 21:1,3–4; 22:20)

NOTES

INTRODUCTION
1. *Church Dogmatics*, Volume III,4 (Edinburgh: T. & T. Clark, 1961), p. 466.
2. Ibid., p. 453.
3. In a personal conversation.

One / THE PRIMEVAL MURDER
1. *Violence: Reflections from a Christian Perspective* (New York: Seabury, 1969), p. 100.
2. Martin Buber in *Between Man and Man* (New York: Macmillan, 1948), p. 31, defined collectivity as "not a binding but a bundling together." I use the word to refer to any bundling together of people, territory, and societal structures which is not itself effectively drawn into a still wider bundling together.
3. *Genesis* (Philadelphia: Westminster, 1961), p. 148. I am indebted to von Rad for some of the insights in chapters on Genesis stories.

Two / CURSING
1. For an excellent treatment of holy war in the Old Testament see Vernard Eller, *King Jesus' Manual of Arms for the 'Armless: War and Peace from Genesis to Revelation* (Nashville: Abingdon, 1973); rev. ed. *War and Peace from Genesis to Revelation* (Scottdale, Pa.: Herald Press, 1981).
2. Gerhard von Rad, *Old Testament Theology*, 2 vols. (Edinburgh: Oliver and Boyd, 1962–65), 1 (1962): 385.

Three / UNDERLINGS OF THE PROSECUTOR
1. Though this story is not found in the oldest New Testament manuscripts and was almost certainly not originally part of John's gospel, the external evidence is strong that from the early years of the church it was regarded as an authentic episode in the ministry of Jesus and thus eventually came to be accepted as canonical. See Edwyn Clement Hoskyns, *The Fourth Gospel*, ed. Francis Noel Davey (London: Faber and Faber, 1947), pp. 563–66.
2. *War and the Gospel* (Scottdale, Pa.: Herald Press, 1962), p. 189.

Four / HITLER AND THE WOMAN CAUGHT IN ADULTERY
1. *Christianity and History* (New York: Scribner's, 1950), p. 40.
2. See A. J. P. Taylor, *The Origins of the Second World War* (New York: Atheneum, 1962), for an analysis that weighs heavily against the usual demonization of Hitler.

3. Herbert Butterfield, *History and Human Relations* (New York: Macmillan, 1952), p. 111.

Five / THE SOURCE OF KILLING

1. *Roots of War* (New York: Penguin Books, 1972), p. 13.

2. In the Three Mile Island nuclear power plant disaster the wide-spreading emission of radioactive substances was accompanied by a huge correlative release of establishment lies, which provided remarkable indication of how what might be called low level, background lies—there abruptly contradicted by events—undergird this nuclear society.

3. The same motifs and dynamic are found in the Nazareth synagogue incident at the beginning of Jesus' ministry (Lk. 4:16–30).

4. *Violence,* p. 103.

5. Yet that very parable, perhaps more than any other, is occasion for our sinning: We are happy not to be like the Pharisee.

Six / "THEY DO NOT KNOW WHAT THEY ARE DOING"

1. *Christianity and History,* p. 122.

2. *Genesis,* pp. 86–87.

3. Quoted in Fletcher Knebel and Charles W. Bailey II, *No High Ground* (New York: Harper & Bros., 1960), p. 116.

4. Robert Jungk, *Brighter Than a Thousand Suns: A Personal History of the Atomic Scientists* (New York: Harcourt, Brace, & World, 1958), p. 201.

5. Ibid., p. 222.

6. Quoted in Knebel, *No High Ground,* p. 229.

7. *The American Character* (Gloucester, Mass.: Peter Smith, 1975), p. 208.

8. *Religio Medici and Other Writings* (New York: Dutton, 1951), p. 75.

9. The continuing development of nuclear power plants illustrates in a subsidiary way these same biblical motifs: the absurd disregard of all that cries out, "You shall not"; the savoring of vast power; acceptance of the lie, "You can get away with it, you will not die"; seizure of a pseudo-dominion that has become a deepening servitude.

10. *The Iliad: or The Poem of Force* (Wallingford, Pa.: Pendle Hill, 1956), pp. 11, 27, 4.

11. Sidney Lens, "The Arms Race: A Primer," *Progressive,* October 1977, p. 42.

12. *The Iliad: or The Poem of Force,* p. 23.

13. *Only One Way Left* (Glasgow: Iona Community, 1956), p. 34.

14. According to one line of argument, Matthew 26:53–54 indicates that the command forbidding the use of the sword was determined by the unique situation in Gethsemane and it therefore cannot be universally applied: "Do you think that I cannot appeal to my Father, and he will at once send me more than twelve legions of angels? But how then should the scriptures be fulfilled, that it must be so?" Jesus, however, did not call in the heavenly army, beside which all weapons there in the garden would have been as nothing. He trusted

in dimensions of God's power far mightier than any such celestial incursion. Thus the scriptures were to be fulfilled. When as disciples we seek to let these verses form our thinking, we see with Jesus the puniness and inutility of weapons; we understand that any situation that jeopardizes us or any temptation to resort to weapons is comparable to that for the first disciples in Gethsemane; we recognize that in Christ's people the scriptures, old and new, must receive additional fulfilment—suffering servanthood, cross, resurrection as derivative extension of his.

Seven / "WHAT HAVE YOU DONE?"
1. NBC-TV, "David Brinkley's Journal," 10 December 1962. Both statements were made at a gathering and interview of the men who flew over Hiroshima.
2. *Give Me Water: Testimonies of Hiroshima and Nagasaki* (Tokyo: A Citizens' Group to Convey Testimonies of Hiroshima and Nagasaki, 1972), pp. 32–34.
3. "Buying Time," *Progressive,* April 1978, p. 13; reprint of "To the Two K's: A Brief Preface to Pushbuttoning," *Fellowship,* March 1, 1963. Ferry later recast the proposal: Close relatives of the national leaders of each superpower would live as hostages in target areas within the rival country; leaders could thus not fire the weapons without realizing that they would be killing persons dear to them. But it seems that no government mad enough to proceed with the nuclear arms race would muster enough sanity to move into such an arrangement.

Eight / THE CENTRAL MURDER
1. *The Death of Christ* (London: Tyndale, 1951), p. 84.
2. Max Thurian, *Marriage and Celibacy* (London: SCM Press, 1959), p. 100.
3. *The Death of Christ*, p. 84.
4. Lasserre, *War and the Gospel*, p. 175.
5. *Um die Zukunft des Menschen im atomaren Zeitalter* (Berlin: Lettner, 1960), pp. 166–68.

Nine / JAGANNATHA
1. "The Reluctant Death of Sovereignty," *Center Magazine,* March 1968, pp. 29, 33.
2. Barnet, *Roots of War*, p. 115.
3. Herbert B. Workman, *Persecution in the Early Church* (Cincinnati, 1906), p. 72.
4. *The Technological Society* (New York: Random House, 1964), p. 284.
5. *Old Testament Theology*, II (1965):15.
6. *Man Against Mass Society* (Chicago: Henry Regnery, 1952), p. 53.
7. "The Lordship of Christ and the Power Struggle," *The Lordship of Christ: Proceedings of the Seventh Mennonite World Conference,* ed. Cornelius J. Dyck (Eklhart, Ind.: Mennonite World Conference, 1962), p. 509.

Ten / THIEVES, ROBBERS, AND THE WOLF

1. Edwyn Clement Hoskyns, *The Fourth Gospel,* ed. Francis Noel Davey, pp. 368–69.

2. *The Day Before Doomsday: An Anatomy of the Nuclear Arms Race* (Garden City, N.Y.: Doubleday, 1977), p. 69.

3. Jim Wallis, *Agenda for Biblical People* (New York: Harper & Row, 1976), p. 2.

Eleven / THE DEVIL'S DICTATION

1. *Jesus the World's Perfecter* (Philadelphia: Muhlenberg, 1961), pp. 81–82.

Twelve / IMAGES OF REBELLION

1. *A Diary of My Times* (London: Boriswood, 1938), p. 71.

2. *Between Man and Man,* p. 31. See note 2, Chapter One

3. *The Meaning of the City* (Grand Rapids: Eerdmans, 1970), p. 19.

4. Scottdale, Pa.: Herald Press, 1962.

5. Grand Rapids: Eerdmans, 1972, pp. 135–62.

6. *Christ and the Powers,* pp. 55–56, 22–23, 24, 36.

7. Ibid., p. 31.

8. *The Interpreter's Dictionary of the Bible* (Nashville: Abingdon, 1962), s. v., "Beast."

9. *Apocalypse: The Book of Revelation* (New York: Seabury, 1977), pp. 95–97.

Thirteen / HERODIANS

1. *Requiem for the Living* (New York: Harper & Row, 1964), p. 99.

Fourteen / NAZISM'S CULMINATION

1. Quoted in Milton Mayer, *They Thought They Were Free: The Germans 1933–45* (Chicago: University of Chicago Press, 1955), p. 339.

2. "Prophetic Faith and Contemporary International Relations," *Biblical Realism Confronts the Nation,* ed. Paul Peachey (Nyack, N.Y.: Fellowship, 1963), p. 83.

3. Quoted in Mark Sherwin, *The Extremists* (New York: St. Martin's Press, 1963), p.110.

4. Thomas Merton in *Faith and Violence* (Notre Dame, Ind.: University of Notre Dame Press, 1968), p. 163, pointed to "the irate clashing of incompatible myth-systems."

Fifteen / ROMANS 13:1–7

1. This clause renders what in the Greek text is a plural noun cognate with the verb meaning *owe,* which is used in the next sentence.

2. *Theological Dictionary of the New Testament,* ed. Gerhard Kittel, 8 vols. (Grand Rapids: Eerdmans, 1964–74), 2 (1964): 562.

3. The question we have been dealing with here of what precisely is God's relation to government as taught in Romans 13:1–7 is surely a far more important issue than the one that has been so widely and vigorously debated by New Testament scholars as to whether or not the *exousiai* of Romans 13:1 refers to spiritual powers behind government.

See John Howard Yoder, *The Politics of Jesus*, pp. 193–214, for a most significant treatment of Romans 13:1–7.

4. John Howard Yoder, ibid., p. 212, illustrates: "The conscientious objector who refuses to do what his government asks him to do, but still remains under the sovereignty of that government and accepts the penalties which it imposes, or the Christian who refuses to worship Caesar but still permits Caesar to put him to death, is being subordinate even though he is not obeying."

Similarly, what is spoken of in verse 2 is an insurgent setting of oneself against the ruling authorities in thought or in deed, not a resistance that may enter into civil disobedience to or nonviolent witness against unjust demands by a government.

Sixteen / GOD'S LAUGHTER

1. *Insight and Outlook: An Inquiry into the Common Foundations of Science, Art and Social Ethics* (New York: Macmillan, 1949), p. 98.

2. Karl Barth, *Church Dogmatics*, Volume IV, 3, I, p. 241.

3. Friends Committee on National Legislation, *Washington Newsletter*, July 1978, p. 1.

4. *The Oxford Universal Dictionary*, 3rd ed. (1955), s.v. "Panic."

Seventeen / RULERS SO-CALLED

1. *The Day Before Doomsday*, p. 18.

2. Barnet, *Roots of War*, p. 82.

3. *Old Testament Theology*, 1:319.

4. *Man Against Mass Society*, pp. 39, 40.

5. "The Subterranean World of the Bomb," *Harper's*, March 1978, pp. 98–99.

6. In *Beyond Tragedy* (New York: Scribner's, 1938), pp. 69–87, Reinhold Niebuhr has a penetrating essay, "Four Hundred to One," based on this story. But it is surely significant that Niebuhr has been taken as possibly the foremost among the four hundred, in spite of much in his theology that weighs against this. Richard J. Barnet in *Roots of War*, pp. 64–65, states that many of the national security managers have been greatly influenced by Niebuhr.

7. *Pensées and The Provincial Letters* (New York: Random house, 1941), p. 112.

8. When on May 10, 1955, the Soviet government basically accepted the disarmament plan that for years had been urged by the United States, Great Britain, and France, this plan was promptly withdrawn by its proposers. Nobel Peace Prize winner Philip Noel-Baker in *The Arms Race: A Programme for World Disarmament* (London: Atlantic Books, 1958), pp. 12–30, tells the wretched

story. Contrary to the illusion so dominant in the West that the Soviets spoiled everything by refusal to accept inspection, Noel-Baker writes, to give here just one example: "This juxtaposition of the proposals made by Russia and the Western Governments in 1957 shows that, *on paper*, the Russians were offering to accept *much more disarmament*, and *much more inspection and control*, than the West" (p. 27).

9. According to elaborate statistical studies conducted by Ernest J. Stern-glass, a professor of radiation physics ("The Death of All Children," *Esquire*, September 1969, pp. 19 ff.), the infant mortality rate in states downwind from the first atomic explosion in Alamogordo, New Mexico, was, for a few years, higher than would otherwise have been expected. During and for a period after the test explosions of about 200 megatons worth of bombs around the world in the 50s and early 60s, the U.S. infant mortality rate was about 1% higher than would have been anticipated otherwise. Damage by strontium 90 to human genetic material can be identified as the main factor. Sternglass points out that a nuclear world war would likely "produce more than a hundred times as much radioactive poison as during all the years of peacetime testing. Based on the excess mortality observed during the period of testing, this would most likely be sufficient to insure that few if any children anywhere in the world would grow to maturity to give rise to another generation."

10. Ed Snyder, "Musings on a Congressional Debate," *Sojourners*, February 1977, p. 18.

11. "Juggernaut: The Warfare State," *Nation*, October 28, 1961, p. 282.

12. Quoted in Robert W. Gardiner, *The Cool Arm of Destruction: Modern Weapons and Moral Insensitivity* (Philadelphia: Westminster Press, 1974), p. 63.

13. Donald Keys, ed., *God and the H-Bomb* (New York: Bellmeadows Press, 1961), p. 73.

14. The contraries are so memorably depicted in the film *The Parable*.

15. "A Biblical Call to Nuclear Non-Cooperation," *The Nuclear Challenge to Christian Conscience: A Study Guide for Churches*, (Washington, D.C.: *Sojourners*, [1978]), booklet 2, p. 15; reprint of "Christian Commitment," *Therefore Choose Life: Essays on the Nuclear Crisis* (London: International Fellowship of Reconcil-iation, 1961).

Eighteen / FORFEITED DOMINION

1. Quoted in George F. MacLeod, *Only One Way Left*, p. 31. The italics are MacLeod's.

2. Katherine Kent Child Walker in *Familiar Quotations*, ed. John Bartlett, 12th ed. (Boston: Little, Brown and Company, 1951), p. 654.

3. *Wir Eichmannsöhne* (Munich: C. H. Beck, 1964), p. 48.

Nineteen / INVALIDATED MODELS

1. *Kill and Overkill: The Strategy of Annihilation* (New York: Basic Books, 1962), p. 107.

2. "Death and Forever: Some Fears of War and Peace," *Atlantic,* March 1962, pp. 88–92.

3. "International Politics and the Nuclear Dilemma," *Nuclear Weapons and the Conflict of Conscience,* ed. John C. Bennett (New York: Scribner's, 1962), p. 21.

4. *Pensées and the Provincial Letters,* p. 177. These words are in *Le Mystère de Jésus.*

Twenty / LATTER-DAY JERUSALEM

1. *An Ethic for Christians and Other Aliens in a Strange Land* (Waco, Tex.: Word, 1973), p. 114.

2. *The Christian Conscience and War* (New York: Church Peace Mission, n.d.), pp. 20–21.

3. *Christianity and History,* pp. 57–58.

4. Edwyn Clement Hoskyns, *The Fourth Gospel,* ed. Francis Noel Davey, p. 525.

Twenty-one / DEATH'S MASQUERADE

1. *Ethics* (New York: Macmillan, 1955), p. 123.

2. This grasping for the boundless ("good and evil") is delineated in the quotation from Gerhard von Rad on p. 30.

3. *A Companion to the Bible,* ed. J. J. von Allmen (New York: Oxford University Press, 1958), p. 470.

4. *A Theology of History* (London and New York: Sheed & Ward, 1963), p. 26.

5. *Theological Dictionary of the New Testament,* ed. Gerhard Kittel, 1 (1964): 395.

Twenty-two / AS IN THE DAYS OF NOAH

1. *War and Peace,* Part Ten, XVII.

2. Hans Urs von Balthasar, *A Theology of History,* p. 34.

3. *Kill and Overkill,* p. 91.

Twenty-three / WHY THE POSSIBILITY FOR THE BOMB?

1. *The Apocalypse Today* (Grand Rapids: Eerdmans, 1959), p. 23.

2. *Stride Toward Freedom: The Montgomery Story* (New York: Harper, 1958), p. 224.

3. This point has been ably made by a number of analysts. See Sidney Lens, "The SALT Trap," *Progressive,* December 1978, pp. 9–10; Robert C. Johansen, "Arms Bazaar," *Harper's,* May 1979, pp. 21–29.

4. For a most significant recent addition to the literature, see Robert C. Johansen, *Toward a Dependable Peace: A Proposal for an Appropriate Security System* (New York: Institute for World Order, 1978).

5. See André Trocmé, *Jesus and the Nonviolent Revolution* (Scottdale, Pa.: Herald Press, 1973), for an important study of Jesus' call in its social breadth.

6. *God's Boycott of Sin* (New York: Fellowship, 1946), p. 73.

7. Butterfield, *Christianity and History,* p. 58.

8. *A Sign for Cain: An Exploration of Human Violence* (New York: Macmillan, 1966), p. 120.

Twenty-five / THE SCANDAL OF DEFENSELESSNESS
1. *The Brothers Karamazov*, Part Two, Book Five, Chapter V.

Twenty-six / DESERTION AND REGATHERING
1. *The Gospel of John*, 2 vols. (Philadelphia: Westminster, 1955), 2:236.
2. It is significant that "deserter" in its most common meaning has to do with running from the military. If people see the country as the center, then desertion will be understood most of all as abandonment of it and will be regarded as supremely reprehensible. When church people oppose amnesty for those classed as deserters in a war, such as the Indochina War, they reveal where the center is for them. If Jesus is Center, desertion from him, of which adherence to the nation-state is a prime form, is what needs chiefly to be dealt with.

Twenty-seven / STANDING WITH THE CENTRAL VICTIM
1. *The Prophets*, 2 vols. (New York: Harper, 1962), 1:26.
2. Neighboring towns of Sodom and Gomorrah, destroyed in the same cataclysm (Gen. 10:19; Deut. 29:23).
3. *Pensées and the Provincial Letters*, p. 176; in *Le Mystere de Jesus*.

Twenty-eight / DEFENDING THE COUNTRY
1. *The Prophets*, 1:171.

Thirty / SHALOM COMMUNITIES
1. *The Original Revolution: Essays on Christian Pacifism* (Scottdale, Pa.: Herald Press, 1971), p. 31.
2. Especially prepared for such use are *A Matter of Faith: A Study Guide for Churches on the Nuclear Arms Race* (Washington, D.C.: Sojourners Magazine, 1981); J. Christopher Grannis, Arthur J. Laffin, and Elin Schade, *The Risk of the Cross: Christian Discipleship in the Nuclear Age* (New York: Seabury, 1981).
3. Peter Ediger, "Explo '72," *Post-American*, Fall 1972, p. 13.

Thirty-one / WATCHFULNESS AND THE TAUT TRAP
1. *History and Human Survival* (New York: Random House, 1970), p. 183.
2. *Death in Life: Survivors of Hiroshima* (New York: Random House, 1967), pp. 19–30.

SELECTED BIBLIOGRAPHY

Barnet, Richard J. *Roots of War.* New York: Penguin Books, 1972.

Butterfield, H. *Christianity and History.* New York: Charles Scribner's Sons, 1950.

Durnbaugh, Donald F. (ed.). *On Earth Peace: Discussions on War/Peace Issues Between Friends, Mennonites, Brethren and European Churches 1935–1975.* Elgin, Ill.: The Brethren Press, 1978.

Eller, Vernard. *King Jesus' Manual of Arms for the 'Armless: War and Peace from Genesis to Revelation.* Nashville: Abingdon Press, 1973. Rev. ed. *War and Peace from Genesis to Revelation.* Scottdale, Pa.: Herald Press, 1981.

Ellul, Jacques. *The Meaning of the City.* Grand Rapids: William B. Eerdmans Publishing Company, 1970.

———. *Violence: Reflections from a Christian Perspective.* New York: The Seabury Press, 1969.

Grannis, J. Christopher, Laffin, Arthur J., and Schade, Elin. *The Risk of the Cross: Christian Discipleship in the Nuclear Age.* New York: The Seabury Press, 1981.

Gray, J. Glenn. *The Warriors: Reflections on Men in Battle.* New York: Harcourt, Brace and Company, 1959.

Hachiya, Michihiko. *Hiroshima Diary.* Chapel Hill: The University of North Carolina Press, 1955.

Johansen, Robert C. *Toward a Dependable Peace: A Proposal for an Appropriate Security System.* New York: Institute for World Order, 1140 Avenue of the Americas, N.Y., N.Y. 10036; 1978.

Lasserre, Jean. *War and the Gospel.* Scottdale, Pa.: Herald Press, 1962.

Lens, Sidney. *The Day Before Doomsday: An Anatomy of the Nuclear Arms Race.* Garden City, N.Y.: Doubleday & Company, Inc., 1977.

Marcel, Gabriel. *Man Against Mass Society.* Chicago: Henry Regnery Company, 1952.

A Matter of Faith: A Study Guide for Churches on the Nuclear Arms Race. Sojourners Magazine, 1309 L Street NW, Washington, DC 20005; 1981.

Trocmé, André. *Jesus and the Nonviolent Revolution.* Scottdale, Pa.: Herald Press, 1973.

Weil, Simone. *The Iliad: or The Poem of Force.* Wallingford, Pa.: Pendle Hill, 1956.

Yoder, John H. *The Original Revolution: Essays on Christian Pacifism.* Scottdale, Pa.: Herald Press, 1971.

———. *The Politics of Jesus.* Grand Rapids: William B. Eerdmans Publishing Company, 1972.